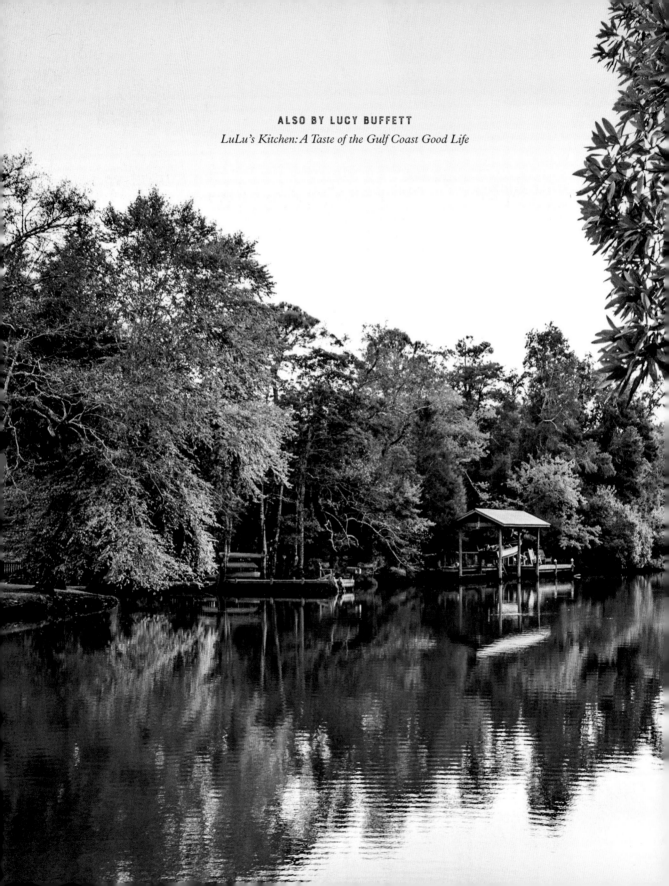

ALSO BY LUCY BUFFETT

LuLu's Kitchen: A Taste of the Gulf Coast Good Life

GUMBO
LOVE

RECIPES FOR GULF COAST COOKING,
ENTERTAINING, AND SAVORING
THE GOOD LIFE

LUCY BUFFETT

FOREWORD BY
THOMAS McGUANE

GRAND CENTRAL
Life & Style

BOSTON • NEW YORK

Grand Central Life & Style
Hachette Book Group
1290 Avenue of the Americas, New York, NY 10104
grandcentrallifeandstyle.com
twitter.com/grandcentralpub

First Edition: May 2017

Grand Central Life & Style is an imprint of Grand Central Publishing. The Grand Central
Life & Style name and logo are trademarks of Hachette Book Group, Inc.

The publisher is not responsible for websites (or their content) that are not owned
by the publisher.

The Hachette Speakers Bureau provides a wide range of authors for speaking events. To find
out more, go to www.hachettespeakersbureau.com or call (866) 376-6591.

Print book interior design by Gary Tooth/Empire Design Studio

Library of Congress Cataloging-in-Publication Data

Names: Buffett, Lucy Anne, author.
Title: Gumbo love : recipes for Gulf Coast cooking, entertaining, and
    savoring the good life / Lucy Buffett ; foreword by Thomas McGuane.
Description: New York : Grand Central Life & Style, [2017] | Includes
    bibliographical references and index.
Identifiers: LCCN 2016056560| ISBN 978-1-4555-6644-0 (hardcover) | ISBN
    978-1-4555-6646-4 (ebook)
Subjects: LCSH: Cooking, American—Southern style. | Cooking—Gulf States. |
    LCGFT: Cookbooks.
Classification: LCC TX715.2.S68 .B798 2017 | DDC 641.5975—dc23 LC record available at
    https://lccn.loc.gov/2016056560

ISBNs: 978-1-4555-6644-0 (hardcover); 978-1-4555-6646-4 (ebook)

Printed in the United States of America

Q-MA

10 9 8 7 6 5 4 3 2 1

For Mac
Who saw what I couldn't see.
Always my sweet okra love and gratitude.

CONTENTS

FOREWORD

BY THOMAS McGUANE

I read Lucy Buffett's cookbook with relish (!) for several reasons: I expected it to arouse my appetite, and I thought it would help me understand the sometimes inscrutable journey of someone I've known and adored for decades but whose adventures often baffled me. At first, Lucy's peregrinations seemed defined by only one thing: a remarkable capacity for work, which enabled her to find and explore her life and bring it to the coherence she now enjoys. It was a winding road, but with the help of this absorbing book I understand it better.

Lucy Buffett is an indelible product of the Gulf Coast, propelled by family stories, appreciation of local habits and tradition, and friends who live on in memory. The celebration of food and its preparation is the thread that led Lucy Buffett to the coherence she sought in her own life, and her search for its meaning.

Years ago I was working on a movie project with Robert Redford, and he said something that has stayed with me: "There is only one interesting story: struggle." Lucy Buffett *struggled* to bring cooking to this high level; she has left a useful trail for other cooks enchanted by her voice and her recipes, and in so doing has found her own story, which is all any of us really want to do.

LETTER FROM LULU

To be a good cook you have to have a love of the good, a love of hard work, and a love of creating. —JULIA CHILD

Dear Friends,

It is with deep humility that I thank you for holding this book in your hands. *Gumbo Love* is my love letter to the northern coast of the Gulf of Mexico—the place of my birth, the place where generations of my people walked the sandy shores, frolicked in the salty waves, sailed the crystal green waters, and cooked pots and pots of seafood gumbo long before I was even a notion.

My intention here is to pay homage to my coastal Southern food culture and continue the conversation I started in *LuLu's Kitchen*, my first book. More than anything, I would simply love to have you "pull up a chair to my kitchen table" and share a little bit of the blessings, memories, and recipes from my Gulf Coast paradise.

If I had been born even slightly inland, I would not be the complex yet hopeful Gulf Coast gal that I am today. Yes, I'm resolutely and stoically Southern, something you can tell the moment I utter a single-syllable word that magically rolls into multiple lazy syllables. But being from the coastal South, in particular, adds a distinct flavor to my Dixie soul that is hard to name or explain…just like it is difficult to truly describe the joy and peace of walking on the sugar-white sandy beach, following the faithful curvy tideline as the irrepressible waves play a hypnotic symphony, lulling my concerns to a mere whisper and awakening a connection to the magnificent wonder and power of life. Perhaps it's the blurry horizon in the faraway distance that beckons a call to adventure or a simple curiosity that sparks hope for a peace floating beyond the water's edge. Whatever saltwater secret it is that makes us coastal Southerners a little "different," a little mystical, it has nurtured a heart connection to a place that I love…a family I cherish…and a cuisine that I am proud to serve and share with you.

Thank you for taking the time to stop by; I hope you enjoy your visit as much as I love welcoming you to my Gulf Coast table!

Always my spicy gumbo love,
Lucy "LuLu" Buffett
Perdido Key, Florida
October 2016

INTRODUCTION

I've spent hours and hours and days and days making gumbo. Plain old flour and oil in a hot skillet and then whisking, whisking, whisking till my arm aches. The oil and flour becomes a deep, dark roux, shiny and beautiful like smooth velvet, almost the color of the ancient cast-iron skillet I make it in. It's hard to describe the transformation that occurs with such simple ingredients and even harder to understand—it's just another of life's many mysteries, like a magic spell passed down from cook to cook, a spell that turns shrimp and crab into tender, weightless, sweet bits of meat and the holy trinity of onions, celery, and peppers into soft morsels in a savory stew that will melt in your mouth like chocolate.

The magic roux is a little bit of a diva—if you rush her, she will rebel, and you'll end up back where you started. She wants to take her time getting ready, and she wants to see just how far you're willing to go to witness her magic. I adjust the heat, keeping the roux just this side of burning, letting the color deepen without scorching. I patiently coax it from light brown to the copper color of a penny and then finally to a deep, dark brown that's almost black. All of a sudden, the roux releases the smell of roasting nuts—she's full of herself now, finally stepping into the room and ready to start the show—and though I'm tempted to pull it off the heat, I let it go just a tad longer, the voice in my head, my lifelong anthem, daring me, *Take it to the edge, sister!*

When one more second will be too long, I sprinkle in the onions and nudge them gently around the pot with my wooden spoon. The onions steam and sizzle. Hot roux spits on my hand and arm. Like I said, she's no easy lady! I stir on. Time for the celery and then the bell pepper. The roux calms down, deigning now to settle in and do her magic, taking every humble ingredient I toss into her mysterious velvety embrace and making it the star of the show.

I beat the odds a lot of times and a lot of ways in my life, and how I cook is how I tell time and how I tell my story. Every passage of my life has been marked by food. Every twist and turn in my personal story has been a leg of my culinary journey. My childhood was a time of Sunday dinners at my grandmothers' homes in Mississippi. Raised in her mother's boardinghouse, my Buffett grandmother would put out a massive spread of fried chicken and roast beef, mashed potatoes, rice and gravy, green beans, stewed squash, speckled butter beans, potato salad, and sliced tomatoes; a sideboard covered in desserts like pound cake with strawberries and dewberry pie; and watermelon iced down in a galvanized tub. Children sat at the children's table, and the men gathered in the garage with the "hidden" bottle of rum. And on Fridays, being a good Catholic, my grandmother made enough seafood gumbo to feed the whole family and even have leftovers to go with Sunday dinner; the smell would wind its way out of the kitchen and down the driveway to greet us in a welcoming cloud that led us right back to her kitchen. She used to say, "You are always underfoot, LuLu. If I can't find you, I know to look in the kitchen." And that's still where you'll find me.

My Peets grandmother was the "dietitian" at a girls' finishing school in Long Beach, Mississippi. That meant she ran the kitchen, planned the menus, and managed the staff. She taught us scrawny and wild Gulf Coast kids about finer fare. At least one Sunday a month, we had to forgo our usual playtime in the red-clay gullies around our modest neighborhood of identical postwar redbrick houses and travel the coast highway to Gulf Park College. It was a beautiful campus with the majestic Friendship Oak overlooking the vast Mississippi Sound. My brother would have to wear a collared shirt and skinny tie, and my sister and I wore white gloves and Mary Janes to the dining hall. A man in a tall white hat carved rounds of beef served with au jus and horseradish sauce, and there were fancy sides like crabmeat au gratin. They even had petits fours for dessert. It was country-club food, even though we were far from country-club people!

Both of these Sunday traditions were authentic Gulf Coast experiences, and my personal cooking and entertaining reflect them both: my cooking, my style, even my home are a little bit rustic, a little bit refined.

A very young wife and mother, I found myself all alone in the kitchen with no help and no experience. My mother, wonderful in so many ways, was cooking "challenged," and my grandmothers were just far enough away that I didn't have their guidance. I did my best with a Junior League cookbook, and I found out for the first time that I actually liked to cook. It wasn't long, though, before no amount of Divine Casserole could keep my young marriage afloat. So with a hundred bucks in my pocket, I put my two girls in my Ford Mustang and a brand-new fifty-dollar vacuum cleaner in the trunk and we headed to Key West. As I crossed the Seven Mile Bridge over those turquoise waters, I figured if it all went south, as my dad would say, I could hock the vacuum for just enough money to get me and my girls back home!

 Key West we moved in with my brother, Jimmy, who lived in an apartment right next to Louie's Backyard, one of Key West's best and most iconic restaurants. Almost the day after I arrived, Jimmy and his friends, including Tom McGuane, who would later become our brother-in-law, took me to a French restaurant, Le Mistral, on Duval Street. I'd had fish stew before, but Chef Renee's bouillabaisse was something completely different. It was thoroughly French, like he was. On the rare payday occasions that we went out to eat growing up, it was Morrison's Cafeteria, Roussos Seafood Restaurant, Constantine's Restaurant, or one of the dives out on the causeway for fried crab claws. This, however, was exotic. The fine wine, the fancy croutons, and the rouille he put on top of the bouillabaisse—it was my first *WOW* moment in food. I don't learn by reading. I've got to get in there with all my senses and then do it myself. This tasting experience awakened something in me— I wanted to try that...I wanted to do that!

And another thing that made the experience at Le Mistral so alluring was the juxtaposition of this sophisticated, finely crafted food being served in an extraordinarily casual environment. We were eating fancy food wearing cutoffs and flip-flops! The dynamic was similar to the contrast between the cooking cultures of my two grandmothers, and it was on its way to becoming a lifelong theme for me. I just fell in love with the freeing lifestyle of Key West and all its small, personal neighborhood restaurants. I immersed myself in the food, with its focus on seafood—lobster, stone crab, yellowtail snapper, hogfish, grouper, conch.

Key West was a place where enjoying life, expressing yourself, and making and savoring good food and drinks were all one and the same. I've carried this point of view with me ever since, and made creating food that captures this spirit my passion and career. Having been barefoot children and then Key West hippies together, Jimmy captures in his music the same attitude I celebrate in my food—songs about friends, about being barefoot and fancy-free, about the adventures and mysteries of life on the water, and, of course, cheeseburgers, margaritas, boat drinks, pitchers of beer, and shrimp beginning to boil.

Life happens. Circumstances took me from Key West back to Alabama and on to New Orleans with another husband who couldn't settle my gypsy soul. So I was off again, cruising on a yacht cooking for Harrison Ford in Belize. When that job finished, instead of going home, I stayed on the yacht, which took me to New York City for several years, catering weddings and Fortune 500 dinner parties, until I eventually made my way to Los Angeles, where I tried my hand at writing screenplays while I catered on the weekends. I quickly got in step with the alfresco cuisine of the West Coast, with its focus on fresh ingredients and simplicity over complicated techniques.

Later I returned to Alabama to care for my mother, who'd had a stroke, and my father, who was suffering from Alzheimer's, but by that time I'd truly gone around the culinary world. I was coming back to the food of my youth, but my interpretation of this food would now be enhanced by all the lessons I'd learned on each leg of my tour. I was home, eons older and wiser than I'd been when I left that day with my vacuum cleaner as my only insurance. To be truthful, though, in terms of money I wasn't that far from where I'd started.

It was a new chapter. So I turned to what had gotten me through all my challenges and adventures before—cooking. And what in the world could I make that would feed the most people? A big ol' pot of gumbo, of course. So that's what I did.

When I opened the first LuLu's Sunset Grill out of a modified bait shop café on Weeks Bay, Alabama, I was the cook, hostess, janitor, server, buser, dishwasher, and office and kitchen manager. I couldn't afford to buy much equipment and had to make do with what I could rustle up. I used my great-aunt Loraine's huge cast-iron skillet to make the roux for my five-gallon batches of gumbo. Do you know how hard it is to break cast iron? Well, I manhandled that thing making so much roux that I broke the handle right off—not that I stopped using it. It didn't matter if it was a hundred degrees outside— people wanted gumbo. We started to run out, so five gallons a day became fifteen gallons. I made batch after batch after batch.

Gumbo was something special from my earliest memories of family love and togetherness, and now here it was, paying my bills, making my customers happy, feeding my children. People kept on coming for the gumbo and the company and the atmosphere of the place, which was a little bit 'Bama river rat den, a little bit Key West dive bar, and a smidge of Friday afternoons in Mom Buffett's kitchen.

As I stirred and stirred and stirred that roux, I got to where I could do it with my eyes closed, and it got to be a ritual for me that I embraced, an intentional moment of stirring together all my crazy adventures that had gotten me to this point, that had brought me home, all the techniques I'd learned, the people I'd met. And when it was time to add the onions, celery, peppers, and other ingredients to the roux, I started tossing in bits and pieces from my mind as well—my worries,

my hopes, my blessings, my intentions—letting them get washed in the mystery of that simmering pot of Gumbo Love, tossing them in almost as if handing them over in a prayer to the gumbo diva herself.

Gumbo became my signature dish and the restaurant's best seller. But behind the scenes it was the cooking of the gumbo that became my therapy, healer, life teacher, and mentor that ushered me from being a young, frantic, overwhelmed single mother fraught with constant anxiety about the future to a woman of confidence and diligence with a supreme faith in the goodness of life. I decided I wouldn't dwell on what I didn't have, but what I could do at that moment, and I knew there was one thing that I could do well: cook. So I cooked and I cooked and I put my hopes and dreams into those pots of gumbo by simply doing what was in front of me—

step-by-step, like ingredients in a recipe. And life unfolded. What I didn't realize at the time was that all those pots of gumbo were gradually building a true organic belief in myself—pot-by-pot, I was becoming the me I had always dreamed of, an empowered woman who embraced most days with hope, curiosity, and laughter.

I like to say every job I ever had prepared me for what I'm doing now, and everything I learned to cook is in every dish I make. All this, plus all the people I care about, plus all the goodness I see around me, is what seasons my gumbo and my life. At some point I started wishing people "Gumbo Love" and signing "Gumbo Love" above my name, because I can't think of a better way to express what sharing goodness means to me. It's my personal secret for success. It is my bliss. Cooking with love, serving with love, and loving life. I am telling you, it comes through in the taste of the food and the good vibes in the air.

I hope this book inspires you to cook up your own Gumbo Love and spread it out to the ones you love with a pot of gumbo or just some "vacation" time spent together on the porch or cozied up on the sofa.

I wish all of you the best. I wish you barefoot weather, cold drinks, and happy cooking. I wish you Gumbo Love!

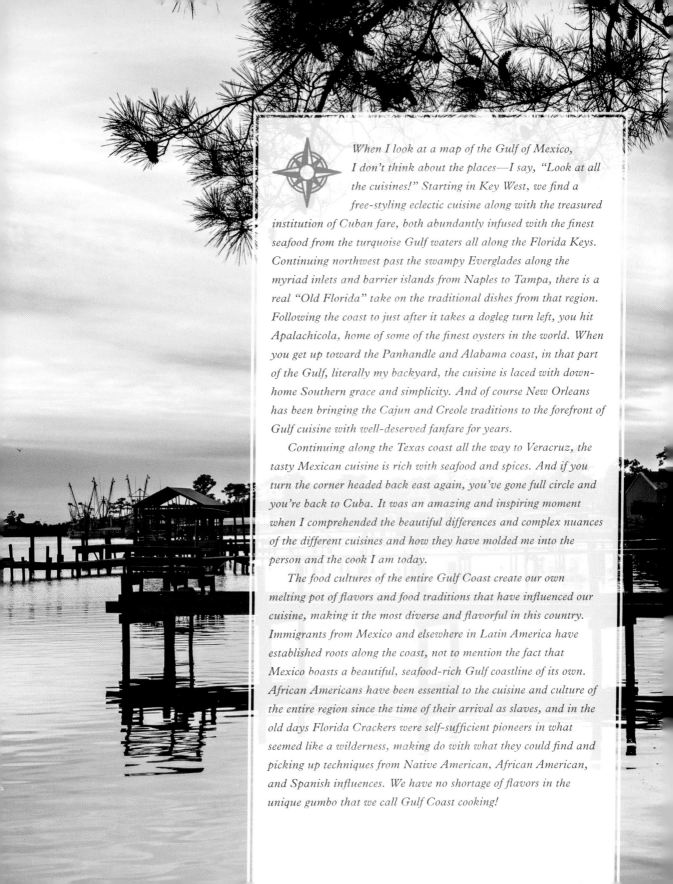

When I look at a map of the Gulf of Mexico, I don't think about the places—I say, "Look at all the cuisines!" Starting in Key West, we find a free-styling eclectic cuisine along with the treasured institution of Cuban fare, both abundantly infused with the finest seafood from the turquoise Gulf waters all along the Florida Keys. Continuing northwest past the swampy Everglades along the myriad inlets and barrier islands from Naples to Tampa, there is a real "Old Florida" take on the traditional dishes from that region. Following the coast to just after it takes a dogleg turn left, you hit Apalachicola, home of some of the finest oysters in the world. When you get up toward the Panhandle and Alabama coast, in that part of the Gulf, literally my backyard, the cuisine is laced with down-home Southern grace and simplicity. And of course New Orleans has been bringing the Cajun and Creole traditions to the forefront of Gulf cuisine with well-deserved fanfare for years.

Continuing along the Texas coast all the way to Veracruz, the tasty Mexican cuisine is rich with seafood and spices. And if you turn the corner headed back east again, you've gone full circle and you're back to Cuba. It was an amazing and inspiring moment when I comprehended the beautiful differences and complex nuances of the different cuisines and how they have molded me into the person and the cook I am today.

The food cultures of the entire Gulf Coast create our own melting pot of flavors and food traditions that have influenced our cuisine, making it the most diverse and flavorful in this country. Immigrants from Mexico and elsewhere in Latin America have established roots along the coast, not to mention the fact that Mexico boasts a beautiful, seafood-rich Gulf coastline of its own. African Americans have been essential to the cuisine and culture of the entire region since the time of their arrival as slaves, and in the old days Florida Crackers were self-sufficient pioneers in what seemed like a wilderness, making do with what they could find and picking up techniques from Native American, African American, and Spanish influences. We have no shortage of flavors in the unique gumbo that we call Gulf Coast cooking!

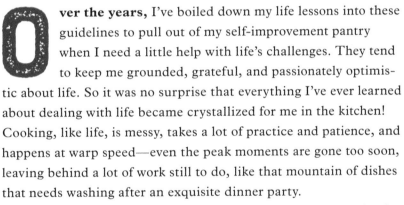

TEN
GRATEFUL INGREDIENTS
FOR A
BRIGHT LIFE
AND A
HAPPY KITCHEN

Over the years, I've boiled down my life lessons into these guidelines to pull out of my self-improvement pantry when I need a little help with life's challenges. They tend to keep me grounded, grateful, and passionately optimistic about life. So it was no surprise that everything I've ever learned about dealing with life became crystallized for me in the kitchen! Cooking, like life, is messy, takes a lot of practice and patience, and happens at warp speed—even the peak moments are gone too soon, leaving behind a lot of work still to do, like that mountain of dishes that needs washing after an exquisite dinner party.

Cooking, in fact, has been one of the greatest teachers in developing my character. It can be instantly rewarding—a grand celebration of flavor. Or it can turn quickly into a life lesson, keeping you humble with lots of opportunities to learn about loss, imperfection, acceptance, perseverance, grief, willingness, and ultimately a simple forgiveness that leaves you with a choice to either throw in the dishtowel or try, try again.

My kitchen has become my sweet, safe haven, and cooking has become one of the most joyous activities in my life. As a matter of fact, I can put these life tools to use more easily in the kitchen than I sometimes can in real life. So don't be surprised if some of these guidelines not only help keep your kitchen running smoothly but also help you out of a real-world jam or two.

1. BELIEVE THAT LIFE IS ALWAYS WORKING FOR YOU, NOT AGAINST YOU.

Things can go wrong in the kitchen—they inevitably do, no matter how prepared you are. But I'm a firm believer that there is always a good reason for everything. We just have to be willing to wade through the challenge and be open to the lesson.

I was once preparing a meal for over a hundred people on a charter yacht in New York City. They were waiting patiently for their dessert, but my key lime pies simply would not set up. I couldn't think anything beyond, *This is a disaster!* I couldn't get beyond the looming sense of failure and dismay. And then one of the waitstaff came up with a brilliant idea: key lime *mousse* with graham cracker morsels! Guess what? We put away the pie plates and started scooping that runny pie, whipped cream, and raspberries into dessert bowls! It was a huge hit. And I learned a great lesson about trusting life and being resourceful, even in the face of what looks like a disaster. Later, that dessert actually became a menu item that was favored by many guests as the best and most interesting take on key lime pie they had ever eaten. I still giggle thinking about that night.

2. YOU ARE WHAT YOU THINK...AND EAT.

The most powerful thing you can do to create a happy life is to keep your thoughts and intentions positive, especially when you are cooking, because your state of mind does affect the food you make. Don't go breaking the bank, but use the freshest and best-quality ingredients you can. Music is as much a part of my cooking experience as the salt and pepper. If listening to some good music helps lift your mood, turn it on, sister! My favorite cooking music ranges from my favorite James Taylor and the Allman Brothers—the music of my youth—to Frank Sinatra, Sara Bareilles, and Beyoncé. Of course, I have to throw in my big brother, Jimmy; nothing's as much fun as cooking in Margaritaville. And to tackle the cleanup, there's nothing that gets it done faster than Aretha and a little *R*E*S*P*E*C*T!*

3. LIFE IS; JUST LIVE IT!

Or maybe the better way to say it is, just *cook* it! Focus on what is working and what you do have in the here and now. You thought you had oregano, but when it's time to add it, you realize you must have used it up last time. Or maybe you have all the ingredients, but you don't have enough of one thing or another. Instead of getting tripped up by what's not there, improvise—be open to the "whatevers" and move forward with what you *do* have. You might even create something with a different slant or flavor that's better than the original. Making do with what you've got is what gets the creative process going. I'd bet most every chef discovered at least one of their favorite recipes simply because they were out of some ingredient and were forced to get creative. I'm convinced that the secret to being a great chef is not how well you can cook but how well you can problem-solve.

4. TRYING TO BE PERFECT IS A SETUP FOR FAILURE.

I am a type A personality, as are both my siblings. Maybe it is genetic or maybe we just found out a lot of times growing up that "a job worth doing is a job worth doing right," echoing the words of our father and his father before him. And as much as we have benefited from living those words and achieving great things in our lives, at times that philosophy has been a harsh master to serve. Because life is not perfect. We are not perfect. We can learn from our mistakes. There is simply no room for anything harsh in my life these days, and I am much more kind to myself than I used to be.

After discovering I loved to cook, I went on a tear replicating complicated recipes from *Gourmet* magazine and any cookbooks I could get my hands on. But while I was living in California, I developed a more relaxed point of view. The amount of effort that went into mastering cooking from a purist's standpoint simply didn't have the payoff for me anymore when it came down to actually eating and enjoying the food. After so much work and worry as I completed each step of every complicated technique, no matter how good the final product, it simply never was good enough to feel worth all the trouble. It was an impossible proposition to create something with taste that matched the intensity of my angst and effort. Don't be afraid to be adventurous in the kitchen—the worst that can happen is you have to throw it away and go out to eat instead—but don't hold yourself to outrageous standards, either. Just be you. Cook what you love! Then others will love what you cook.

5. LIFE HAPPENS AND LIFE GOES ON. THE SUN WILL RISE AGAIN—IN FACT, IT WILL RISE EVERY SINGLE MORNING—EVEN WHEN IT'S HIDING BEHIND A CLOUD OR LOST IN THE FOG, IT'S THERE. "Hang tough," are the words of an old boss of mine. I learned a lot from my days with him in Los Angeles. "Hang tough" became a mantra I still use today to get me to a place of change or acceptance when I'm out of sorts with the rhythm of life. Sometimes you have to just stop. Other times, you have to keep on keeping on. And occasionally the time comes when you've got to cut bait and start over again.

In the kitchen, the cake may fall. The roast might dry out. The oven might even go up in flames! In my case, Hurricane Ivan might even send a barge crashing into my restaurant, but what do you know? The next day there was still cold beer in the cooler and no one had gotten hurt. We managed to rebuild the part of the restaurant that had been damaged, and we had a new name for it—the Barge Bar—to remind us that the day after a storm is almost always (even cruelly so) glorious and sunny, and that when things go horribly wrong, it's better to try again than to give in.

6. WHEN YOU DON'T KNOW WHAT TO DO, DO NOTHING. If I'm out of options or running in circles trying to find a solution or make something happen, I've found that I'm trying too hard. I need to breathe. I need a moment to get still so I can hear what life wants me to do. Kitchens can be chaotic. Ingredients here and there, a spill, different times and temps for different dishes. When you feel the heat building and the countertop starting to spin, stop what you're doing and take a deep breath to get your bearings. Have a cup of coffee. Take a sip of wine if that helps. Or a bite of ice cream. Just be still and be in the moment and you'll be surprised—the knife you were looking for is right there in front of you. One way to avoid some of the chaos is to prepare all your ingredients and implements ahead of time with veggies chopped, bowls lined up, and whatever tools you need at the ready.

7. RUN TOWARD WHAT YOU FEAR; CLOSE YOUR EYES, HOLD YOUR NOSE, AND JUMP INTO IT. I know, this sounds crazy, huh? But it works to get past what you think you might be afraid of. I've done this more times than I can count—cook fish and Thai food I've never heard of, tasted, or seen for none other than Harrison Ford on a boat in Belize? Yes, please! With no restaurant experience whatsoever, risk everything

and open a restaurant pretty much in the middle of nowhere? Can't wait! Whether you fear frying, cooking seafood, or making roux for gumbo, just go for it. It might take a few tries and tweaks to get it right, but you can do it! You might even be good at it. There's nothing more satisfying than doing something you've never done before and, with a little practice, actually succeeding.

8. SAY "THANK YOU" EVERY DAY FOR YOUR BLESSINGS AND BLESS YOUR CHALLENGES WITH GRATITUDE.

Yep, that's right. Even be grateful for those folks and experiences that are sometimes hard. Because nothing can change negativity faster and more sweepingly than gratitude. Maybe the cashier at the grocery store was a grouch, maybe your children turned up their noses at what you put on the table, maybe the waiter got your order wrong and didn't really seem to care—sometimes it's hard to be gracious. But it's amazing how powerful "thank you" can be for the recipient and the person saying it. Sometimes I even stop what I'm doing and thank the kitchen fairies (oh yes, I believe in fairies!), especially when I feel they have abandoned me. *Thank you for making sure I had plenty of flour and oil for my roux—since I scorched it and have to start all over!* I went to Peru recently to the Sacred Valley and learned that the Incan word for "Mother Earth" is *Pachamama*. Isn't that the most beautiful word? While there, before each meal, our blessing would be thanks to the Divine Creator, but we also thanked Pachamama because no matter what you eat, it has come from the earth. All our food and sustenance comes from our beautiful planet. I had an aha moment that connected heaven and earth for me and inspired more reverence for the food that I cook and eat.

9. SAY "I'M SORRY" WHEN NECESSARY AND BE KIND TO YOURSELF.

"Fall on the sword and then move on" is one of my favorite anthems. But just as important, we need to let ourselves off the hook for not being perfect. We are so hard on ourselves—even in the kitchen. We feel bad when our tart doesn't look like Martha's, when we have every intention of making home-made biscuits but go frozen instead, when our timing gets a little off and we end up with warm salad and cold lasagna. Away with the guilt—food that's not perfect but that's prepared with love tastes better than you think. Stop making apologies about your food and let everyone enjoy it, including yourself.

10. YOU ARE THE COOK OF YOUR OWN KITCHEN.

Take responsibility for your successes and your failures. You know what they say about too many cooks in the kitchen. Everyone has their own way they like to do things; everyone thinks their gumbo or their mama's gumbo is *the* best. But you've got to make your own gumbo. Your recipe comes from using your own favorite ingredients, your own family traditions, what you've learned from your own experiences—good and bad—in the kitchen. That doesn't mean someone else's gumbo is wrong. In fact, with an open mind you may be able to pick up things here and there that you'd like to add to your own. Sometimes you're going to have to improvise. Listen to your cooking instincts; the kitchen diva is always whispering in your ear. I've finally figured out my life's recipe, but it took me a whole lot of time in the kitchen to get there.

HOW TO GUMBO LULU:

A FEW NOTES ON GULF COAST COOKING ESSENTIALS

One of the reasons I wrote this book was to share my favorite Gulf Coast recipes with folks so they could cook them at home in an authentic yet easy way. I wanted to take the mystique out of the mix so you won't be deterred from attempting recipes you may not have tried before, especially the gumbos. Here are a few notes that may help familiarize you with some of the essential elements and assuage any fears you might have, so you can spread a little of your own Gumbo Love to your friends and families.

ROUX

You can't cook an authentic Gulf Coast gumbo without roux! Roux, pronounced "rue," is basically flour cooked in some kind of fat, used to create a depth of flavor and to thicken gumbo, soup, or sauce. The French use butter and flour as the base for roux when making their famous sauces. Lard was the fat used by country cooks, but the gumbo of my childhood used bacon fat; a tin pot of bacon grease lived on top of every stove. These days I don't eat much bacon, so I use vegetable oil for my roux.

You can make roux of varying colors depending on how long you brown the flour in the fat. For gumbo, though, I like to get it really dark—I mean brown-black dark—and for that, you have to take it to the edge of scorching. That's what gives gumbo that smoky-rich flavor. Making a roux has the reputation of being difficult, but it just takes time and patience. Don't get too worked up over it. Follow the roux directions carefully in the gumbo recipes, but don't worry if you mess up and have to start over. You will be in good company, because every gumbo cook and chef, including this one, has scorched a roux and had to start over. It's like paying your dues or an initiation into a pretty elite club—besides, it's only a little oil and flour!

CREOLE SEASONING

You'll find this ingredient in so many of my recipes because Creole seasoning is a staple in the South; it's our version of seasoned salt with a lively bite to it from the cayenne pepper. We sprinkle it on everything—a little in the guacamole, in our grits, in burger meat. It gives almost anything a spicy pop of flavor. Below is the recipe I use, at home and in my restaurants. It is super simple to make a batch of it and keep it by the stove. That being said, there are plenty of good Creole seasoning products available at most every supermarket. All rely on pretty much the same ingredients but each has its own nuance. I encourage you to make some of my Crazy Creola Seasoning—or make things easy on yourself and use a store-bought version. If you do make my Crazy Creola, feel free to experiment with the ingredients and make it your own brand of crazy!

LULU'S CRAZY CREOLA SEASONING
MAKES ½ CUP

1 tablespoon sea salt

2 tablespoons granulated garlic or garlic powder

4 teaspoons granulated onion or onion powder

¼ cup paprika

1½ teaspoons freshly ground black pepper

2 teaspoons cayenne pepper

2 teaspoons white pepper

½ teaspoon dried thyme

½ teaspoon dried oregano

Combine all the ingredients and store in an airtight container.

——— CREOLE MUSTARD ———

Creole mustard is a standard condiment in the land of Gumbo Love. I simply can't cook much without it because it is used in salad dressings, sauces, and marinades and spread on sandwiches.

It is a beautiful, creamy, golden-yellow condiment with flecks of the dark-brown spicy and pungent mustard seeds that are the source of down-home peppery mustard greens. With the seeds, we make this exceptional spicy mustard, not too hot and not too mild, with loads of flavor. The famous brand is Zatarain's, which hails from Louisiana and is widely available in supermarkets across the country. If you can't find it locally, you can buy it online to add to your new gumbo pantry shelf. But please don't skip a recipe just because you can't find Creole mustard! You can substitute another variety of spicy brown whole-grain mustard or even Dijon mustard.

——— FILÉ POWDER ———

Hank Williams sang about filé gumbo in the 1950s in his hit song "Jambalaya on the Bayou," which quickly became a proud folk anthem for Gulf Coast people and flung the word *filé* into the national lexicon. But if you weren't from the swampy Louisiana coast stretching east toward the Florida Panhandle, you probably hadn't a clue what gumbo was, much less filé. Choctaw Indians in Louisiana were the first to grind leaves from the sassafras tree to make filé (pronounced FEE-lay) powder to thicken and flavor their gumbo. African American slaves eventually brought okra to the New World, and okra became the more popular thickener for gumbo. Like tomatoes, though, okra was harvested only in the summer. Filé powder became the gumbo essential for wintertime gumbos featuring ingredients like duck, sausage, and oysters, and that has remained a tradition among Gulf Coast gumbo cooks. I've been told by a reliable source, my fifth-generation Cajun hairdresser, that a true Acadian gumbo would *never* use okra—only filé powder, regardless of the season.

Filé powder is usually added at the end of the recipe, about ten minutes before you take the gumbo off the heat. It is also common practice to have a small bowl on the table that gets passed around for sprinkling on individual bowls. Filé is just another example of the natural blessings we enjoy in the coastal South. What a bounty all these gumbo recipes feature! Filé finds a noble place in the kingdom of gumbo, with the likes of blue crab and shrimp from the Gulf, juicy sweet tomatoes, peppers, bright green okra, luscious greens, and homegrown traditions of sausage, hot sauce, and Creole seasonings.

HOT SAUCE

Hot sauce in the South is a passionate pastime. Home cooks develop their own special concoctions. Most restaurants bottle their own brand as well, and LuLu's is no exception. Ours is called LuLu's Perfect Pepper Sauce, and it is bottled by the Panola Pepper Sauce folks in Lake Providence, Louisiana. They have a great line of hot

sauces and other regional ingredients. And if you are ever in that lazy northeastern corner of Louisiana that sits right in the midst of the Mississippi Delta, don't miss the opportunity to visit their facility. It's a hoot of a field trip, and you're in for a treat if you get to meet the owner, Mr. Grady "Bubber" Brown, whose mother was the inspiration for his hot sauce company. The sauce he makes for me is from his mother's recipe, and it is a cooked sauce rather than a fermented pepper-mash sauce.

For all my recipes that call for hot sauce, I use LuLu's Perfect Pepper, but there are plenty of wonderful alternatives out there. Experiment with the recipes using your favorite hot sauce—hopefully giving LuLu's Perfect Pepper a try, too (it's available on my website, as is my Clearly Crazy hot sauce, which you can use on any recipe calling for pepper vinegar)—and keep in mind that some sauces are hotter than others. When you're using a more powerful sauce, adjust the amount to your preferred level of heat.

SEAFOOD/SHRIMP STOCK

The most popular gumbo is the classic seafood gumbo. You can toss any kind of available seafood into the pot. I typically use crab, shrimp, and oysters. To enhance the flavor, I make a stock from the shrimp shells or fish carcasses and vegetable trimmings. But please don't let the idea of making your own stock deter you from making a gumbo. On page xxx you'll find a simple recipe for a versatile shrimp stock that can be used for anything calling for shrimp, seafood, or fish stock, but *you do not have to use a homemade stock*. In a pinch for time, I have used chicken broth and even plain water, and back when seafood stocks were not readily available in grocery stores, the go-to ingredient in many recipes was bottled clam juice. In other words, don't be afraid to improvise or do the best you can when it comes to stock.

These days there are plenty of quality ready-made seafood stocks easily available out on the market. This is a true testament to the rise in popularity of dishes like gumbo, jambalaya, and seafood bisque, among others, beyond our Gulf Coast region. The millions of tourists who grace our shores every year come for the beaches, water recreation, and the coastal cuisine. More and more of them are now taking a little bit of our Gulf Coast paradise with them by cooking up some of our classic recipes themselves at home.

SHRIMP STOCK

If you are lucky enough to get shrimp with the heads on, rejoice. Shrimp heads make the stock even richer and more flavorful. When making stock, I fill an empty liter Coke bottle (label removed) with water and freeze it ahead of time. When the stock has cooled down a bit, about 30 minutes or so, I plunge the frozen bottle into the middle to help cool the stock from the inside out. This is also how I cool down a pot of gumbo before refrigerating it.

MAKES ABOUT 4 QUARTS

Heads, tails, and shells from about 5 pounds
peeled wild-caught Gulf shrimp

6 quarts water

2 lemons, sliced into ¼-inch rounds

2 bay leaves

3 onions, coarsely chopped

6 celery stalks, coarsely chopped

1 bunch green onions, coarsely chopped

Handful of fresh parsley with stems, washed thoroughly

1 teaspoon whole black peppercorns

1 whole garlic clove

White wine

1. At least several hours before you plan to make the stock, fill a clean, empty 1-liter soda bottle with water to about 2 inches from the top, seal, and freeze it.

2. Run cold water over the shrimp shells to rinse. Place all the ingredients in a medium stockpot. Bring to a boil over high heat.

3. Reduce the heat to medium, or until the stock is simmering. Skim off the foam that rises to the top. Cook for a couple of hours, skimming again about every 15 minutes.

4. Place the stockpot in an empty sink. Fill the sink with water and ice around the stockpot. Let the stock cool completely, uncovered. When the stock has cooled down a bit, about 30 minutes or so, put the frozen soda bottle in the middle to cool the stock from the inside out. Strain the stock, discarding the solids, transfer to storage containers, and refrigerate or freeze immediately.

NOTES ON HANDLING SEAFOOD

Seafood from the Gulf is an essential ingredient in the cuisine of the Deep Coastal South, reigning supreme with our colorful culture of recreation, bartering, and storytelling. For centuries, going fishing has been a mythic rite of passage for young boys and, more recently, girls as well. I admit, I do have a pink rod and reel and a tackle box. Coastal professionals and businesspeople are well familiar with getting paid on a Monday with an ice chest full of pretty shrimp or a plastic bag filled with freshly caught "spec" (speckled trout) fillets. And let's not forget that tall fish tales are frequently the topic of the conversation every day at the diamond-in-the-rough waterfront dive bars and restaurants deliciously scattered along the Gulf Coast like treasure on a treasure map.

That's all fun and games, but what do you do with the seafood when you get it home? Raw seafood requires special handling; it's highly perishable. Here are a few helpful hints for working with fresh seafood. It goes without saying that fresh off the boat is the best, and I'm passionate about using wild-caught seafood only. Sure, some of the imported seafood is a lot cheaper, but I prefer to support the local Gulf shrimpers and fishermen whose family seafood businesses have become threatened by imported products.

As far as freshness, unless you're blessed to have a local fishmonger in your area, you're probably purchasing your fish from the supermarket. Some of that product is flown in fresh, but most has been flash-frozen, which is perfectly acceptable to use with any of my recipes calling for shrimp or fish. A lot of it is flash-frozen right on the boats while they are still out in the middle of the Gulf. One of the wonderful things about seafood is that it does freeze beautifully. So if you are hankering for some blackened snapper, grilled mahi-mahi, or fried shrimp, don't be deterred because you can find only frozen product.

With all seafood, it is important to keep it iced until you use it. If I'm preparing for a big party and have purchased a large amount of seafood, I simply keep it in plastic bags iced down in a cooler on the kitchen floor or the back deck. I drain the cooler and re-ice when necessary; you don't want your seafood languishing in water for a long time. Even with the seafood that I buy at the market to prepare at home, I put the bag of seafood in a large bowl of ice and put it in the fridge. As the ice melts, I drain and re-ice until I'm ready to use it.

When it's time to cook, I completely rinse the seafood in a colander. Rinsing seafood every time you pull it out of the refrigerator is the best way to keep it fresh tasting and fresh smelling. If I'm using frozen product, the best way to defrost it is to place it in a colander in the sink and let cold water run over it until it has thawed. After rinsing, I pat the seafood dry with paper towels before cooking it.

For fresh crab, if you're not catching your own, you are most likely buying it in a tub labeled "Jumbo Lump," "Lump," or "Claw" crabmeat. It may also say on the tub that it is "hand-picked" and "wild-caught." This meat is from crab that has already been steamed, and the meat has been picked fresh from the crab. You do not have to cook the crabmeat. If fish is the seafood on the menu for the day, I will soak it in a little milk for twenty minutes or so, then pat it dry before I use it. I think the milk bath diffuses what some folks call the "fishy" taste and smell. All the fish recipes I've included are for the light, white-fleshed, warm-water fish we have around the Gulf Coast. You can substitute one light, white-fleshed fish for another based on the fish that's in season where you live or what you can find in your local market. A good rule of thumb is to always pan sauté or deep-fry delicate fish such as trout, redfish, and snapper, and save the grilling for firmer varieties such as mahi-mahi, tuna, and wahoo. So, fish lovers, be brave—dive in and bring a little beach food to your backyard! Get the blender roaring and have yourself a Gumbo Limbo good time!

CHAPTER 1

LIFE IS SWEET: EAT DESSERT FIRST

IT MAY seem strange to begin a cookbook with the desserts, but being a lifetime rule breaker and someone who actually reads magazines from the back cover to the front, this seems entirely the right place to start this book. And these days, when I now get up at the hour I used to come home, I feel more freedom to be quirky and untraditional without the guilt and regret that accompanied most of my wanton, rebellious youth. These days, I simply tend to choose my rebellions more wisely—like having dessert first.

It was my very staid and stoic mother, Loraine Peets Buffett, who showed me the beauty of having dessert first. In the last years of her life, "Peets," as she was called, became notorious in the local cafés for beginning a meal by ordering dessert first, only of course after the requisite Tanqueray and tonic had been delivered to her table. This practice began after she had a devastating stroke that left her right side paralyzed and her speech impaired. In genuine Southern matriarchal style, she miraculously recovered, determined to enjoy whatever life she had left, even though it would require even more grit than before.

True to family tradition, enjoying good food remained a focal point of her life; "going out" for lunch, especially to the original LuLu's restaurant, was the highlight of her day. As I was munching on a shrimp quesadilla appetizer during one such lunch, she was haphazardly digging into an order of Krispy Kreme bread pudding with a big soupspoon (after the stroke, she had to learn to feed herself and write using her left hand). Eventually she got the spoon to her mouth with great gusto, and with the signature sparkle in her cornflower-blue eyes, she giggled. "Mmmmmmm. Mmmm. You never know." They were all the words she could muster, but I knew exactly what she meant.

I can't even approach the subject of dessert without being flooded with warm, sweet memories of my mama. For her, "dessert first" became a way of choosing the good life in the everyday things. Life can be incredibly messy, frustrating, and challenging. We humans are so imperfect, and just when we think we might be getting something right, a hurricane swoops in and blows our plans right out of the water. It's inevitable that we'll be dealt some hard hands, so all we can do is play them as gracefully as we can.

On those days when the best I can do is put one foot in front of another, I now choose the sweet path. I *choose* to ignore grumpy people and mutter a simple "Bless their hearts!" as I choose to recognize the silver linings in my own challenges. I choose to believe that despite appearances to the contrary, I know life is working for me, not against me. I'm going to choose to fill that bone-dry glass of negativity and angst with gratitude for my blessings, family, friends, animals, and opportunities. I'm going to choose the sweet approach to life!

SOUTHERN POUND CAKE
WITH STRAWBERRIES

SERVES 12 TO 16

1½ cups (3 sticks) unsalted butter, at room temperature, plus more for the pan

3 cups all-purpose flour, plus more for the pan

3 cups plus 2 tablespoons sugar

3 cups sliced fresh strawberries

½ teaspoon baking powder

½ teaspoon sea salt

5 large eggs, at room temperature

1 cup whole milk

2½ teaspoons vanilla extract (or use almond or any other flavored extract)

Fresh whipped cream (recipe follows), for garnish

Fresh Whipped Cream

1 cup heavy cream

1 teaspoon vanilla extract or flavored liqueur

3 tablespoons sugar

GROWING UP SOUTHERN, pound cake was part of my sweet-tasting experience, as there was always some kind of pound cake sitting on my grandmother's counter. The traditional story about pound cake is that the ingredients consist of "a pounda" butter, sugar, eggs, and flour. This is my rendition of the classic dessert, and there are really no words to describe the sweet vanilla aroma and rich buttery taste of love infused in every bite.

1. Preheat the oven to 325°F. Butter and flour a 10-inch tube pan (a tube pan is preferred, but if you use a Bundt pan instead, you'll need to make sure to leave 1 inch of space at the top of the pan, so you may end up with a small amount of leftover batter).

2. Sprinkle 2 tablespoons of the sugar over the sliced strawberries. Cover and refrigerate until ready to serve the cake.

3. Whisk together the flour, baking powder, and salt and set aside.

4. In a large bowl, beat the butter on medium speed with an electric mixer until creamy. Add the remaining 3 cups sugar, ½ cup at a time, and beat until fluffy. Add the eggs one at a time, beating well after each addition.

5. Reduce the mixer speed to low and alternate adding the flour mixture and the milk, starting and finishing with the flour mixture. Add the vanilla and mix to incorporate.

6. Pour the batter into the prepared pan. Bake for 1 hour and 10 minutes, or until a toothpick inserted into the center comes out clean. Cool in the pan on a wire rack for 15 minutes, then turn the cake out onto the rack to cool completely. Serve each piece with a spoonful of the chilled strawberries and a dollop of fresh whipped cream.

FRESH WHIPPED CREAM

1. Place a medium metal bowl in the freezer to chill.

2. When ready to prepare the whipped cream, place the cream and vanilla in the chilled bowl. With an electric mixer, whip the cream on medium speed, gradually adding the sugar. The cream will begin to thicken.

3. Whip the cream until it begins to form stiff peaks. Be careful not to overwhip or the cream will separate.

SOUTHERN
TRES LECHES
(TRIPLE MILK CAKE)

**SERVES 10 TO 12
NORMAL FOLKS,
OR 6 HUSBANDS**

Nonstick baking spray

2 cups all-purpose flour

2 teaspoons baking powder

½ teaspoon baking soda

1 teaspoon ground cinnamon

Pinch of sea salt

¾ cup (1½ sticks) unsalted butter,
at room temperature

1¾ cups sugar plus 2 tablespoons

6 large eggs, at room temperature,
separated

1½ cups whole milk, at room
temperature

1 teaspoon almond or vanilla extract

Zest of 1 orange (about 2 teaspoons)

½ teaspoon cream of tartar

1 (14-ounce) can sweetened
condensed milk

1 (12-ounce) can evaporated milk

1 cup buttermilk

1 cup heavy cream

1 tablespoon Cointreau or other
orange-flavored liqueur

Fresh raspberries or mango slices,
for garnish

I'M A SUCKER for any creamy dessert, and when I discovered *tres leches* cake, I was a goner. There is a great Cuban place called Versailles in the Miami airport where I always duck in for a *café con leche* and a piece of *tres leches* cake when I have a long layover. Putting my Southern spin on it, I decided to try making this dessert with buttermilk and orange zest and, being true to my gene pool, a little Cointreau. I couldn't be happier with the end result: the buttermilk cuts the sweetness with a tanginess that is perfectly complemented by the essence of orange and the touch of spirits!

1. Preheat the oven to 350°F. Lightly grease a 9 x 13-inch baking pan with nonstick baking spray and place a medium metal bowl in the freezer.

2. In a medium bowl, sift together the flour, baking powder, baking soda, cinnamon, and salt. Set aside.

3. In a large bowl, cream the butter with an electric mixer, slowly adding 1½ cups of the sugar a little at a time. Beat for 3 minutes, stopping to scrape down the sides of the bowl several times. Slowly add the egg yolks one at a time and beat for 2 to 3 minutes more.

4. Alternate adding the flour mixture and the whole milk, beginning and ending with the flour mixture, creating a smooth batter. Add almond extract and orange zest and mix well.

5. In a medium bowl, using an electric mixer with clean beaters (see Note), beat the egg whites on high until they begin to froth. Add the cream of tartar, then gradually add ¼ cup of the remaining sugar. Beat until the egg whites hold stiff peaks.

6. Gently fold the beaten egg whites into the batter, a third at a time, until they are thoroughly mixed in—be careful not to overmix, as you want to keep your batter fluffy.

7. Pour the mixture into the prepared pan. Bake for 25 to 30 minutes, or until a toothpick inserted into the center of the cake comes out clean.

8. Remove the cake from the oven and let it cool completely on a wire rack. Don't worry if the cake deflates a little; it is supposed to have a dense texture. When completely cooled, invert the cake onto a serving platter (or serve it directly from the pan).

9. With a toothpick or fork, poke holes all over the entire cake, poking all the way to the bottom of the serving platter or pan.

10. Combine the condensed milk, evaporated milk, and buttermilk in a glass measuring cup with a spout. Slowly pour three-quarters of the milk mixture over the cake and let it soak in for 15 minutes. Reserve the remaining milk mixture as a garnish when plating the cake.

11. While the cake is soaking, pull the metal bowl out of the freezer. Pour the heavy cream into the bowl and beat with an electric mixer. When the cream reaches a frothy consistency, add the Cointreau and the remaining 2 tablespoons sugar. Whip until the cream is thick and holds stiff peaks. Be careful not to overwhip or the cream will separate.

12. Spread the whipped cream over the cake, cover with plastic wrap, and refrigerate for 1 hour.

13. When ready to serve, pour a little of the reserved milk mixture onto each dessert plate before placing a piece of cake on the plate; or, once the cake is plated, drizzle a little of the reserved milk mixture over each piece of cake. Garnish with fresh raspberries or mango slices. Because of the milk, do not leave the cake out of the refrigerator for more than 4 hours. In the refrigerator it will last 4 to 5 days, soaking up all that yummy goodness.

NOTE: *When beating the egg whites, make sure there is no grease or any other residue on the beaters or in the bowl or any bit of egg yolk in with the whites, as this will hinder the ability of the egg whites to foam and reach soft peaks.*

FRESH STRAWBERRY
— AND —
CHOCOLATE ANGEL FOOD
TRIFLE

SERVES 8 TO 10

Pudding

3½ cups whole milk

1 vanilla bean, or 2 teaspoons
vanilla extract

¾ cup sugar

2 large eggs, at room
temperature

1 egg yolk

3 tablespoons cornstarch

Pinch of sea salt

2 tablespoons unsalted butter

Trifle

4 cups leftover Chocolate Angel
Food Cake (page 9), torn into
bite-size pieces

3 cups fresh whipped cream
(see page 3)

3 cups fresh strawberries,
hulled and halved, plus a few whole
strawberries for garnish

THIS RECIPE IS another throwback to my beloved mother's cooking days. Never one to waste anything, she must have found a trifle recipe in one of her magazines and one day included it in her skimpy cooking repertoire when she had some leftover angel food cake. Even though she used instant everything, including pudding mix and ready-made whipped topping, it tasted sweet and creamy and delicious, and I still remember how pretty it looked in her trifle dish (which I still use). Reinventing this dish from my childhood, I found that using a chocolate angel food cake gave it that special little LuLuTwist, and when combined with fresh Baldwin County strawberries, vanilla pudding made from scratch, and some sweet whipped cream, it reminded me of Neapolitan ice cream and the barefoot summer days of my youth.

To make the pudding:

1. Pour 3 cups of the milk into a medium saucepan. Split the vanilla bean and scrape the seeds into the milk. (If you are not using a vanilla bean, wait to add the vanilla extract until later as directed.) Add the scraped bean pod and ½ cup of the sugar to the milk. Heat the milk mixture over medium heat, stirring continuously, until the sugar has dissolved. Cover, remove from the heat, and let sit for at least 15 minutes.

2. While the milk is heating, whisk together the eggs, the egg yolk, the remaining ¼ cup sugar, the remaining ½ cup milk, the cornstarch, and the salt.

3. Slowly pour about 1 cup of the warm milk through a strainer into the egg mixture, stirring continuously, to slowly temper the eggs and bring them to the same temperature as the warm milk, keeping them from curdling. Gradually pour the remaining milk through the strainer into the egg mixture.

4. Transfer the mixture to a clean large saucepan and cook the pudding over medium heat, stirring continuously, until it thickens. Remove from the heat. Add the butter and the vanilla extract (if you did not use a vanilla bean). Whisk until the mixture is smooth, then pour into a bowl or individual cups. Let cool for 10 minutes, then cover with plastic wrap, pressed directly against the surface of the pudding to prevent a skin from forming, and let cool to room temperature, then refrigerate for 4 hours or overnight.

To assemble the trifle:

5. In a clear bowl or trifle dish, start with a bottom layer of pudding, then add cake pieces so they can soak in the pudding. Follow with a layer of whipped cream, then a layer of berries. Repeat the process, ending with the whipped cream. Cover with plastic wrap and refrigerate for at least 4 hours. Garnish with whole strawberries before serving.

CHOCOLATE
ANGEL FOOD CAKE
WITH STRAWBERRIES AND CREAM

SERVES 12 TO 16

1½ cups sugar

¾ cup sifted cake flour

¼ cup unsweetened cocoa powder

1½ cups egg whites
(from 10 to 12 large eggs),
at room temperature

1 teaspoon cream of tartar

¼ teaspoon sea salt

2 teaspoons vanilla extract

¼ teaspoon almond extract

1 cup sliced fresh strawberries

1 cup fresh whipped cream
(see page 3)

1. Preheat the oven to 325°F.

2. In a small bowl, sift together ¾ cup of the sugar, the cake flour, and the cocoa powder. Set aside.

3. In a large bowl, beat the egg whites with an electric mixer until frothy (see Note, page 5). Add the cream of tartar and salt. With the mixer at high speed, very slowly add the remaining ¾ cup sugar a couple of tablespoons at a time. Beat the egg whites until soft peaks form.

4. Add the vanilla and almond extracts and beat gently for a few seconds to evenly distribute.

5. In small amounts, sift the flour mixture over the egg whites and gently fold in by hand until completely combined, but still maintaining a very light consistency. Be very careful not to overmix.

6. Spoon the batter into an ungreased 10-inch tube pan. (I use a two-piece, detachable-bottom tube pan for best results. If you use a standard Bundt pan, be sure to leave at least 1 inch of space at the top of the pan or the batter may overflow.) Smooth the top with a spatula and pat gently to pop any air bubbles hiding beneath the surface.

7. Bake for 50 to 55 minutes, or until the top springs back when lightly pressed.

8. Remove from the oven and let it cool completely on a wire rack, up to overnight. You can also place the tube pan on the neck of an empty wine bottle so that air can get under the cake, helping it cool more quickly.

9. When you are ready to serve, gently run a thin knife around the sides of the pan and then around the bottom to release the cake. Top each piece with fresh strawberries and garnish with a dollop of fresh whipped cream.

Pete Buffett's

Lazy "V" Cake   375° - 20-25 min
            "Spray"   Jelly Roll Pan

1 cup water   ⎤ 1 qt Saucepan
2 Sticks Butter   ⎦ bring to boil
4 Tablespoon Cocoa

                                1½ tsp Cinnamon

2 C sugar
2 C Plain Flour
Put dry ingredients in large mixing
bowl, stir to mix, add hot mixture
to this, beating to mix,

2 eggs   ⎤ mix + add
½ C Buttermilk ⎦ to above mixture
1 tea Vanilla
Pour into greased Jellyroll pan (9 X 15) (10 X 15)
bake 375° - 20-25 min -

make icing 5 min before cake is
finished baking -

1 stick butter   ⎤ in above
6 Tablespoon milk or Cream ⎦ Saucepan
4 Tab Cocoa   bring to boil
Add in small mixing bowl - (same
beaters)
1 box powdered sugar + pour
hot mixture - Mix Well - add 1 Tea
Vanilla + 1-2 Cups finely chopped nuts
Pour over hot Cake - Enjoy -
★ I freeze this in pan. Then remove
from freezer + cut in Pieces. Wrap in
saran + refreeze.

LAZY V CHOCOLATE FUDGE CAKE

MAKES ONE 9 X 15-INCH SHEET CAKE

Cake

Nonstick baking spray

1 cup (2 sticks) unsalted butter

¼ cup unsweetened cocoa powder

1 cup water

2 cups sugar

2 cups all-purpose flour

1½ teaspoons ground cinnamon

¼ teaspoon sea salt

2 large eggs, at room temperature

½ cup buttermilk

1 teaspoon vanilla extract

Frosting

½ cup (1 stick) unsalted butter

6 tablespoons heavy cream

¼ cup unsweetened cocoa powder

3 cups confectioners' sugar, sifted

1 teaspoon vanilla extract

1 cup pecan pieces

LIKE ME, MY MOTHER, PEETS, had a mighty respectable sweet tooth. Though she wasn't crazy about cooking, she could make a pretty good dessert when inspired. After she and my dad retired, they hosted pier parties every weekend with tons of fabulous food and frozen drinks while guests swam, sunned, and gossiped. It was during that period that I remember Mama started making this cake. I never knew the name of it; I just recalled how lusciously sweet and chocolaty rich it was. It would freeze beautifully, and she always had some available for any spontaneous gathering or pieces wrapped in plastic for the kids.

Fast-forward thirty years: Long gone are those memorable Buffett pier parties, and I'm sitting in my office at LuLu's going through mail when I find an envelope that some folks from the Carolinas had left for me at my restaurant. I open what I think is a letter, and I gasp as I gaze at my mother's undeniably perfect penmanship in a recipe for the long-forgotten chocolate sheet cake titled "Peets Buffett's Lazy V Cake." I was caught between tears and giggles—transported back to the days when we would solve the problems of the world over coffee, and completely amused by the name of the cake, because I had never heard her refer to it that way.

The methods and ingredients she used are unconventional and not at all the way I might approach this type of cake, but it worked. Is it any surprise that the daughter would do it differently than her mother? And yet, I am finding lately that there are so many things I do as she did—I seem to become more and more like her. I'd give a million dollars to have another cup of coffee with her. To this day, there doesn't seem to be any rhyme or reason why this cake is called Lazy V, and that's just one of many things I wish I could ask her.

To make the cake:

1. Preheat the oven to 375°F. Grease a 9 x 15-inch baking pan with nonstick baking spray.

2. Combine the butter, cocoa powder, and water in a medium saucepan and heat over medium heat, stirring continuously, until the butter has melted and the ingredients are well combined. Remove from the heat.

CONT.

3. In a large bowl, sift together the sugar, flour, cinnamon, and salt.

4. Add the hot butter mixture to the dry ingredients and beat until smooth.

5. In a small bowl, beat the eggs, buttermilk, and vanilla. Add a little of the warm chocolate batter to the egg mixture to temper the eggs. Mix until well combined.

6. Slowly add the egg mixture to the chocolate batter and beat until smooth.

7. Pour the batter into the prepared baking pan. Bake for 20 to 25 minutes, or until a toothpick inserted into the center of the cake comes out clean.

8. Frost the cake while it's still hot.

To make the frosting:

9. In a medium saucepan, combine the butter, cream, and cocoa powder and heat over medium heat, stirring continuously, until the butter has melted and the ingredients are well combined. Remove from the heat.

10. Add the confectioners' sugar and beat until smooth.

11. Stir in the vanilla and pecans.

12. Pour the hot frosting over the hot cake and spread it to the edges of the cake.

NOTE: *You can actually freeze this cake in the pan. It will last in the refrigerator for 1 to 2 weeks or in the freezer for up to 2 months.*

BUTTERMILK ORANGE CHESS PIE

SERVES 6 TO 8

All-purpose flour, for dusting

Dough for 1 piecrust (recipe follows)
or 1 store-bought piecrust

1½ cups sugar

3 tablespoons yellow cornmeal

½ teaspoon sea salt

4 large eggs, at room temperature

⅓ cup buttermilk

1½ teaspoons vanilla extract

1¼ teaspoons orange zest

2 tablespoons orange juice

2 tablespoons unsalted butter, melted

Fresh whipped cream
(see page 3)

Piecrust

2½ cups all-purpose flour

1 tablespoon sugar

¾ teaspoon sea salt

1 cup (2 sticks) unsalted butter,
cut into ¼-inch pieces and placed
in freezer

8 tablespoons ice water

1. Preheat the oven to 325°F.

2. Lightly dust your work surface with flour. Roll out the pie dough, always working from the center, into a round to fit a 9-inch pie pan. Fold the edges of the dough over the pan and crimp with your fingers.

3. In a large bowl, whisk together the sugar, cornmeal, and salt.

4. In a medium bowl, stir together the eggs, buttermilk, vanilla, orange zest, and orange juice until combined.

5. Add the egg mixture to the sugar mixture and stir until well combined. Stir in the melted butter. Pour the mixture into the piecrust.

6. Bake for 40 to 50 minutes, or until the center of the pie is set. Let cool completely on a wire rack. Serve at room temperature or cover and refrigerate. To serve, garnish with a dollop of fresh whipped cream.

——— PIECRUST ———
MAKES ENOUGH FOR 1 (9-INCH)
DEEP-DISH DOUBLE-CRUST PIE

1. In a food processor, combine the flour, sugar, and salt and pulse for a few seconds to distribute the sugar and salt.

2. Add the butter chunks and pulse until a coarse meal forms.

3. Gradually blend in enough ice water to form moist clumps (you may not need all the ice water).

4. Gather the dough into a ball, then divide it in half. Form each half into a ball, then flatten each into a disk. Wrap each disk in plastic. Chill for at least 2 hours or overnight in the refrigerator before rolling out. You can also freeze the dough and use it later.

LUCY B. GOODE'S
BLUEBERRY ALMOND BREAD PUDDING

SERVES 8

Pudding

1½ teaspoons unsalted butter

7 cups cubed stale bread of your choice (I like to use brioche or French bread, and if I'm feeling terribly decadent and they are available, I use almond croissants)

¾ cup fresh blueberries

¼ cup slivered or sliced unsalted almonds

3 large eggs, at room temperature

3 cups whole milk

½ cup granulated sugar

1 teaspoon vanilla extract

1 teaspoon ground cinnamon

Topping

¼ cup all-purpose flour

¼ cup packed brown sugar

4 tablespoons (½ stick) cold unsalted butter, chopped into cubes

¼ cup finely chopped salted almonds

Garnish

½ cup Lucy's Favorite Salted Caramel Sauce (page 29)

Fresh whipped cream (see page 3)

Fresh blueberries

To make the pudding:

1. Preheat the oven to 350°F. Coat a 9-inch square baking pan with the butter.

2. Place a third of the bread cubes in a single layer in the bottom of the prepared baking pan. Add half the blueberries and half the almonds. Top with another third of the bread cubes. Add the remaining blueberries and almonds. Top with the remaining bread cubes.

3. In a medium bowl, whisk together the eggs, milk, granulated sugar, vanilla, and cinnamon. Pour the milk mixture over the bread and blueberry mixture in the pan, making sure the bread is completely covered by the milk mixture.

To make the topping:

4. In a medium bowl, mix together the flour and brown sugar. Cut the butter into the flour and brown sugar with a pastry blender or fork until coarse crumbs form.

5. Stir in the almonds. Sprinkle the topping evenly over the bread pudding.

6. Bake for 40 minutes, or until the bread pudding is golden brown and cooked through.

7. Remove from the oven and let cool for at least 30 minutes. Drizzle the salted caramel sauce over the top and serve with fresh whipped cream and blueberries.

NOTE: *The bread pudding can be made a day in advance and stored, covered, in the refrigerator. Just reheat the pudding and add the salted caramel sauce, fresh whipped cream, and fresh blueberries before serving.*

CHOCOLATE BROWNIE FLAN

SERVES 8

Caramel

1 cup sugar

Fudgy Brownies

4 tablespoons (½ stick) unsalted butter, plus more for the pan

¼ cup all-purpose flour, plus more for the pan

4 ounces semisweet chocolate, chopped

½ cup sugar

Pinch of sea salt

1 teaspoon vanilla extract

1 large egg, at room temperature, beaten

Vanilla Custard

3 large eggs

5 egg yolks

1 (12-ounce) can evaporated milk

1 (14-ounce) can sweetened condensed milk

1 cup whole milk

2 tablespoons vanilla extract

Pinch of sea salt

Fresh raspberries and blueberries or orange slices, for garnish

ONE OF MY favorite places on the planet is Louie's Backyard, the famous waterfront restaurant in Key West, Florida. My children grew up eating maraschino cherries at the Afterdeck bar there. They serve the most amazing crème brûlée with a brownie hidden in the middle. This is my homage to that dessert and to that wonderful place, but I drifted toward a Cuban influence with a traditional flan and caramel.

This recipe actually consists of three components—caramel sauce, brownie, and custard—combined in a custard cup or ramekin and baked. It may seem complicated, but don't be deterred: each component is simple, and the result is well worth it.

To make the caramel sauce:

1. In a small heavy saucepan, heat the sugar over medium-high heat, whisking continuously until the sugar is completely melted and begins turning brown. Reduce the heat to medium-low and cook until the sugar has turned golden brown, being careful not to overcook and scorch the caramel.

2. Remove the pan from the heat and quickly divide the caramel among eight custard cups or ramekins, coating the bottom of each (tilt the cups, if necessary, to coat the bottoms). Be careful not to touch the caramel. This stuff can burn like lava! Let the caramel cool; it will solidify like hard candy.

To make the brownies:

3. Preheat the oven to 350°F. Butter and flour an 8-inch square brownie pan.

4. In a small saucepan, melt the butter and chocolate together over low heat, stirring until completely melted and smooth. Remove the pan from the heat and transfer the chocolate mixture to a large bowl to cool.

5. Whisk the sugar, salt, vanilla, and egg into the chocolate mixture until well combined. Slowly add the flour and stir until just blended.

6. Pour the batter into the prepared pan and bake for 15 to 20 minutes, or until the brownies are just barely done and still a little soft to the touch. (This recipe will make very thin brownies because we are looking to use only a little bit in the middle of the custard.)

LIFE IS SWEET: EAT DESSERT FIRST

CONT.

7. Let the brownies cool completely. Cut into small squares that will fit into the custard cups or ramekins. You can make the brownies ahead of time and wrap them in plastic until ready to use.

To make the custard:

8. In a medium bowl, whisk together the eggs and egg yolks.

9. Whisk in the evaporated milk, condensed milk, whole milk, vanilla, and salt until well combined.

To assemble:

10. Place a brownie in each of the eight custard cups on top of the hardened caramel.

11. Pour the custard over the brownies in each cup. Place the cups in a large baking pan and fill the pan with warm water to come about two-thirds up the sides of the custard cups. Carefully place the pan in the oven so as not to spill the water into the custard.

12. Bake for 45 minutes at 350°F, or until the custard is set. Carefully remove the baking pan from the oven and then transfer the cups from the pan to a wire rack to cool. When the flan is completely cool, refrigerate for at least 4 hours or overnight.

13. You can serve the flan in the cups or you can unmold each flan by running a thin knife around the edge of the custard cup, placing a dessert plate on top of the cup, and flipping it over. Tap the cup and the custard should slide out with the caramel sauce oozing over the flan. Garnish with fresh raspberries, blueberries, or orange slices.

STRAWBERRIES-SOUR CREAM-BROWN SUGAR

SERVES 6 TO 8

1 pound fresh whole strawberries

1 carton sour cream

1 box brown sugar

WHEN I FIRST moved to Key West, my neighbors Karen and Scott Beauprie kindly invited me to go with them to an Easter potluck at Fort Zach Beach, part of an exquisite Florida state park where the locals often gather. John Correa, who is the chef and owner of the popular Café Solé, was cooking a leg of lamb on one of the park-provided grills. It was a postcard-perfect day, and I met lots of new folks who brought beautiful dishes to complement Chef's perfect lamb entrée. Being a consummate sugar lover, after lunch, I was in search of dessert but there didn't seem to be any until John pulled out a large carton of beautiful strawberries, a huge commercial container of sour cream, and a big bag of brown sugar. He proceeded to pour the strawberries into a large yellow plastic bowl, open the container of sour cream, pour the brown sugar on a paper plate, and then plop it all in the middle of one of the old weathered park picnic tables.

I watched a free-for-all rush to the table by the kids and adults alike; they would take a whole strawberry, dip it into the sour cream, dredge it through the brown sugar, and then pop it into their mouths. I was amazed and immediately enamored, especially when I tried one for myself. It tasted as incredible as any time-intensive fancy French dessert. If a classically trained and celebrated chef could serve this dish at Easter, I figured I could share it here. Great for kids, picnics, boat-nics, and for any family supper, this is one of my go-to quick-and-easy desserts for any occasion.

1. Wash and hull the strawberries. Dry them well and place in a bowl.

2. Place the sour cream in a bowl and the brown sugar in another bowl.

3. To serve, place the three bowls on the table and let your guests dig in. If you're not a fan of free-for-alls, you can put some of all three on individual plates.

FLOATING ISLAND

SERVES 8

Crème Anglaise

4 cups whole milk

¾ cup sugar

1 vanilla bean, split

6 egg yolks, at room temperature

Meringues

6 egg whites, at room temperature

¼ teaspoon cream of tartar

Pinch of sea salt

½ cup sugar

Caramel

1 cup sugar

Raspberries, for garnish (optional)

MY MAMA INTRODUCED me to this fancy dessert on an overnight trip to New Orleans when I was a child. Once I became a foodie and a cook, I found it again in the first cookbook by my culinary hero, Julia Child. Even though this dessert has three steps, each step has at the most only four ingredients. It may look complicated, but in truth it's quite simple if you prep the ingredients ahead of time and have all your equipment ready. Basically it consists of a crème anglaise, which is a fancy French name for custard cream, topped with a cloud-shaped meringue and drizzled with caramelized sugar. So yummy and sure to impress!

To make the crème anglaise:

1. In a medium saucepan, combine the milk and sugar. Split the vanilla bean lengthwise, scrape the seeds into the saucepan, and add the pod as well. Cook the milk mixture over medium heat for about 15 minutes, or until it begins to simmer but not boil. Remove from the heat, cover, and steep for 15 minutes.

2. In a medium metal bowl, whisk the egg yolks.

3. Slowly pour the warm milk mixture through a strainer into the egg yolks, whisking continuously, to temper the eggs.

4. Transfer the mixture to a clean saucepan and cook over low heat, stirring continuously, until it thickens and coats the back of a wooden spoon, but not letting it boil. (I advise using a candy thermometer and cooking the custard until it reaches 170°F.)

5. Remove the pan from the heat and strain the custard once again into a medium metal bowl. Place the bowl inside a larger bowl filled with ice to help cool the custard down. Stir occasionally until the custard is cool, then refrigerate.

To make the meringues:

6. Preheat the oven to 250°F. Line a baking sheet with parchment paper.

7. In a large metal bowl, beat the egg whites with an electric mixer until foamy. Add the cream of tartar and salt. Add the sugar 1 tablespoon at a time until the egg whites are shiny and form stiff peaks.

CONT.

8. Spoon the meringue into 8 cloud-shaped mounds on the prepared baking sheet and bake for 30 to 35 minutes. The meringues should feel a little firm but still springy and should not be browned.

9. Remove the meringues from the oven and let them cool completely.

To make the caramel:

10. In a small heavy saucepan, heat the sugar over medium-high heat, whisking continuously until the sugar is completely melted and begins turning brown. Reduce the heat to medium-low and cook until the sugar has turned golden brown, being careful not to overcook and scorch the caramel. Remove from the heat, as the caramel will continue to cook in the pan. Be careful not to touch the caramel. This stuff can burn like lava!

To serve:

11. Pour the crème anglaise into eight individual shallow bowls or dessert plates. Place 1 meringue cloud on top of the crème anglaise in each bowl. Dip a fork into the caramel and drizzle it back and forth over each meringue. If the sauce begins to thicken, simply reheat it over low heat until it returns to drizzling consistency. Garnish with fresh raspberries, if desired.

NOTE: *The easiest way to do this is to first prepare the crème anglaise, then prepare the meringues, and then assemble those two components in bowls before starting to make the caramel. Keep the bowls close to the stovetop, near the caramel, so that it is easy to immediately drizzle the caramel over the meringues before the caramel has a chance to harden.*

SALTED BUTTERSCOTCH BLONDIES

MAKES 9 TO 12 BARS

Bars

Nonstick baking spray

1½ cups all-purpose flour

1 teaspoon baking powder

1 teaspoon sea salt

1¼ cups packed brown sugar

½ cup (1 stick) unsalted butter,
at room temperature

1½ teaspoons vanilla extract

2 large eggs, at room temperature

1 cup butterscotch chips

¾ cup chopped pecans

Icing (optional, but encouraged)

5 tablespoons unsalted butter

½ cup packed brown sugar

¼ teaspoon sea salt

3 tablespoons whole milk

1½ cups confectioners' sugar

⅛ teaspoon butterscotch flavoring
(optional, but yum)

Medium-coarse sea salt,
for sprinkling

To make the bars:

1. Preheat the oven to 350°F. Lightly grease a 9-inch square baking pan with nonstick baking spray.

2. In a medium bowl, combine the flour, baking powder, and salt and set aside.

3. In a large bowl, beat the brown sugar, butter, and vanilla with an electric mixer on medium speed until creamy. Add the eggs one at a time and beat until smooth.

4. Gradually add the flour mixture, stirring by hand until just barely combined. Gently fold in the butterscotch chips.

5. Spread the batter into the greased pan. If you are not planning to use icing, go ahead and sprinkle the pecans on top of the batter. If you are using icing, wait to sprinkle the pecans on top of the icing after baking.

6. Bake for 30 to 35 minutes, or until a toothpick inserted into the center comes out clean. Remove from the oven and let cool completely before icing.

To make the icing:

7. In a small saucepan, combine the butter, brown sugar, salt, and milk and bring to a simmer over medium-low heat. Remove from the heat.

8. Add the confectioners' sugar and mix until smooth. Stir in the butterscotch flavoring (if using). Immediately spread or drizzle the icing on top of the uncut cooled bars still in the pan. Sprinkle with the chopped pecans and medium-coarse sea salt to taste and cut into bars to serve.

STRAWBERRY COBBLER

SERVES 8 TO 10

Crust

3¾ cups all-purpose flour

2 tablespoons sugar

1¼ teaspoons sea salt

1½ cups (3 sticks) unsalted butter, cut into ¼-inch chunks and placed in the freezer

12 tablespoons ice water

Nonstick baking spray

Filling

8 cups fresh strawberries, hulled and halved

3 cups sugar

½ cup all-purpose flour

1 teaspoon sea salt

1 tablespoon fresh lemon juice

2 tablespoons unsalted butter

1 large egg

¼ cup water

1 tablespoon sugar

2 tablespoons unsalted butter, melted, for brushing

Lemon Buttermilk Sorbet (page 27), for serving

I CREATED THIS nontraditional cobbler to celebrate the absolute lusciousness of the Louisiana strawberry. Like its cousin the Creole tomato, the Louisiana strawberry is big and full of sweet juice. Strawberries in general are going to make more juice in a filling than blueberries or peaches. That being the case, we found that using a double crust is key to finding the right balance between filling and crust. And what we do a little differently to achieve that optimum cobbler is to use the prebaked crust in the middle of the cobbler instead of on the bottom. Any sweet strawberry will work for this recipe, but if you ever find yourself in New Orleans walking along the French Market in March or April, you won't be able to stop yourself from plucking a strawberry from a basket and popping it into your mouth. The delight is indescribable.

To make the crust:

1. Combine the flour, sugar, and salt in a food processor and pulse a couple of times to thoroughly combine.

2. Add the cold butter and pulse until a coarse meal forms.

3. Add 6 tablespoons of the ice water and pulse three or four times. Add the remaining 6 tablespoons ice water and pulse until the dough begins to form a ball and pulls away from the sides of the bowl.

4. Remove the dough from the bowl and divide it in half. Form each half into a ball, then flatten it into a disk. Wrap each disk in plastic. Chill for at least 2 hours or overnight in the refrigerator before using.

5. Preheat the oven to 375°F. Grease two 9 x 13-inch baking pans with nonstick baking spray.

6. On a floured surface, roll out one chilled dough disk into a roughly 9 x 13-inch rectangle about ⅛ inch thick. Trim the dough to fit inside the prepared baking pan; the dough should cover the bottom of the pan only, not go up the sides of the pan.

7. Use a fork to prick the dough all over, then bake for about 10 minutes, or until the edges are just turning brown. Remove the crust from the oven and set aside to cool.

CONT.

For the filling:

8. While the crust is baking, in a large heavy saucepan, combine the strawberries, 3 cups of the sugar, the flour, and the salt. Stir and let the mixture sit until the strawberries start releasing their juices, creating a syrup. Add the lemon juice and mix well.

9. Cook the strawberry mixture over low to medium heat until it begins to thicken, 15 to 20 minutes. Remove from the heat, stir in the butter, and let the mixture cool completely.

To assemble:

10. Spread half the strawberry mixture into the second prepared pan. Turn the prebaked crust out of the first pan and place it over the strawberry layer. Evenly spread the remaining strawberry mixture over the crust.

11. Roll out the second disk of dough as directed in step 7 and place it over the strawberry mixture. Prick the dough with a fork or cut small slits in it to allow steam to escape.

12. Whisk together the egg and water. Brush the dough with the egg wash and sprinkle the remaining 1 tablespoon sugar over the top.

13. Bake for 30 to 35 minutes, or until the crust is golden brown. Remove the cobbler from the oven. Brush the melted butter over the top of the baked cobbler. Let cool to slightly warm or room temperature and serve with my lemon buttermilk sorbet.

LEMON BUTTERMILK SORBET

MAKES 1½ QUARTS

Zest of 2 lemons

½ cup fresh lemon juice

2 cups sugar

½ cup water

4 cups buttermilk

½ teaspoon vanilla extract

Fresh raspberries,
for garnish

1. In a small saucepan, combine the lemon zest, lemon juice, sugar, and water. Heat over medium heat, stirring, just until the sugar has melted. Remove from the heat and let cool.

2. In a large bowl, whisk together the cooled lemon juice mixture, buttermilk, and vanilla until combined. Cover and refrigerate for at least 4 hours or overnight to chill.

3. Process the mixture in a 2-quart old-fashioned or electric ice cream maker according to manufacturer's instructions.

4. Transfer the sorbet to an airtight container with a lid and freeze to the desired firmness.

5. Serve bowls of sorbet garnished with fresh raspberries or serve alongside Strawberry Cobbler (page 25).

LUCY'S FAVORITE
SALTED CARAMEL SAUCE
— AND —
EASY-PEASY CHOCOLATE SAUCE

THERE IS NOTHING easier and perhaps more enjoyed than making an ice cream sundae for the grandchildren, guests, and, um, I'll admit it, to take to bed for my right-before-the-sandman snack. I keep these two dessert sauces in my fridge at all times. The caramel sauce is born from my love of sweet and salty. The chocolate sauce is a treasured recipe of my friend Dilana Norman. I think she has been reluctant to share her secret because when she serves it, folks think she has been working for hours in the kitchen, but the surprise is that it almost cooks itself.

MAKES 2 CUPS

2 cups sugar

¾ cup (1½ sticks) unsalted butter, chopped into pieces, at room temperature

1 cup heavy cream, at room temperature

2 teaspoons sea salt

— LUCY'S FAVORITE SALTED CARAMEL SAUCE —

1. In a small saucepan, melt the sugar over medium-high heat, whisking continuously. Keep a close eye on the sugar as it melts, swirling the pan occasionally.

2. When the sugar has completely melted and turned an amber color, carefully add the butter a few pieces at a time, whisking continuously. It will bubble up, but just keep whisking until all the butter has melted.

3. Remove the pan from the heat and while whisking vigorously, slowly pour in the cream. The caramel is going to bubble aggressively again, so be careful but stay firm with it.

4. Whisk until all the cream is combined and then whisk in the salt.

5. Set the sauce aside to cool for 15 minutes, then pour it into a glass jar to cool completely.

6. You can refrigerate the sauce for up to 2 weeks, but you will have to warm it before serving.

½ cup (1 stick) unsalted butter

⅔ cup evaporated milk, plus
more if needed to thin

2¼ cups confectioners' sugar

1 (4-ounce) semisweet or bittersweet
chocolate bar

EASY-PEASY CHOCOLATE SAUCE

1. Place all the ingredients in the top of a double boiler.

2. Slowly cook the sauce over medium heat for a full 30 minutes—
do not stir the sauce.

3. Remove the sauce from the heat and whisk well to blend until smooth.
If the sauce needs to be thinned, use evaporated milk—do not add water.

4. Serve warm. You can refrigerate the sauce for up to 2 weeks, but you will
have to warm it in the microwave before serving.

CHAPTER 2

STARTERS AND SNACKS

SOUTHERN hospitality is a magical thing, and of course food plays an essential role in its power. Entertaining is in our DNA, but sometimes when the doorbell rings and you're not quite ready to receive company, even a Southern social butterfly can get that sinking oh-no feeling. And when you are expecting someone to stop by to say hello, the anticipation can occasionally be an anxious rather than excited feeling. Yet with a little pimento cheese and a glass of iced tea (or something stronger, when necessary), it's amazing how quickly any negative feelings fade into the background. There's simply something sweet and human about fixing a drink for someone or spreading a little cheese on a cracker and passing it to another person. It creates an instant connection, a heart token, a peace offering, and a sense of welcome. It's not a fix-all for the world's problems, but for me it's a starting point of love.

In my refrigerator I tend to keep a passel of homemade goodies for just such occasions, such as garlic herb cheese spread or boiled shrimp I can put out with some remoulade. One of the easiest, tastiest little bites I keep on hand are roasted fresh-crop pecans from the B & B Pecan Co., right around the corner from me in Fairhope, Alabama. Pecan orchards line the roads I drive every day between home and LuLu's. In fact, that's how we tell when spring has finally sprung. Once you start seeing the tiniest hint of a green leaf on the bare gray pecan branches, you know the last frost has finally come and gone.

When I host a dinner party, I'm running behind schedule more times than not—luckily, guests don't want to sit down right away anyway. Everyone usually ends up in the kitchen while I'm still whirling around getting everything coordinated. With my attention caught between working in the kitchen and engaging with my guests, I'll put out a little shrimp dip on the counter or something else that complements the flavors of the main dish and whets the appetite, my own version of a chef's amuse-bouche, which literally translates to "entertains the mouth." What better way to start a dinner party than with a happy mouth? What better way to say "I'm so glad you're here!" than by giving your guests some good food that makes them smile? What better magic potion to transform yourself from frazzled to fabulous than having your guests gathered around you in the kitchen *ooh*ing and *aah*ing over a fantastic appetizer you made just for them?

ROSEMARY
ROASTED
PECANS

MAKES 4 CUPS

4 tablespoons (½ stick) unsalted butter

1 teaspoon sea salt

½ teaspoon sugar

⅛ teaspoon cayenne pepper

1 pound fresh-crop pecan halves

1 tablespoon finely chopped fresh rosemary

I KNOW PECANS because I used to run a Nut House! No joke—I was the manager of a pecan candy concession at the 1984 Louisiana World Exposition in New Orleans, and the pecans came from right down the road from my house in Alabama. It's a fall ritual to "pick up" pecans from trees that are in my neighbor's yard and then take an afternoon to crack them, rocking on the porch of my barn and plucking out the nutmeat in large pieces, or what they call "mammoth halves." Roasted pecans are a seasonal tradition and an essential part of the Southern pantry. I give them for Christmas presents, especially to those friends and family who have everything. You can flavor them with any savory spice and herb or any sweet fruit essence, and they make a perfect coffee-table snack. In this recipe, I use fresh rosemary from my garden. You can also use cashews and walnuts instead of or along with the pecans.

1. Preheat the oven to 325°F.

2. In a large heavy skillet (10 to 12 inches), combine the butter, salt, sugar, and cayenne and heat over medium-low heat, stirring occasionally, until the butter has melted.

3. Add the pecan halves and stir well until all the pecans are coated. Stir or shake the skillet a few times and cook until the pecans are heated through, 3 to 4 minutes.

4. Stir in the rosemary, making sure it is well distributed, then transfer the pecans to a baking sheet, spreading them in a single layer.

5. Bake for 10 minutes, or until the nuts are a beautiful golden brown. Remove from the oven and let cool completely. Store in an airtight container.

2 pounds large wild-caught Gulf shrimp, boiled (see page 39)

3 celery stalks, with leaves, coarsely chopped

4 green onions, coarsely chopped

½ small sweet onion, coarsely chopped

4 garlic cloves

Leaves from 4 large sprigs fresh tarragon

¼ cup fresh lemon juice

¼ cup red wine vinegar

1 teaspoon hot sauce

1 tablespoon prepared or freshly grated horseradish

½ cup Creole or Dijon mustard

1 tablespoon tomato paste

½ teaspoon sea salt

½ teaspoon LuLu's Crazy Creola Seasoning (page xxviii) or other Creole seasoning

¼ teaspoon white pepper

1 teaspoon sugar

1 tablespoon paprika

Small handful of fresh parsley with stems (about 1 cup)

¼ cup vegetable oil

1 head red- or green-leaf lettuce, rinsed, dried, and coarsely torn or chopped

2 hard-boiled eggs, peeled and quartered (optional)

1 cup halved cherry tomatoes (optional)

CLASSIC
SHRIMP
REMOULADE

THIS IS MY take on a New Orleans classic dish using a red remoulade sauce. Over the years, there have been many renditions of this traditional cold dressing for seafood, many using a mayonnaise base. But my version, inspired by *The New Orleans Cookbook* by Rima and Richard Collin, is an emulsion of olive oil and Creole mustard with fresh herbs and spices, including paprika, which gives it its reddish color. With this recipe, I'm a purist. It may seem long and arduous, but in fact, it's just a lot of ingredients tossed into a food processor. It is truly easy if you gather all your ingredients at once.

1. Peel and refrigerate the cooked shrimp until ready to use.

2. In a food processor, combine the celery, green onion, sweet onion, garlic, tarragon, lemon juice, vinegar, hot sauce, horseradish, mustard, tomato paste, salt, Creole seasoning, white pepper, sugar, paprika, and all but 2 tablespoons of the parsley. Pulse several times to thoroughly combine.

3. With the food processor running, gradually add the vegetable oil and process until the mixture has the consistency of a sauce, about 1 minute.

4. Arrange the lettuce on top of a serving platter or divide it among individual salad plates. Add the shrimp and spoon the sauce over the shrimp.

5. Garnish with the remaining parsley and top with the egg wedges and tomato halves, if desired.

EASY
BOILED SHRIMP

**MAKES 2 POUNDS
SHRIMP**

---

3 tablespoons sea salt

2 bay leaves

¼ teaspoon liquid crab boil,
or 2 tablespoons LuLu's Crazy
Creola Seasoning (page xxviii) or
other Creole seasoning

1 lemon, sliced

8 cups water

2 pounds large wild-caught
Gulf shrimp in the shell

1. Combine the salt, bay leaves, crab boil, lemon slices, and water in a medium stockpot and bring to a boil over high heat.

2. Add the shrimp and cook for 3 to 5 minutes. Remove from the heat and drain. Cover the shrimp with ice. When the shrimp are cool to the touch, drain; discard the ice, lemon, and bay leaves. Place the shrimp in an airtight container and refrigerate until ready to use.

SPICY
SHRIMP CEVICHE

SERVES 8

2 pounds poached wild-caught
Gulf shrimp (recipe follows)

⅓ cup finely chopped red onion

½ cup finely chopped celery

1 cup quartered cherry tomatoes

¾ cup peeled, seeded, and
chopped cucumber

1 teaspoon finely chopped
seeded jalapeño

2 teaspoons finely chopped garlic

2 teaspoons finely chopped
fresh ginger

⅓ cup finely chopped fresh cilantro,
plus ¼ cup for serving, if desired

Juice of 5 limes (about 1 cup)

Juice of 2 lemons (about ½ cup)

Juice of 1 orange (about ½ cup)

2 tablespoons extra-virgin olive oil

½ teaspoon sea salt

¼ teaspoon white pepper

½ teaspoon sugar

1 avocado, pitted, peeled, and
sliced (optional)

2 limes, quartered (optional)

1. Chop the shrimp into thirds or bite-size pieces, or leave them whole if you prefer, and place in a large bowl.

2. Add the red onion, celery, tomatoes, cucumber, jalapeño, garlic, ginger, cilantro, lime juice, lemon juice, orange juice, olive oil, salt, white pepper, and sugar and stir well.

3. Transfer to an airtight container and refrigerate overnight. While the mixture marinates, occasionally turn the container to evenly coat the shrimp in the liquid.

4. Transfer the shrimp and liquid to a glass bowl to serve or divide among eight martini glasses. If desired, garnish with avocado, cilantro, and lime.

POACHED
SHRIMP

MAKES 2 POUNDS SHRIMP

2¼ pounds large wild-caught headless Gulf shrimp in the shell

8 cups water

½ cup tequila or rum

1 lemon, sliced into rounds

½ white onion, coarsely chopped

6 garlic cloves

2 tablespoons sea salt

1 tablespoon whole black peppercorns

4 fresh cilantro sprigs

I USE THIS method to cook shrimp that have been peeled. It takes only a few minutes, so be careful not to overcook the shrimp. Poaching lets them absorb the flavors from the poaching liquid, which is called court bouillon in fancy French cooking and typically uses wine. Staying in step with my beloved Gulf Coastal Caribbean and Mexican influences, I use tequila or rum!

1. Peel and devein the shrimp. Keep refrigerated until ready to use.

2. Place the water in a large heavy skillet or saucepan. Add the tequila, lemon, onion, garlic, salt, peppercorns, and cilantro. Cover and bring to a boil over medium heat. Boil for 5 minutes.

3. Reduce the heat until the liquid is simmering. Add the shrimp, cover, and cook for **3 minutes only!** Pour the shrimp into a strainer and immediately cover with ice. When the shrimp are cool, remove and discard the lemon rounds, garlic, and cilantro. Refrigerate in an airtight container until ready to use.

OYSTER LOVE

It was a haunting experience to walk through the abandoned ancient streets of the French Quarter in my favorite Southern city, a place I have lived and consider a second home. My brother greeted many of the National Guardsmen patrolling the soundless streets, patting their backs and thanking them. There were a few local business owners beginning the cleanup of their stores. But the city sounds of traffic, buses, and garbage trucks were missing, and bins of garbage were overflowing on every corner. All of us, even the soldiers, were stunned, completely shaken by the haunting silence of a once vibrant city.

We had heard that Ralph Brennan, the famous restaurateur, was determined to help the city get back to normal, and the only way he knew how to do that was to open his kitchen and start feeding people. Against a lot of odds and with the difficulty of acquiring product and finding people to work,

Soon after Hurricane Katrina, I flew to New Orleans with my brother and husband to view the damage, deliver supplies, and check on the Margaritaville restaurant and its staff in the French Quarter. Jimmy had acquired special permission, and though my own home had been flooded in Alabama, the news stories coming out of New Orleans were hard to fathom. I felt immensely lucky compared to the legions of displaced residents who seemed to have simply vanished. I knew their lives would never be the same. It was eerie to land at the Louis Armstrong International Airport, generally busy with lots of flights but on this day still closed to commercial flights with the terminal being used as a medical triage center and no planes any-where. Driving from the airport into the city was a similar experience, with only a few cars on the interstate.

he had opened one of his restaurants, the Red Fish Grill, hoping to lead the way to the beginning of a resolute recovery for both his beloved restaurant industry and New Orleans.

The atmosphere in the Red Fish Grill that day was reminiscent of a typical New Orleans jazz funeral. Most of the folks were locals who had come by to show their support or lament their losses. Shock and grief hung in the air, and yet incongruously the smell of fried food hit you as you walked in the door. Jazz music was playing in the background, and there was the hum of conversation. Folks were hugging, crying, drinking...and eating! For Gulf Coast people, nothing soothes a grieving soul better than good food.

That day, we felt honored to be patrons of the Red Fish Grill and to spread a little Gumbo Love to the folks in New Orleans. We shared our sorrows, but we quietly celebrated the life, heart, and culture of a grand city. Ralph brought to the table a platter of BBQ oysters. I can taste them to this day because they have a revered place in my heart as the best oysters I have ever tasted. Maybe it was because at that heartbreaking moment, when the devastation of New Orleans was everywhere, those BBQ

oysters represented the phoenix beginning to rise out of the ashes. The preparation of a humble platter of oysters became one of the many foundational blocks to rebuilding a great city.

Later, I could recall only that they had been fried and then covered with hot sauce, blue cheese, and honey, then run back under the broiler. I was astounded at how the crazy ingredients created an explosion of inspiration with every bite. I would never have thought to put those ingredients together,

but that is how life works. In every challenge, even a literal disaster, the creative impulse of life will shine through. Whether it's a blade of grass growing through a crack in the asphalt or a chef concocting a delicious dish in the face of a disaster because that is all he knows how to do, life continues. After that meal, I knew New Orleans would rebuild. It would take heart, determination, grit, grief, love, and willingness, but that's what Gulf Coast people are made of.

GULF OYSTERS BROCHETTE
DRIZZLED WITH HONEY AND BLUE CHEESE

MAKES 16 SKEWERS

1 quart fresh medium-size shucked Gulf oysters (about 2 pounds)

14 to 16 bacon slices, frozen

2 cups fine-ground white cornmeal

2 tablespoons LuLu's Crazy Creola Seasoning (page xxviii) or other Creole seasoning

1 tablespoon freshly ground black pepper

1½ teaspoons sea salt

About 6 cups peanut or canola oil, for frying

½ cup honey

Bad Girl Buffalo Sauce (page 285)

Stilton Blue Cheese Dressing (page 285)

¾ cup chopped fresh parsley

NOTE: *You will need 16 (6-inch) bamboo skewers.*

AS YOU READ on pages 44 and 45, my beloved New Orleans rose from the flood/ashes after Hurricane Katrina. This recipe is my homage to the spirit of New Orleans, Ralph Brennan, and his BBQ oysters. Inspired by the flavors I encountered that day at the Red Fish Grill, I combined them with another New Orleans favorite: skewering the oysters to make oysters brochette. I prepare this only on special occasions and for special folks. It does take some time and effort to execute—but it's a dish that always brings people together. I like to set up a little fry station before a dinner party and make these to order, often tasking a guest or two to be the honey and sauce "drizzlers." Everyone gathers around, and the ritual has become to make a toast "to New Orleans" before the brochettes get grabbed up and disappear.

1. Preheat the oven to 225°F.

2. Drain the oysters, discarding the liquid, then return the oysters to the refrigerator.

3. Chop the frozen bacon into ¾-inch squares, using the meaty parts and discarding any pieces that are mostly fat. Return the bacon pieces to the freezer until ready to use.

4. In a medium bowl, combine the cornmeal, Creole seasoning, pepper, and salt. Set aside.

5. In a large heavy skillet (10 to 12 inches) or electric skillet, heat the oil over medium heat until it registers 360°F on a candy/deep-fry thermometer, or until a little flour flicked into the oil sizzles. Line a baking sheet with paper towels and set it nearby.

6. While the oil is heating, prepare the brochettes. Remove the bacon from the freezer and the oysters from the refrigerator. Thread 4 squares of bacon and 3 oysters onto each 6-inch skewer, alternating between the bacon and the oysters. Be sure to leave a little space on the skewers between each item. This will help you bread the skewers evenly and completely fry the oysters and bacon. Gently dredge the skewers through the cornmeal mixture, shaking off any excess.

7. Fry a few skewers at a time for 1 to 1½ minutes, or until the bacon is crispy. As you finish them, transfer the skewers to the prepared baking sheet and keep warm in the oven.

8. When ready to serve, place the skewers on a platter or individual plates and drizzle with the honey, buffalo sauce, and blue cheese dressing to your preference. Sprinkle with the parsley and enjoy!

PAN-BROILED
GULF OYSTERS
WITH LEMON-GARLIC BUTTER

SERVES 2 TO 4

Rock salt

24 Gulf oysters on the
half shell

Lemon-Garlic Butter Spread
(recipe follows)

½ cup plain dried breadcrumbs

½ cup shredded
Parmesan cheese

Lemon-Garlic Butter Spread

1 cup (2 sticks) unsalted butter,
at room temperature

Zest of 1 lemon

1 tablespoon finely chopped
fresh parsley

2 tablespoons finely chopped garlic

2 tablespoons finely chopped
green onion

1 teaspoon LuLu's Crazy Creola
Seasoning (page xxviii) or other
Creole seasoning

½ teaspoon Worcestershire sauce

½ teaspoon sea salt

1 teaspoon hot sauce

I SERVE THESE at Christmas, and when I can't find a good ol' guy to shuck for me, I use already-shucked oysters. I have a collection of real oyster shells that I reuse, and I have a set of ceramic shells that work beautifully as well. You can always put the oysters in individual ramekins and broil them in batches or even use a large baking dish and set it in the middle of a casual table for guests to dig into with cocktail forks.

1. Preheat the oven to broil.

2. Spread rock salt over two rimmed baking sheets to cover. Place a dozen oysters on the half shell on each sheet.

3. Top each oyster with 1 teaspoon of the lemon-garlic butter spread. Sprinkle with breadcrumbs and a little Parmesan.

4. Broil for 3 to 5 minutes, or until the tops are golden brown and the butter is bubbling. Serve immediately.

——— LEMON-GARLIC BUTTER SPREAD ———

Stir all the ingredients together until thoroughly combined.

NOTE: *You'll have a little bit of spread left over—use it to make some decadent garlic bread or spread it on a warm croissant.*

NOTES ON OYSTERS

OysteRs—with a capital *R*—are coastal delicacies and an acquired taste for those who didn't cut their teeth (or actually chip a tooth) on a pearl after biting into the middle of one of those babies like I did when I was a kid. As a youngster, I had to have my oysters fried, but as my legs grew longer, I learned the blessed secret that lives within that strangest-looking bivalve: the exotic and scrumptious taste of the ocean. I can slurp them off a shell naked or with a squeeze of lemon, but they must be shivering cold. Along the Gulf Coast, raw oysters are usually served with a traditional red horseradish cocktail sauce, but I also enjoy the simplicity and tartness of a mignonette sauce featuring red wine vinegar with shallots.

If you are lucky enough, as I am, to live in an area where you can get a sack of oysters from a place like Bon Secour Fisheries right down the road, and have a lot of good ol' boys who love to drink beer, shoot the sh*t, and shuck—then you know a little about my brand of paradise. And though I've eaten oysters on every coast of this country and in several others, some of the best oysters in the world hail from the northern Gulf Coast, from Texas to Louisiana, along my Alabama home, and all the way to Apalachicola down past the Florida Panhandle. I still eat oysters only during months with the letter *R* in them. I know that with refrigeration and air travel, good oysters can be had all year-round, but old habits die hard. And there is something special about the reward of oyster season as we abandon our watersports when the weather turns cool. Having friends over to sit by an outdoor fire to eat oysters on the half shell or toss them on a grill is one of my favorite ways to entertain when the temp starts dropping. A really good bottle of pink champagne or an icy-cold longneck bottle of beer is the only way to go with oysters.

Live oysters in the shell come in boxes or burlap bags of varying sizes; some are measured by the pound and others by the piece. Because each oyster can be decidedly unique and also come in clusters, it can be hard to compute a serving size. I usually count on either a 40-pound bag or two 20-pound boxes, which serve ten people about a dozen each. Though I prefer to eat mine wild and straight from the Gulf, there are wonderful processing procedures these days to accommodate a longer shelf life, and purveyors can freeze them individually (IQF) with good results for mail-order business. So no worries! There are many good online resources for Gulf seafood when you're hankering for a vacation oyster fix.

ICY-COLD
GULF OYSTERS
ON THE HALF SHELL
WITH
CLASSIC COCKTAIL AND MIGNONETTE SAUCES

SERVES ABOUT 10

1 large burlap bag Gulf oysters
in the shell (about 40 pounds or
120 oysters)

Crushed ice

Classic Cocktail Sauce (page 281)

Mignonette Sauce (recipe follows)

Lemon wedges

1. Dump the oysters into an outdoor sink or galvanized washtub and cover with crushed ice. Make sure the oysters are icy cold before serving.

2. Find a good-looking dude who loves to shuck and talk sh*t but who is also well versed in the art and culinary science of oyster shucking. Fix him a big strong drink or pop the top on an icy-cold brew for him. Make sure he has the right tools ready for the chore: shucking glove, oyster knife, and a couple of clean rags. Stack up some cheap trays from the dollar store nearby.

3. Put on some vintage rock-and-roll and watch him shuck! It's important to keep his glass or koozie replenished and treat him like a king until his chore is finished.

4. On a picnic table, set out the cocktail sauce, mignonette sauce, and a bowl of lemon wedges with a couple of rolls of paper towels and let guests help themselves.

MAKES ABOUT 2¼ CUPS

1½ cups red wine vinegar

½ cup pink champagne

3 tablespoons finely chopped shallots

1 teaspoon truffle salt or sea salt

2 teaspoons freshly ground
black pepper

MIGNONETTE SAUCE

1. Combine all the ingredients in a small nonreactive bowl. Let the mignonette sit for at least 20 minutes before serving.

2. Drink the rest of the champagne as you enjoy the oysters.

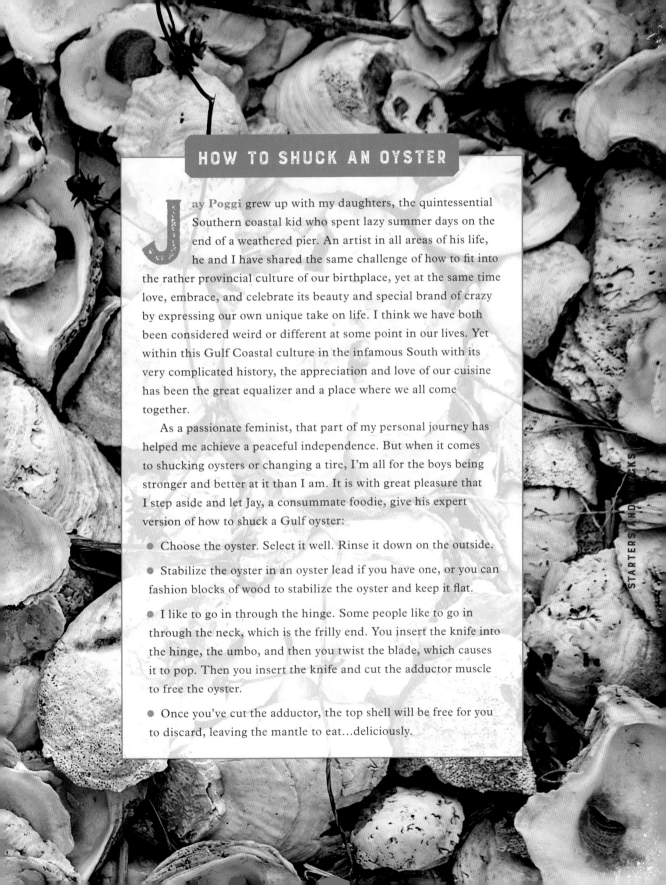

HOW TO SHUCK AN OYSTER

Jay Poggi grew up with my daughters, the quintessential Southern coastal kid who spent lazy summer days on the end of a weathered pier. An artist in all areas of his life, he and I have shared the same challenge of how to fit into the rather provincial culture of our birthplace, yet at the same time love, embrace, and celebrate its beauty and special brand of crazy by expressing our own unique take on life. I think we have both been considered weird or different at some point in our lives. Yet within this Gulf Coastal culture in the infamous South with its very complicated history, the appreciation and love of our cuisine has been the great equalizer and a place where we all come together.

As a passionate feminist, that part of my personal journey has helped me achieve a peaceful independence. But when it comes to shucking oysters or changing a tire, I'm all for the boys being stronger and better at it than I am. It is with great pleasure that I step aside and let Jay, a consummate foodie, give his expert version of how to shuck a Gulf oyster:

- Choose the oyster. Select it well. Rinse it down on the outside.

- Stabilize the oyster in an oyster lead if you have one, or you can fashion blocks of wood to stabilize the oyster and keep it flat.

- I like to go in through the hinge. Some people like to go in through the neck, which is the frilly end. You insert the knife into the hinge, the umbo, and then you twist the blade, which causes it to pop. Then you insert the knife and cut the adductor muscle to free the oyster.

- Once you've cut the adductor, the top shell will be free for you to discard, leaving the mantle to eat…deliciously.

STONE CRABS

WITH
KEY LIME-MUSTARD SAUCE

SERVES ABOUT 4

5 pounds cooked large
stone crab claws

Key Lime–Mustard Sauce
(page 283)

MY FIRST INTRODUCTION to stone crabs was when I was a young pup in the seventies in Key West. Being a gal from the northern Gulf Coast, I was supremely familiar with the beautiful blue crab. But I was unprepared for how exquisite a treat its eloquent cousin would be, residing in the warmer and more turquoise headwaters along the Florida straits. The stone crab's body is inedible and relatively small compared to its large, plump claws, where the sweet meat resides. When they are in season, you are allowed to take only one of the claws. This way the crab can defend itself from predators and feed itself with its remaining claw—and it will actually regrow its missing claw!

The best way to enjoy this coastal delicacy is to book a table at Joe's Stone Crab, the famous Miami Beach restaurant. Or come down to Key West and have dinner at my house. I always have them as a starter when I entertain, and I serve them with my version of the classic key lime–mustard sauce. If you do buy your own, the claws come presteamed and ready to eat whether you're buying them from the crabber or from a large seafood supplier. The crabbers cook them in large batches right after harvesting them.

Lay out some newspaper on a picnic table. Place the crabs on the table with a large bowl for the shells and small bowls of key lime–mustard sauce, along with wooden mallets, claw crackers, and cocktail forks. Folks will quickly become experts at cracking open the claws and plucking out the luxurious crabmeat.

BAD GIRL
BUFFALO WINGS

SERVES 4 TO 6

8 to 12 cups canola or peanut oil, for frying (optional)

2½ pounds chicken wings (about 14 small wings), wing tips removed and remaining wings cut at the joint to make 2 pieces

1 teaspoon sea salt

1 teaspoon freshly ground black pepper

3 tablespoons unsalted butter, melted, for baking (optional)

Bad Girl Buffalo Sauce (page 285)

Stilton Blue Cheese Dressing (page 285), for serving

Celery sticks, for serving

WINGS ARE EVERYONE'S favorite snack food, and my Bad Girl Buffalo Sauce is sinfully good because it starts with a roux. And anything that starts with a roux is going to be some kind of bad*ss. I've included directions for both frying and baking the wings—you can decide just how bad you want to be!

To fry the wings:

1. Preheat the oven to broil on high. In a Dutch oven, heat the oil over medium-high heat until it registers 355°F on a candy/deep-fry thermometer, or until a little flour flicked into the oil sizzles. Line a baking sheet with paper towels and set it nearby.

2. Season the wings with the salt and pepper.

3. Working in batches, fry the wings for 12 to 15 minutes, making sure the skin is crispy. Between batches, you may need to give the oil a few minutes to get back up to 355°F. As you finish them, transfer the wings to the prepared baking sheet to drain.

4. Line a large baking sheet with aluminum foil. Pour the buffalo sauce into a large bowl. Add the fried wings a few at a time to the sauce, making sure they are completely covered.

5. Use tongs to transfer the sauce-covered wings to the foil-lined baking sheet. Broil the wings until they start to brown and caramelize, 4 to 6 minutes. You can broil for a longer or a shorter time, depending on how crispy you like your wings.

6. Serve with blue cheese dressing and celery.

To bake the wings:

1. Preheat the oven to 425°F.

2. Season the wings with the salt and pepper.

3. Line a large baking sheet with aluminum foil. Put the wings on the pan and drizzle them with the melted butter to coat.

4. Bake the wings for 30 minutes. Flip them over and bake for 15 minutes more, or until the skin is crispy.

5. Remove the wings from the oven and turn the broiler to high. Line a clean baking sheet with foil.

6. Pour the buffalo sauce into a large bowl. Add the baked wings a few at a time to the sauce, making sure they are completely covered.

7. Use tongs to transfer the sauce-covered wings to the clean foil-lined baking sheet. Broil the wings until they start to brown and caramelize, 4 to 6 minutes. You can broil for a longer or a shorter time, depending on how crispy you like your wings.

8. Serve with blue cheese dressing and celery.

FRESH HERB
AND
GARLIC CHEESE SPREAD

MAKES 1¼ TO 1½ CUPS

1 (8-ounce) package cream cheese,
at room temperature

½ cup (1 stick) unsalted butter,
at room temperature

1 garlic clove, finely chopped

½ teaspoon finely chopped fresh dill

1 tablespoon finely chopped
fresh chives

3 tablespoons grated
Parmesan cheese

1 tablespoon finely chopped
fresh parsley

1 teaspoon finely chopped
fresh basil

2 teaspoons finely chopped
fresh tarragon

½ teaspoon finely chopped
fresh thyme

¼ teaspoon sea salt

½ teaspoon freshly ground
black pepper

THE FIRST TIME I served a fancy cheese spread to guests was as a novice cook. The wonderful Boursin cheese had made it into the new gourmet section of the Delchamps family grocery market in my little hometown of Fairhope, Alabama, and it became a quick go-to for my Friday-afternoon wine gatherings with friends. Recently when I was brainstorming a specialty burger, I thought about how good it would be to have one with Boursin cheese, so I set out to figure out how to create my own version of the delectable spread with its fragrant garlic-herb flavor. And voilà! Here is my version, infused with fresh herbs from my garden.

1. In a food processor, combine the cream cheese and butter. Pulse several times until thoroughly blended and fluffy.

2. Add all the remaining ingredients and pulse a few times to evenly distribute the herbs and spices.

3. Transfer the cheese mixture to an airtight container and refrigerate until ready to use. Serve at room temperature with crackers, raw vegetables, or on a burger (see page 248).

TAILGATE SHRIMP AND CRAB DIP

MAKES 6 CUPS

1½ (8-ounce) packages cream cheese, at room temperature

1 cup mayonnaise

2 tablespoons Creole mustard

¼ cup sour cream

2 dashes of Worcestershire sauce

3 dashes of hot sauce

1 tablespoon LuLu's Crazy Creola Seasoning (page xxviii) or other Creole seasoning

½ teaspoon freshly ground black pepper

1 teaspoon finely chopped fresh dill

1 teaspoon finely chopped fresh parsley

½ teaspoon lemon zest

1 teaspoon fresh lemon juice

¼ teaspoon red pepper flakes

½ cup finely chopped green onions

½ cup grated Parmesan cheese

2 teaspoons prepared or freshly grated horseradish

1 pound Easy Boiled Shrimp (page 39), peeled

1 pound cooked fresh lump blue crabmeat, drained and picked through for shells, handled carefully to keep the meat in big chunks (see Notes on Handling Seafood, pages xxx–xxxi)

Crackers, chips, or crudités, for serving

1. In a food processor, combine the cream cheese, mayonnaise, mustard, and sour cream. Pulse several times to blend.

2. Add the Worcestershire, hot sauce, Creole seasoning, black pepper, dill, parsley, lemon zest, lemon juice, and red pepper flakes. Pulse until well blended.

3. Add the green onion, Parmesan, and horseradish. Pulse until well blended and transfer to a large bowl.

4. Use a knife to chop the shrimp into medium pieces and fold into the cream cheese mixture.

5. Add the crabmeat to the cream cheese mixture and gently fold it all together until well combined.

6. Transfer to an airtight container and refrigerate for 1 to 2 hours or overnight. Serve with crackers, chips, or crudités.

HONEY ALE
PIMENTO CHEESE

MAKES 2 CUPS

¼ cup honey ale or dark beer

1 (4-ounce) jar pimentos, drained and chopped

1 pound extra-sharp cheddar cheese, shredded

1 tablespoon finely chopped garlic

2 tablespoons grated sweet onion

½ teaspoon sea salt

½ teaspoon freshly ground black pepper

½ cup mayonnaise

3 or 4 dashes of hot sauce

THIS FAVORITE SOUTHERN entertaining staple reminds me of my grandmother Bessie Peets. There was always a little pimento cheese in her refrigerator, and I loved to help her make tea sandwiches when she had her bridge "girls" over. They were more likely to be drinking cordials than tea, however! The honey ale or dark beer in this recipe gives the cheese a special tang that complements a salty cracker or a slice of rustic farm bread. It can also be found gracing a humble bun with a juicy burger (see page 247).

1. In a small saucepan, bring the beer to a simmer for about a minute. Remove from the heat and let cool completely. (I'm not sure why, but heating the beer for this recipe makes it taste better.)

2. In a large bowl, combine the pimentos, cheese, garlic, onion, salt, and pepper.

3. Fold the beer and mayonnaise into the cheese mixture. Add the hot sauce and stir well. The mixture should be a little runny.

4. Refrigerate for at least 2 hours or overnight so the flavors can marry and the mixture can thicken. Make sure the pimento cheese sits out for at least half an hour before serving so that it can soften and become easy to spread.

FIVE-OLIVE SALAD
WITH FRESH HERBS

MAKES 4 CUPS

5 (10- to 12-ounce) jars of a variety of pitted olives

1 (3.5-ounce) jar capers

6 garlic cloves, sliced

Whole sprigs of fresh herbs (I use oregano, basil, tarragon, and sage)

1 cup extra-virgin olive oil

1 cup lemon olive oil, or 1 cup extra-virgin olive oil plus the rind of 1 lemon sliced into slivers

Crackers or bread, for serving

ONE NIGHT SOME friends brought even more friends to my house for dinner, so I needed an extra dish to stretch my menu. Inspired by the classic olive salad from the famous Central Grocery in New Orleans, I hurriedly threw this recipe together with olives I had in my refrigerator and herbs from my garden. I put it out on the table with a loaf of crusty artisan bread and my guests raved about it, so I decided I should write it down and share it here. Instead of loaves and fishes, it was loaves and olives that managed to help feed a much larger crowd than I had anticipated! It's okay to play with this recipe and get creative. You can't mess it up.

1. Drain the olives and capers and chop the olives into large pieces, leaving some of them whole.

2. Transfer the olives and capers to a large bowl. Add the garlic, herbs, olive oil, and lemon olive oil (or olive oil and and slivered lemon rind, if using) and stir gently to combine.

3. Transfer to a glass jar or serving bowl and serve with crackers or bread.

BLACK BEAN & CORN SALAD DIP
WITH PLANTAIN CHIPS

MAKES 8 CUPS

⅔ cup fresh lime juice

¼ cup extra-virgin olive oil

½ cup rice vinegar

4 teaspoons finely chopped garlic

2 teaspoons sea salt

3 tablespoons honey

2 teaspoons chili powder

2 teaspoons LuLu's Crazy Creola Seasoning (page xxviii) or other Creole seasoning

1 tablespoon hot sauce

4 (15-ounce) cans black beans, drained and rinsed

4 cups fresh or frozen corn kernels

2 cups quartered cherry tomatoes

1 cup finely chopped sweet onion

1 cup finely chopped green bell pepper

½ cup finely chopped fresh cilantro

Plantain chips, homemade (recipe follows) or store-bought, for serving

Plantain Chips

4 green plantains

About 6 cups vegetable oil, for frying

2 tablespoons LuLu's Crazy Creola Seasoning (page xxviii) or other Creole seasoning

Zest of 2 limes or lemons

½ teaspoon sea salt

1. In a jar, combine the lime juice, olive oil, vinegar, garlic, salt, honey, chili powder, Creole seasoning, and hot sauce. Cover with the lid and shake until the dressing is well blended.

2. In a large bowl, stir together the black beans, corn, tomatoes, onion, bell pepper, and cilantro.

3. Toss the black bean salad with the dressing and transfer to an airtight container. Refrigerate for at least 2 hours or overnight.

4. Serve with store-bought plantain chips or take an adventure and make your own!

—————— PLANTAIN CHIPS ——————

1. Cut the ends off the plantains. Score the skin of each plantain lengthwise four to six times. Soak the plantains in a bowl of hot water for 5 to 10 minutes. This makes the skins easier to peel.

2. In a large heavy skillet (10 to 12 inches) or electric skillet, heat the oil over medium heat until it registers 375°F on a candy/deep-fry thermometer, or until a little flour flicked into the oil sizzles. Line a baking sheet with paper towels and set it nearby.

3. While the oil is heating, peel the plantains and use a knife or mandoline to slice them very thinly lengthwise.

4. Fry the plantain chips in batches of 5 or 6 so the oil is not overcrowded; cook evenly for 2 to 3 minutes, or until they float to the top and begin to brown. As you finish them, transfer the fried plantains to the prepared baking sheet. Sprinkle with the Creole seasoning, lime zest, and salt and serve immediately.

HOLY GUACAMOLE

MAKES 6 CUPS

7 ripe medium avocados (see Note)

2 tablespoons fresh lime juice (from 1 lime)

1 teaspoon ground cumin

1 teaspoon sea salt

1 teaspoon freshly ground black pepper

2 tablespoons finely chopped fresh cilantro

1 teaspoon finely chopped garlic

1 teaspoon finely chopped seeded jalapeño

½ cup chopped Roma (plum) tomatoes

1 tablespoon finely chopped red onion

Tortilla chips, for serving

1. Pit, peel, and chop the avocados into chunks and place in a large bowl with the lime juice. Smash the avocado into a chunky consistency with a fork or potato masher.

2. Add the cumin, salt, pepper, cilantro, garlic, jalapeño, tomatoes, and onion and mix together. Serve immediately with tortilla chips.

NOTE: *You can ripen avocados in a paper bag overnight. If you keep one of the avocado pits in the guacamole, it will help keep it from turning brown. If you are not able to serve immediately, covering with plastic wrap so that the wrap is pressed directly against the surface of the guacamole will also help prevent browning.*

SALSAS

I AM A SUCKER for any kind of salsa!!! These are some of my favorites that I use as a little side condiment for any main dish.

WATERMELON SALSA
MAKES 4 CUPS

2 cups chopped watermelon

2 cups chopped fresh homegrown, heirloom, or pretty, ripe tomatoes

¼ cup chopped sweet onion

Juice of 1 lime (about 2 tablespoons)

1 small jalapeño, seeded and finely chopped

½ cup finely chopped fresh cilantro

Sea salt

Combine all the ingredients in a medium bowl or airtight container. Cover and refrigerate for 2 hours or overnight before serving.

CHERRY TOMATO SALSA
MAKES 4 CUPS

2 pints cherry tomatoes, quartered

¼ cup finely chopped fresh cilantro

½ cup finely chopped yellow onion

1 jalapeño, with seeds, finely chopped

Juice of 1½ limes (about 3 tablespoons)

½ teaspoon sea salt

Freshly ground black pepper

Combine all the ingredients in a medium bowl or airtight container. Cover and refrigerate for 2 hours or overnight before serving.

NOTE: *If you'd like a milder salsa, remove and discard the seeds of the jalapeño.*

MAKES 2 CUPS

1 ear sweet white corn, still in the husk

2 or 3 large green tomatoes, coarsely chopped

½ cup finely chopped red onion

½ red jalapeño, seeded and finely chopped

½ teaspoon honey or sugar

1 garlic clove, finely chopped

½ teaspoon ground cumin

¼ teaspoon sea salt

¼ cup finely chopped fresh cilantro

Juice of 1 lemon (about 2 tablespoons)

Juice of 1 lime (about 2 tablespoons)

———— GREEN TOMATO SALSA ————

1. Place the ear of corn in the microwave and cook for 8 minutes on high. Wearing oven mitts, carefully remove the corn. Cut off the top of the corn cob, then hold the stalk and shake it vigorously over the sink until the cob slips easily out of the husk, completely free of silk. Let cool, then cut the kernels from the cob into a medium bowl.

2. Add the tomatoes, onion, jalapeño, honey, garlic, cumin, salt, cilantro, lemon juice, and lime juice. Stir to combine.

3. Transfer to an airtight container and refrigerate for 2 hours or overnight before serving.

NOTE: *I learned this easy method for shucking an ear of corn from Ken on YouTube! He is adorable and his method works. Check him out!*

MAKES 3 CUPS

2 cups chopped fresh pineapple

1 cup finely chopped peeled seedless cucumber

½ cup finely chopped red onion

½ teaspoon lime zest

2 tablespoons finely chopped fresh cilantro

2 teaspoons finely chopped seeded jalapeño

Juice of 2 limes (about 4 tablespoons)

½ teaspoon sea salt

¼ teaspoon chili powder

1 tablespoon extra-virgin olive oil

———— PINEAPPLE-CUCUMBER SALSA ————

Combine all the ingredients in a medium bowl or airtight container. Cover and refrigerate for 2 hours or overnight before serving.

GUMBO LOVE AND OTHER HEARTWARMING SOUPS

IT TAKES courage to make a gumbo, and you've got to rustle up plenty more qualities along the way to achieve a successful end result. But like any character-building exercise, your experience and wisdom deepens with every step, until you reach a profound sense of satisfaction by the end of the process. A simmering pot of contentment is your reward, and the knowledge that you made this nurturing goodness from the humblest of ingredients and your own ability. It is literally and figuratively a pot full of flavor that can feed your loved ones for days and that's just brimming with all the courage, mindfulness, and love you put into it.

It all starts with *preparation*—you must gather all the ingredients and prep them: chop the vegetables, clean the seafood, and sauté the meats and sausages. When done in an orderly fashion, this preparation simplifies the steps to come. It eliminates the chaos and fear. With practice and focus, you quickly learn you were more afraid of the fear itself than the task at hand.

Next is the queen bee—the roux! Making a roux simply requires *a little focus and paying attention*, seasoned with *faith*—you have to shake off the doubt and believe in yourself before diving headfirst into the *perseverance* part, which keeps you doing what you have to do, stirring long after your arm has gone numb from pain. Then there's the *listening*, where you tune in to your wisdom and experience to take the roux just to the edge of burning before you toss in the vegetables. Next is the easy *follow-directions* part, where you do what you're told to do: you add the stock, along with the rest of the ingredients and seasonings, and mix it all together. Then comes the hard part for lots of us: *you let it go.* You leave it alone, letting it simmer, with an occasional stir. You get out of the way. You trust the age-old cooking process and let the magic happen.

Then some *discernment* is employed to determine when the gumbo is "just right." You do some tweaking, adjusting the seasoning here or adding a little more stock there. And finally comes the

giving: you serve it up and joyfully share your heart love with a humble pot of peasant fish stew. Following that is *acceptance*: you accept all the appreciation that flies your way serenaded by all the *ooooh*s, *ahhhh*s, and groans of delicious delight coming from your guests. Now it's time for the *rest* part: you take off your apron and let others help clean up. And last, your heart swells with *gratitude* as you enjoy the feeling of family and a job well done.

Making gumbo taught me how to become a woman and has become a rite of passage for the young women in my family. Perhaps that's why I so revere the process and appreciate the tradition. What I learned by being at my grandmother's knee, I have passed along to my own children and nieces over the years. It seems that whenever they want to impress a new beau, husband, in-laws, or friends, they turn to the family ritual of making a gumbo. It used to be via minute-by-minute long-distance phone calls, but most recently I'm able to advise with in-living-color real-time Facetime, the most frequent questions from my novice gumbo makers being, "Is it dark enough yet?" "Did I do it right?" "When should I put the shrimp in?" And when there has been that dreaded scorch in the roux, I've reassured them that "life happens. It's just a pot of gumbo. Take a deep breath and a little break. Then start over."

Over the years the gumbo pot has taken on even more meaning; it's close to mythic in a humorous sort of way. When I look back over a life of many starts and stops, I find it curious yet not surprising that my current success is built upon the very first five-gallon pot of gumbo I ever cooked for LuLu's. It was one of those dramatic Southern March days. A front had rolled in from the Gulf and the sky was purple, raining buckets; I had agreed to take over a miserable but beautiful waterfront dive. I thought I could transform it and put a little life into it. It was my reluctant answer to what I was going to do to support myself after moving back home from Los Angeles to take care of my ailing parents.

I was scared, and opening day was twenty-four hours away. I had prepared the best I could, considering I had never even worked in a restaurant, much less owned one. The last thing to do was to cook a pot of gumbo. With the roof leaking—water was literally pouring through the light fixtures in the kitchen—I was seriously wondering what in the world I'd gotten myself into, taking on a restaurant. Even though friends who had long enjoyed my cooking had urged me to do so, I had sworn I would *never, ever* open a restaurant, one of the hardest businesses imaginable. But here I was, sitting in this dilapidated kitchen working on a dream with not much more

than a wing and a prayer, when Joni and Van, two of those sweet friends, came by to give me a hand. What a welcome sight! We started to work, and their kindness and my sheer determination went into that pot of gumbo, along with a barrel of laughs and some old-fashioned fun by the end of the day. Before it was over, there were a few empty bottles of hooch on the tables as we cranked up some soul music...singing, dancing, and creating our own brand of sunshine on what was a scary, dark, and dismal day. We shifted the energy, and they helped me see beyond the rain and the worry as we celebrated my new venture.

That first pot was the foundational piece of what is now a phenomenally successful restaurant that has enabled me to realize my dharmic purpose of becoming an independent woman this go-round on this beautiful blue planet. I am able to have a positive influence and do "good" for my family and community. So for me, a pot of gumbo has deep meaning—it is not only my culinary legacy but my ticket to success. It was born of love with an intention to share that love. That's why gumbo is special to me. That's why it's more than a humble tasty seafood soup or a menu item. It's tradition and work ethic...it's heart and soul...it's family and heritage...it's magic and art...it's ceremony and laughter...it's respect and escapism. It is the song of my elders and the future of my "songlines." It's all that and more, but at the heart of it, at its genesis, it's simply love...Gumbo Love.

SUMMER SEAFOOD GUMBO

SERVES 14 TO 16

3 pounds medium wild-caught Gulf shrimp, heads on

2 pounds cooked blue crab claw meat, picked through for shells, handled carefully to keep the meat in big chunks (see Notes on Handling Seafood, pages xxx–xxxi)

4 large ripe tomatoes, or 1 (28-ounce) can whole tomatoes with their juices

¾ cup vegetable oil or bacon grease

1 cup all-purpose flour

2 large onions, coarsely chopped

1 bunch celery, coarsely chopped, including leaves

2 green bell peppers, coarsely chopped

8 cups shrimp or seafood stock (see page xxx), heated

2 to 3 teaspoons sea salt, or to taste

1 tablespoon freshly ground black pepper

¼ teaspoon cayenne pepper

2 tablespoons dried thyme

4 bay leaves

1 teaspoon dried oregano

1 teaspoon dried basil

CONT.

OVER THE YEARS, this is the recipe that I've cooked the most and that has remained a featured specialty at my restaurants. As far as the seafood goes, I use shrimp and crab, but if it's cool enough for oysters and there are some sweet and pretty ones available, or it's crawfish season, I will toss those in, too. And though I usually use only sausage in my winter gumbo, it's no crime to add a little andouille to the pot as well.

1. Peel and devein the shrimp. (If you're making your own stock, reserve the heads and shells to make the stock.) Refrigerate the shrimp and crabmeat until ready to use.

2. If using fresh tomatoes, fill a medium saucepan with water. Bring to a boil. Carefully drop the tomatoes into the boiling water and cook for 1 minute. Remove with a slotted spoon and let them cool. The skins will slip off easily. Remove the cores and coarsely chop the tomatoes over a bowl to retain as much juice as possible. Set aside. (If using canned tomatoes, chop each tomato into eighths and return them to the juice in the can.)

3. To make the roux, in a large stockpot (about 10 quarts), heat the vegetable oil over medium-high heat. When the oil is hot, gradually add the flour, whisking continuously, and cook, stirring and adjusting the heat as necessary to keep it from burning, until the roux is a dark mahogany color, 25 to 35 minutes. Be careful: if the roux burns, you will have to start all over again!

4. Carefully add the onion to the roux and stir with a large wooden spoon for 2 to 3 minutes. (The onion will sizzle and steam when it hits the hot roux, so caution is advised. All seasoned gumbo cooks have roux battle scars on one or both arms.)

5. Add the celery and cook, stirring continuously, for 2 to 3 minutes.

6. Add the bell pepper and cook, stirring continuously, for 2 to 3 minutes more. The mixture should resemble a pot of black beans in color and texture.

7. Add the heated stock and the tomatoes with their juices. Stir in the salt, black pepper, cayenne, thyme, bay leaves, oregano, basil, Creole seasoning,

2 tablespoons LuLu's Crazy
Creola Seasoning (page xxviii) or
other Creole seasoning

¼ cup hot sauce

2 tablespoons Worcestershire sauce

4 blue crab bodies, if available
(optional)

2½ pounds fresh okra, chopped
into ¼-inch pieces, or thawed
frozen cut okra

2 cups finely chopped green onions

½ cup finely chopped fresh parsley

½ cup fresh lemon juice

Cooked white rice, for serving

French bread and butter, for serving

hot sauce, and Worcestershire sauce. Stir well. Bring the gumbo to a boil and cook for 5 minutes, then reduce the heat to maintain a slow simmer. Add the crab bodies (if using) and simmer, uncovered, for about 1 hour.

8. Add the okra and bring the gumbo to a boil. Cook for 5 minutes. Reduce the heat to maintain a slow simmer and cook, uncovered, for 30 minutes, or until the okra has lost its bright green color and cooked down like the other vegetables. If the gumbo gets too thick, add a little water. If it is too thin, continue to simmer it, uncovered.

9. Gumbo is always better the day after it has been cooked, although I've never had a complaint when I served it the day I made it. At this point, you can cool the gumbo. Turn off the heat and let it sit for about 30 minutes. Then place the pot, uncovered, in an empty sink. Fill the sink with cold water and ice around the stockpot (try not to get any in the stockpot itself). Stir every 15 minutes to facilitate cooling. (The gumbo will spoil if improperly cooled—see page xxx for tips on cooling the gumbo.) When completely cool, refrigerate the gumbo in the stockpot, uncovered.

10. When ready to serve, slowly bring the gumbo to a simmer over medium-low heat. Thirty minutes before serving, add the green onion, parsley, and lemon juice to the gumbo. Cover and cook for 15 minutes. Add the shrimp and crabmeat, mix well, and cook for 2 minutes. Cover and turn off the heat. Let it sit for at least 15 minutes more to cook the seafood. The gumbo will stay hot for a long time. Remove and discard the bay leaves. Taste and adjust the seasonings; serve over cooked white rice with French bread and butter.

LUCY'S
WINTER GUMBO

SERVES 14 TO 16

1 whole chicken

6 bay leaves

1 pound andouille sausage or other smoked sausage, chopped into ⅛-inch-thick rounds or half-moons

¾ cup vegetable oil

1 cup all-purpose flour

2 large onions, coarsely chopped

1 bunch celery, coarsely chopped, including leaves

2 green bell peppers, coarsely chopped

2 to 3 teaspoons sea salt

2 teaspoons freshly ground black pepper

1 tablespoon dried thyme

1 teaspoon dried oregano

½ teaspoon dried sage

1 tablespoon LuLu's Crazy Creola Seasoning (page xxviii) or other Creole seasoning

2 tablespoons Worcestershire sauce

2 cups finely chopped green onions

½ cup finely chopped fresh parsley

1 quart fresh oysters, drained

2 pounds medium wild-caught Gulf shrimp, peeled and deveined

2 to 3 tablespoons hot sauce

3 tablespoons filé powder (optional)

Cooked white rice, for serving

French bread and butter, for serving

BEFORE REFRIGERATION AND the invention of electric freezers, the foods people ate were much more strictly determined by the seasons. Since tomatoes and okra are grown in the summer months along the subtropical zone of the Gulf Coast, gumbo cooks had to come up with an alternative in the winter months. Tomatoes were eliminated, and to add thickness and taste, filé powder was used. Filé is made from ground sassafras leaves, and its use in gumbos dates back to the Choctaw Indians. Winter gumbos also use more fowl, game, meats, sausages, and oysters, which are at their best when harvested from colder waters. In this winter gumbo, I use almost any tasty ingredient available. I combine chicken with pork sausage, and I include both oysters and shrimp. After all, for me, gumbo is all about anything goes!

1. Place the whole chicken in a large stockpot. Add water to cover and 2 of the bay leaves and bring the water to a boil. Cook until the chicken is tender. Remove the chicken from the pot and set aside to cool. Reserve 8 cups of the liquid in the pot to use as broth.

2. When the chicken is cool enough to handle, remove and discard the skin and bones. Chop the chicken into large bite-size pieces and set aside.

3. In a large heavy skillet (10 to 12 inches), cook the sausage over medium heat until browned. Use a slotted spoon to transfer the sausage to a paper towel-covered plate. Pat well with paper towels to soak up extra grease.

4. To make the roux, in a large stockpot (about 10 quarts), heat the vegetable oil over medium-high heat. When the oil is hot, gradually add the flour, whisking continuously. Continue to stir the roux, adjusting the heat as necessary to keep it from burning, for 25 to 35 minutes, or until the roux is a dark mahogany color. Be careful—if the roux burns, you will have to start all over again!

5. Carefully add the onion to the roux and cook, stirring with a large wooden spoon, for 2 to 3 minutes. (The onion will sizzle and steam when it hits the hot roux, so caution is advised. All seasoned gumbo cooks have roux battle scars on one or both arms.)

GUMBO LOVE AND OTHER HEARTWARMING SOUPS

CONT.

6. Add the celery and cook, stirring continuously, for 2 to 3 minutes.

7. Add the bell pepper and cook, stirring continuously, for 2 to 3 minutes more. The mixture should resemble a pot of black beans in color and texture.

8. Slowly add the reserved 8 cups of chicken broth and stir well.

9. Add the chicken and sausage and stir well.

10. Add the remaining 4 bay leaves, the salt, black pepper, thyme, oregano, sage, Creole seasoning, and Worcestershire. Stir well. Bring the gumbo to a boil and boil for 5 minutes. Reduce the heat to maintain a slow simmer and cook, uncovered, for about 1 hour. If the gumbo gets too thick, add a little water. If it is too thin, continue to let it simmer uncovered. Because there is pork sausage in this gumbo, skim off any excess oil that rises to the top.

11. Gumbo is always better the day after it has been cooked, although I've never had a complaint when I served it the day I made it. At this point, you can cool the gumbo. Turn off the heat and let it sit for about 30 minutes. Then place the pot, uncovered, in an empty sink. Fill the sink with cold water and ice around the stockpot (try not to get any in the stockpot itself). Stir every 15 minutes to facilitate cooling. (The gumbo will spoil if improperly cooled— see page xxx for tips on cooling the gumbo.) When completely cool, refrigerate the gumbo in the stockpot, uncovered.

12. When ready to serve, slowly bring the gumbo to a simmer over medium-low heat. Thirty minutes before serving, add the green onion and parsley to the gumbo. Cover and cook for 15 minutes. Add the oysters and shrimp and stir well. Simmer for 2 minutes, or until the oysters begin to curl.

13. Add the hot sauce, using more or less to taste. Cover and turn off the heat. Let it sit for at least 10 minutes more. It will stay hot for a long time. Remove and discard the bay leaves. Adjust the seasonings and stir in the filé powder (if using), or set it out on the table so everyone can add it to their bowl of gumbo to their preferred thickness and taste. Serve over cooked white rice with French bread and butter.

TRUE ACADIAN (CAJUN) GUMBO

SERVES 8

¾ cup vegetable oil

1 cup plus 2 tablespoons all-purpose flour

1 cup finely chopped yellow onion

½ cup chopped celery

½ cup finely chopped green bell pepper

8 cups seafood stock (see page xxx), heated

1 teaspoon sea salt

½ teaspoon cayenne pepper

2 tablespoons finely chopped green onions

1 tablespoon finely chopped fresh parsley

1 pound medium wild-caught Gulf shrimp, peeled and deveined

1 pint (or more) shucked raw Gulf oysters and their liquor (liquid)

1 pound cooked lump blue crabmeat, picked through for shells, handled carefully to keep the meat in big chunks (see Notes on Handling Seafood, pages xxx–xxxi)

1 tablespoon filé powder

4 cups cooked white rice, for serving (optional)

I'M KNOWN TO change my hair color often, and when I heard about a fantastic "blond" colorist in Atlanta, I just had to try him. As I am with most folks, I was quick to open up to him about all the chapters of my life, revealing to him that I was a cook and restaurant owner. When he opened his mouth to exclaim, "Girl, I love to cook!" I knew he had to be from the swampy lands nestled inside the Louisiana coast and the home of the Cajun descendants for centuries. Sure enough, he was a proud Cajun, and it was only a matter of minutes before we were talking the secret language of gumbo.

That day, not only did I get a great color job, I also got a master class on what makes a true Cajun gumbo. In his version, which of course was his mama's, there would never, ever be any okra or tomato used—ever. Inspired by his passion to stay true to his heritage, this is my best recollection of his version of a true Acadian, or Cajun, gumbo.

1. To make the roux, in a large stockpot (about 10 quarts), heat the vegetable oil over medium-high heat. When the oil is hot, gradually add the flour, whisking continuously. Continue to stir the roux, adjusting the heat as necessary to keep it from burning, for 25 to 35 minutes, or until the roux is a dark mahogany color. Be careful—if the roux burns, you will have to start all over again!

2. Raise the heat to medium and carefully add the onion, celery, and bell pepper to the roux, stirring them in with a wooden spoon. (The vegetables will sizzle and steam when they hit the hot roux, so caution is advised. All seasoned gumbo cooks have roux battle scars on one or both arms.) Cook until the vegetables are tender, 10 to 15 minutes.

3. Add the stock very slowly in a thin stream, stirring continuously. Add the salt and cayenne and bring to a simmer, stirring frequently. Reduce the heat to low and simmer for 1 hour.

4. Gumbo is always better the day after it has been cooked, although I've never had a complaint when I served it the day I made it. At this point, you can cool the gumbo. Turn off the heat and let it sit for about 30 minutes. Then place the pot, uncovered, in an empty sink. Fill the sink with cold water and

ice around the stockpot (try not to get any in the stock-pot itself). Stir every 15 minutes to facilitate cooling. (The gumbo will spoil if improperly cooled—see page xxx for tips on cooling the gumbo.) When completely cool, refrigerate the gumbo in the stockpot, uncovered.

5. When ready to serve, slowly bring the gumbo to a simmer over medium-low heat. Thirty minutes before serving, stir in the green onion and parsley. Cover and cook for 15 minutes. Add the shrimp, oysters, and crab and cook for 3 to 5 minutes more. Stir in filé powder at the time of serving. Serve over white rice (optional, but encouraged).

CHICKEN AND SAUSAGE FILÉ GUMBO

SERVES 8 TO 10

4 pounds bone-in, skin-on chicken thighs

2 large onions, coarsely chopped, trimmings reserved

1 bunch celery, coarsely chopped, including leaves, trimmings reserved

2 green peppers, coarsely chopped, trimmings reserved

1 pound smoked andouille sausage or other smoked sausage, cut into rounds about ⅛ inch thick

¾ cup vegetable oil or bacon grease

1 cup all-purpose flour

1 tablespoon sea salt

1 tablespoon freshly ground black pepper

2 tablespoons dried thyme

4 bay leaves

1 teaspoon dried oregano

1 teaspoon dried basil

1 tablespoon LuLu's Crazy Creola Seasoning (page xxviii) or other Creole seasoning

2 cups chopped green onions

½ cup finely chopped fresh parsley

2 tablespoons Worcestershire sauce, or to taste (optional)

¼ cup hot sauce, or to taste (optional)

3 tablespoons filé powder

Cooked white rice, for serving

French bread and butter, for serving

1. Place the chicken thighs in a large stockpot and cover with 3 quarts water. Bring to a boil. Reduce the heat to medium to maintain a vigorous simmer.

2. Add the trimmings from the chopped vegetables to the pot with the chicken and cook, skimming foam from the top of the stock as needed, for 40 minutes, or until the chicken is cooked through.

3. In a large heavy skillet (10 to 12 inches), cook the sausage over medium heat until browned. Use a slotted spoon to transfer to a paper towel–lined plate. Pat well with paper towels to soak up extra grease. Set aside.

4. Remove the chicken thighs from the stock and let them cool. Pour the stock through a large strainer into a clean container, discarding the solids. When the chicken is cool enough to handle, remove and discard the skin and bones. Chop the chicken into large pieces and set aside.

5. To make the roux, in a large stockpot (about 10 quarts), heat the vegetable oil over medium-high heat. When the oil is hot, gradually add the flour, whisking continuously. Continue to stir the roux, adjusting the heat as necessary to keep it from burning, for 25 to 35 minutes, or until the roux is a dark mahogany color. Be careful—if the roux burns, you will have to start all over again!

6. Carefully add the chopped onion to the roux and cook, stirring continuously with a large wooden spoon, for 2 to 3 minutes. (The onion will sizzle and steam when it hits the hot roux, so caution is advised. All seasoned gumbo cooks have roux battle scars on one or both arms.)

7. Add the celery and cook, stirring continuously, for 2 to 3 minutes more.

8. Add the bell pepper and cook, stirring continuously, for 1 to 2 minutes more. The mixture should now resemble a pot of black beans in color and texture.

9. Add the strained stock, salt, black pepper, thyme, bay leaves, oregano, basil, and Creole seasoning. Stir well.

10. Stir in the chopped chicken and sausage. Bring the gumbo to a boil and cook for 5 minutes. Reduce the heat to maintain a slow simmer and cook, uncovered, for 1 to 2 hours. (If you like a chunkier texture, cook for about 1 hour. If you want a smoother texture, cook for 2 hours.) If the gumbo gets too thick, add a little water. If it is too thin, continue to let it simmer

uncovered. Because there is pork sausage in this gumbo, skim off any excess oil that rises to the top.

11. Gumbo is always better the day after it has been cooked, although I've never had a complaint when I served it the day I made it. At this point, you can cool the gumbo. Turn off the heat and let it sit for about 30 minutes. Then place the pot, uncovered, in an empty sink. Fill the sink with cold water and ice around the stockpot (try not to get any in the stockpot itself). Stir every 15 minutes to facilitate cooling. (The gumbo will spoil if improperly cooled—see page xxx for tips on cooling the gumbo.) When completely cool, refrigerate the gumbo in the stockpot, uncovered.

12. When ready to serve, slowly bring the gumbo to a simmer over medium-low heat. Thirty minutes before serving, add the green onion and parsley to the gumbo. Cover and cook for 15 minutes.

13. Add the Worcestershire, the hot sauce (if using), and the filé powder. Remove from the heat and let sit for 10 minutes. Remove and discard the bay leaves. Taste and adjust the seasonings as desired. Serve over cooked white rice with French bread and butter.

GUMBO Z'HERBE
— OR —
GREEN GUMBO

SERVES 10 TO 12

12 cups chicken or vegetable broth

1 pound andouille sausage or other smoked sausage, cut into ⅛-inch-thick rounds or half-moons (optional)

1 cup vegetable oil

1½ cups all-purpose flour

2 large onions, coarsely chopped

1 bunch celery, including leaves, coarsely chopped

2 green bell peppers, coarsely chopped

4 garlic cloves, finely chopped

2 bay leaves

1 tablespoon LuLu's Crazy Creola Seasoning (page xxviii) or other Creole seasoning

1 ham hock (optional)

3 pounds assorted greens, such as turnip, collard, mustard, or kale greens, chopped (about 14 cups)

Sea salt (optional)

4 to 6 cups cooked white rice

Filé powder (optional)

TRADITIONALLY, THIS CAJUN/CATHOLIC gumbo was made on Holy Thursday and served on Good Friday during Lent. Some cooks would add a ham hock for flavor and remove it before serving to keep the gumbo free of meat. Gratefully, eating meat is now allowed on Fridays, but if you're a traditionalist or a vegetarian, you can omit the ham hock altogether. However, if you're a sin-now, pray-later kind of eater like me, then chop up all the ham hock meat and add it back in. And if you're already breaking the rules, well, then you may as well throw in some andouille sausage, too! This gumbo is a great way to use up a pile of greens you don't know what to do with or to make when you want some authentic gumbo and there's no fresh seafood available.

1. In a large stockpot, bring 10 cups of the broth to a simmer.

2. In a large heavy skillet (10 to 12 inches), cook the sausage (if using) over medium heat until browned. Use a slotted spoon to transfer it to a paper towel–lined plate. Pat well with paper towels to soak up extra grease. Set aside.

3. To make the roux, in a large stockpot (about 10 quarts), heat the vegetable oil over medium-high heat. When the oil is hot, gradually add the flour, whisking continuously. Continue to stir the roux, adjusting the heat as necessary to keep it from burning, for 25 to 35 minutes, or until the roux is a dark mahogany color. Be careful—if the roux burns, you will have to start all over again!

4. Carefully add the onion to the roux and cook, stirring with a large wooden spoon, for 2 to 3 minutes. (The onion will sizzle and steam when it hits the hot roux, so caution is advised. All seasoned gumbo cooks have roux battle scars on one or both arms.)

5. Add the celery and cook, stirring continuously, for 2 to 3 minutes more.

6. Add the bell pepper and cook, stirring continuously, for 1 to 2 minutes more. The mixture should resemble a pot of black beans in color and texture.

7. Add the garlic and cook for 1 to 2 minutes more.

8. Slowly stir in the hot broth and add the bay leaves and Creole seasoning.

GUMBO LOVE AND OTHER HEARTWARMING SOUPS

CONT.

9. Add the ham hock and sausage (if using), and all the assorted greens (the greens will cook down in size, so pile them all in). If you are not using a ham hock or sausage, taste and season the gumbo with salt. Reduce the heat to low, cover the pot, and simmer gently for 1 hour and 15 minutes, stirring about every 20 minutes and skimming off any fat and foam from the surface as necessary.

10. Remove the ham hock. The meat should be falling off the bone. Remove and discard the skin, fat, and bone, and chop the meat into pieces before returning it to the pot.

11. Gumbo is always better the day after it has been cooked, although I've never had a complaint when I served it the day I made it. At this point, you can cool the gumbo. Turn off the heat and let it sit for about 30 minutes. Then place the pot, uncovered, in an empty sink. Fill the sink with cold water and ice around the stockpot (try not to get any in the stockpot itself). Stir every 15 minutes to facilitate cooling. (The gumbo will spoil if improperly cooled—see page xxx for tips on cooling the gumbo.) When completely cool, refrigerate the gumbo in the stockpot, uncovered.

12. When ready to serve, slowly bring the gumbo to a simmer over medium-low heat. If desired, use the remaining 2 cups broth to adjust the consistency of the gumbo, thinning it as needed. Remove and discard the bay leaves. Serve over cooked white rice. If desired, set filé powder out on the table so everyone can add it to their gumbo to their preferred thickness and taste.

SAVING GRACE

I'm not much for doing anything unless it has heart or touches mine! Big pots of bubbling soups and simmering gumbos gently scream "nurturing" to me! Mastering a pot of gumbo was my personal gateway from frivolous teen to responsible single mother of two. I was the last-born of three children with an age difference that sometimes left me lonely as a youngster, who then developed into a wild teenager.

A rule-breaking rebel with an unusually quick mind that bored easily with the learning-by-rote system of the Catholic education of my youth, I was hard to keep on track. It was only the perilous promise of angering my very passionate father or disappointing my overworked mother that kept me even a little bit in line. And of course, there were the Irish nuns! But even those stern and precious creatures with their funny brogue and somber habits had little impact on my jitterbug creative nature. I was always turning in assignments late or under the wire. It was more fun to dream, play make-believe, hang out with friends, or listen to music. The consistent message I got from the adult world was that I was not living up to my potential.

There is now a diagnosis and treatment for my "scatterbrained" work habits, but back in the day, when life was happening faster than my little limbs could carry me, I found a kind of solace in the summers I spent in Pascagoula, Mississippi, at the Formica-topped corner table in my grand-mother's modest kitchen. Every day I would watch her cook up a massive meal and on most Fridays, a big pot of gumbo. It was the only place where I could "sit still."

Though my grandmother was a typical wife and mother of her generation, she was the ruler of her little kingdom on Parsley Street, mainly because my much-revered seafaring grandfather, a ship's captain, was away from home sometimes for as long as a year, sailing to exotic, faraway places. Her response was to take stern charge of her own home and make her kitchen her throne. She was undoubtedly the boss of us all, including my grandfather.

As I watched her orchestrate a meal, she was completely empowered, holding my complete attention. I was enraptured; my brain slowed down, and I could follow every step. When she asked me to do little chores, like shell the peas or scrape the last bit of cake batter into a heat-worn tube pan, I felt connected to that place within me that said, *I'm worth it…I'm worth all the trouble I may cause.*

Looking back, I know now that those little chores were touching my heart—inspiring my art. Those childhood days watching my grandmother create beautiful meals out of a bunch of meager ingredients or using a whole day to cook a pot of gumbo on the top of her simple gas stove left an imprint on my soul, planting the seeds for my passion for cooking. More important, the whole process of cooking held my attention. That was epic. I could concentrate and take it all in. And it happened pretty fast. I liked fast! Even with an all-day-long gumbo, you knew pretty quickly if it was working your way or not. In fact, timing was everything, and the sheer quickness of the process of cooking felt in tune with my rapid thinking.

There was no *delayed* gratification. I really liked that! I had a hard time with big projects that took lots of time and lots of steps to complete. When I watched my grandmother cook, the immediate sense of accomplishment was obvious by the smile that would break across her face after dipping a tasting spoon into the pot. From my young eyes, I could see that cooking could be fun—plus, the best treat was that it usually tasted delicious! And when it didn't work, when something didn't taste so good, which was rare for her, she cussed a little bit but didn't fret too long; instead, with clenched-jaw determination, she just started all over again. I didn't know it then, of course, but significant life lessons were taking form in my psyche as I watched my grandmother cook gumbo.

I don't even remember my first pot of gumbo, but I'm sure the recipe was from the first cookbook I ever owned: the Mobile, Alabama, Junior League's *Jubilee!* I was familiar with the haunting tales and perils of making a roux, but I wasn't daunted because of the years I had spent spectating in my grandmother's kitchen. I figured I had the basic parts down. There were many pots that followed, with lots of starts, failures, and start-overs, as I developed my own techniques and used the ingredients that tasted good to me. And to this day, every time I cook a pot of gumbo, it's like cooking it for the first time because I learn something new. In the end, like anything you master, it simply takes practice.

In the South, when you ask a person, "What's your favorite gumbo?" Nine out of ten will say, "My mama's." No two gumbos are alike, even if the same recipe has been followed, because a pot of gumbo is not just a pot of soup. A pot of gumbo comes with an ancient secret permission to be who you are and express what you feel. There's happy gumbo to celebrate and there's sad gumbo to heal.

Any gumbo cook will tell you there's a magic that happens when you cook a pot of gumbo. As a young mother of two tiny girls, I was buoyed in more ways than one by that magic and those hard-learned lessons that came with it. Cooking helped me "stay the course" in my life. It was the life ring that always connected me to my own heart and brought me back to my family. Cooking was the way that I expressed my love to them and the way I apologized to them for being flawed. And cooking quenched my thirst for creative expression. Looking back, it seems kindly predestined that as I timidly teetered on the brink of adulthood, already jump-starting the process by birthing two babies by the time I was eighteen, that a pot of gumbo would be my saving grace.

COASTAL CRAB AND CORN BISQUE

SERVES 6

5 tablespoons unsalted butter

1 tablespoon extra-virgin olive oil

2 cups finely chopped onion

2 tablespoons finely chopped garlic

1 cup finely chopped celery

3 tablespoons all-purpose flour

2 cups seafood stock (see page xxx)
or chicken broth

2 cups heavy cream

2 cups milk

2 bay leaves

¼ teaspoon LuLu's Crazy
Creola Seasoning (page xxviii) or
other Creole seasoning

1 teaspoon sea salt

¼ teaspoon white pepper

¼ teaspoon freshly ground
black pepper

1 teaspoon liquid crab boil

2 cups fresh corn kernels (or frozen,
if necessary)

½ cup chopped green onions

1 teaspoon Worcestershire sauce

2 tablespoons sweet white wine,
such as sake

1 pound cooked fresh lump blue
crabmeat, picked through for shells,
handled carefully to keep the meat in
big chunks (see Notes on Handling
Seafood, pages xxx–xxxi)

½ teaspoon seasoned salt

Pinch of ground nutmeg

THIS BISQUE FEATURES two of our region's sweetest delicacies: Silver Queen corn and blue crab. It's only natural that they would pair so beautifully together in this rich, silky soup. Crab and corn bisque is a standard on the menu of many local restaurants and in households year-round. Tourists can't wait to get here to order it, and locals can't get enough of it, either. What a lot of our visitors may not realize, however, is just how easy it is to re-create, so don't wait to come see us to try this classic favorite.

1. In a medium stockpot, melt 3 tablespoons of the butter with the olive oil over low heat.

2. Add the onion, garlic, and celery. Cover and cook over medium heat, stirring occasionally, for 3 minutes, or until the vegetables have softened.

3. Add the remaining 2 tablespoons butter and cook, stirring, until the butter has melted.

4. Add the flour and cook, stirring, as the vegetables begin to brown.

5. Add 1½ cups of the stock, the cream, and the milk and stir well.

6. Add the bay leaves, Creole seasoning, sea salt, white pepper, black pepper, and liquid crab boil.

7. Cover and simmer over low heat, being careful not to let it boil.

8. Add the corn, ¼ cup of the green onion, the Worcestershire, and the wine. Simmer for about 5 minutes.

9. Add the crabmeat and seasoned salt. Cover and simmer for about 20 minutes.

10. Stir in the nutmeg, the remaining ¼ cup green onion, and the remaining ½ cup stock. Simmer for 5 minutes more, remove and discard the bay leaves, and then serve.

DADDY'S
NAVY BEAN SOUP

SERVES 8

1 pound dried navy beans

1 smoked ham hock

2 bay leaves

8 cups chicken broth

2 tablespoons extra-virgin olive oil

1 large onion, coarsely chopped

6 celery stalks, coarsely chopped

½ red bell pepper, chopped

1 large carrot, chopped

6 garlic cloves, finely chopped

4 tablespoons finely chopped
fresh rosemary

4 tablespoons finely chopped
fresh thyme

½ teaspoon freshly ground
black pepper

2 tablespoons Worcestershire sauce

2 cups kale, washed and torn
into medium pieces

½ cup finely chopped fresh parsley

Sea salt

MY DADDY HAD a repertoire of about ten dishes that he could cook as well as any seasoned chef. One of our wintertime favorites was his navy bean soup. As was his nature, he was meticulously organized, and every vegetable was chopped into almost uniform-size pieces. That was probably due to his upbringing by a sea captain who required that all things be "shipshape," a term that still rings with his voice in my head and has truly been an ingredient in my success as a restaurant owner. But with my tendency to rebel and do things "my own way," along with a heaping cup of my mother's "*C'est la vie!*" nature, I simply chop everything as easily and as effortlessly as possible. When I cook this soup, it transports me back many years and tastes just like home, sitting by my parents' roaring fireplace and looking out at a blazing orange sun, slipping into the horizon over a frigid Mobile Bay in January.

1. Pick through the beans to remove rocks or odd beans. Rinse the beans under cold water, then put them in a large bowl. Cover the beans with 3 inches of water and set them aside on the counter for 6 to 8 hours or overnight.

2. Drain and rinse the beans. In a medium stockpot, combine the beans, ham hock, bay leaves, and 6 cups of the broth. Bring to a boil over medium-high heat, then reduce the heat to medium-low and cover.

3. While the beans cook, in a large heavy skillet (10 to 12 inches), heat the olive oil. Add the onion and sauté for 4 to 5 minutes. Add the celery, bell pepper, and carrot and sauté for 4 to 5 minutes more.

4. Add the garlic and sauté for 2 minutes more, stirring continuously and scraping up all the "good stuff" from the bottom of the pan. If the vegetables start to stick or burn, add a little broth to the pan.

5. Scrape the vegetable mixture into the pot with the beans and stir well. Reduce the heat to low. Add 2 tablespoons of the rosemary, 2 tablespoons of the thyme, the black pepper, and the Worcestershire. Simmer on low for 1 hour, or until the beans are soft, adding the remainder of the broth if the soup gets too thick.

CONT.

6. Add the kale, the parsley, and the remaining 2 tablespoons each of rosemary and thyme and simmer for 15 minutes more.

7. At this point, the meat from the ham hock should be falling off the bone. Remove the hock. Remove and discard any skin, fat, or bone, and chop the meat. Return the meat to the pot. Since the ham hock is salty, taste the soup before adding any salt. Remove and discard the bay leaves. Serve immediately.

NOTE: *Any type of ham or sausage can be used instead of a ham hock—or you can eliminate the meat altogether, use vegetable broth instead of chicken broth, and serve this as a vegetarian dish.*

EASY CHICKEN
TORTILLA SOUP

SERVES 8

Tortilla Strips

Organic olive oil cooking spray

Fresh corn tortillas

Sea salt

Stock

1 (3- to 4-pound) whole chicken

1 medium onion, halved or cut into large pieces

1 carrot, chopped into chunks

2 celery stalks, chopped into chunks

4 to 6 fresh cilantro stems

2 bay leaves

2 teaspoons sea salt

1 teaspoon whole black peppercorns

Soup

2 tablespoons extra-virgin olive oil

2 cups chopped onion

1 teaspoon sea salt

8 garlic cloves, finely chopped

½ large bell pepper, coarsely chopped

1 teaspoon finely chopped seeded jalapeño

1 (14.5-ounce) can diced tomatoes, with their juices

THIS IS A very easy and fast soup. I let my guests serve themselves from a big pot on the stove and have all the garnishes in bowls along the countertop in the kitchen so they can choose whatever suits their fancy.

To make the tortilla strips:

1. Preheat the oven to 350°F. Coat a baking sheet with olive oil spray.

2. Cut the tortillas into 3-inch strips.

3. Place the tortilla strips on the baking sheet, scattering them so there is room for them to bake without sticking to one another too much.

4. Spray the tortilla strips with olive oil spray and sprinkle a little salt over the top.

5. Bake for 15 to 16 minutes, or until golden brown. Remove and set aside.

To make the stock:

6. Fill a large stockpot with 6 to 8 quarts of water. Add the chicken, onion, carrot, celery, cilantro, bay leaves, salt, and peppercorns. Cover the pot and bring to a boil over medium-high heat. Reduce the heat to medium and simmer for 1 hour, or until the chicken is cooked through.

7. Remove the chicken from the pot and strain the stock into a large bowl, discarding the solids. Measure out 8 cups of the warm stock to use for the soup. Let the rest of the stock cool completely and refrigerate or freeze for later use.

8. When the chicken has cooled, remove and discard the bones and skin. Chop the meat into medium to large pieces. (I get 4 to 5 cups of chicken meat from one chicken.)

To make the soup:

9. In a large stockpot, heat the olive oil over medium heat.

10. Add the onion and ½ teaspoon of the salt and sauté until the onion is golden brown.

11. Add the garlic, bell pepper, and jalapeño and cook for 1 minute.

¼ cup fresh lime juice

1 cup whole-kernel corn (I prefer fresh corn, but you can use frozen)

2 teaspoons ground cumin

1 teaspoon chili powder

¼ teaspoon freshly ground black pepper

¼ cup chopped fresh cilantro

Garnishes

Shredded Monterey Jack or cheddar cheese

Radish slices

Lime slices

Jalapeño slices

Avocado slices

Chopped green onions

Fresh cilantro

Sour cream

12. Add the tomatoes and the 8 cups chicken stock. Bring to a boil.

13. Add the lime juice, the corn, and the chopped chicken. Reduce the heat to medium-low.

14. Add the remaining ½ teaspoon salt, the cumin, chili powder, black pepper, and cilantro. Cook for 15 minutes. Cover and reduce the heat to low until ready to serve.

15. Serve in large soup bowls and top with the tortilla strips. Let your guests choose from among the suggested garnishes.

NEVER-FAIL OLD-FASHIONED
VEGETABLE BEEF SOUP

SERVES 8

2 tablespoons extra-virgin olive oil

1 to 1½ pounds beef stew meat or chuck roast, chopped into bite-size pieces

1 teaspoon sea salt, plus more as needed

½ teaspoon freshly ground black pepper, plus more as needed

2 large sweet yellow onions, chopped

3 to 4 large carrots, sliced into medium rounds or half-moons

6 celery stalks, chopped

1 green bell pepper, chopped

4 to 6 cups beef broth

1 (28-ounce) can whole tomatoes, drained and coarsely chopped

3 bay leaves

1 tablespoon dried oregano

2 teaspoons dried basil

1 teaspoon dried thyme

2 large baking potatoes, peeled, chopped into 1-inch pieces, and placed in a bowl of water

1 bunch green onions, finely chopped

½ bunch parsley, finely chopped

THIS IS A weekly wintertime staple in my house. It's so easy, light, and healthy yet nurturing on so many levels. I like lots of texture in my vegetable soup, so I coarsely chop the vegetables in medium to large pieces since they will "cook down" during the long simmering that melds the flavors into a delicious soup.

1. In a medium stockpot, heat 1 tablespoon of the olive oil over medium heat.

2. Add the beef, salt, and black pepper and cook for 3 to 4 minutes. Turn the beef pieces to the other side and cover the pot. Cook for 2 to 3 minutes. Transfer the braised beef and any cooking juices to a bowl and set aside.

3. Add the remaining 1 tablespoon olive oil to the hot pot. Add the onion and sauté over medium heat for 3 to 4 minutes, until translucent. Cover the pot. Stir every couple of minutes.

4. Add the carrots, cover, and cook, stirring often, for 4 to 5 minutes.

5. Add the celery, cover, and cook, stirring often, for 3 to 4 minutes more, or until the celery has softened.

6. Add the bell pepper, cover, and cook, stirring often, for 2 to 3 minutes.

7. Return the beef and its cooking juices to the pot. Add 4 cups of the broth, the tomatoes, bay leaves, oregano, basil, and thyme. Cover and bring the soup to a boil, then reduce the heat to low and simmer, stirring occasionally, for 1 hour.

8. Drain and rinse the potatoes and add them to the soup. Cook for 30 minutes, or until the potatoes are cooked through. Be careful not to overcook the potatoes. If the soup is too thick, add a little more broth. If it is too thin, let it cook, uncovered, for 15 minutes to let some of the liquid evaporate.

9. Add the green onion and parsley and cook, covered, for 10 minutes.

10. Remove and discard the bay leaves. Taste and season with salt and black pepper as desired. Serve.

STIR THE POT AND STAY THE COURSE

I think that one of the reasons cooking stole my heart when I was young was because there is no delayed gratification. You follow a recipe step-by-step and you know pretty quickly if something is going to work out or not. Patience is not one of my virtues, and I've had to learn a lot of life's lessons the hard way. I've always turned to cooking for comfort, and more than once I've been able to gain understanding of a problem or a situation simply by poring over the steps of a complicated recipe—breaking it down into increments until I see the big picture.

I'm quick to say, "I have a lot of good start-up energy, but I'm short on completion energy." It may be hard to believe, but since I was a child, I've had a hard time finishing anything. It takes all my due diligence to get grounded enough that I can take things one step at a time. I'm completely engaged in the beginning of any new project or relationship, but when it gets tough, or, more accurately, when it gets tedious, I tend to get going—off in a different direction entirely. Now, that can be useful in business. When a plan is not working and probably won't work, it's easy for me to change directions. I think it's one of the components that have helped me create and sustain a successful restaurant. But it can be a

worthy challenge to accomplish an end result. Along the way, I've learned to ask for help when I need it and pull people in who do certain things better than I do. But in the long run, there are simply going to be times when you are the only cook in the kitchen and you have to go it alone.

The biggest lesson I've learned is that no one, no place, or no thing can make me happy. That's all an inside job. The big disappointments that life inevitably slings in my path, usually when I least expect it—those are the times when I have to dig deeply and find my own way. And when my own humanity comes barreling out in rude and mean-spirited ways or when I simply mess up, I've learned to take stock and employ the dreaded *R* word: *responsibility*. I own my failings, make amends, and practice the really hard part, forgiving myself. In the wise words of my brother, I "breathe in. Breathe out. Move on."

Plain and simple, it's called growing up... sometimes you have to do things that you just don't want to do, and follow-through is necessary to accomplish anything to completion, something I have to work on daily. I rely upon a sailing term from the menfolk of my family, "stay the course," to get the simplest to the most difficult projects completed. When I'm up to my ass in alligators in the middle of a complicated or long-term venture, it's so easy to get confused or distracted, and that's when I have to stop and ask myself, *What was my original motivation?* I go over the steps that got me to that place, just like following a recipe. Then I let those thoughts simmer as I ask myself: *What was the crystalline moment when I had the thought in the first place? What did it feel like? What did I want to accomplish in the beginning?* These questions remind me why I started the project and help me get back on track, get my spoon back into the pot, and give me the fortitude to "stay the course."

FRENCH ONION SOUP
WITH FRESH ROSEMARY

SERVES 6 TO 8

½ cup (1 stick) unsalted butter

4 onions, thinly sliced lengthwise
(6 to 8 cups)

½ teaspoon sea salt

1 tablespoon sugar

6 garlic cloves, finely chopped

3 tablespoons all-purpose flour

¾ cup white wine

8 cups beef broth

2 bay leaves

3 fresh rosemary sprigs

¼ teaspoon freshly ground
black pepper

2 tablespoons Worcestershire
sauce

8 ounces Gruyère or Swiss cheese,
shredded (about 3 cups)

Toasted Garlic Bread Rounds

4 tablespoons (½ stick)
unsalted butter

2 garlic cloves

1 loaf French bread, cut into
1-inch-thick slices

THERE ARE THOSE occasional days in Key West during December when a front is moving through and the temperature drops to a startling sixty-five degrees. You can always tell who is a local because they are bundled up like they are in Anchorage, Alaska. In fact, it is sometimes a welcome relief when I can turn on the gas fireplace in my old 1930s Arts and Crafts–style conch house. It takes the chill out of the air—with the doors wide open. There is nothing like winter in paradise, and on those days I'm moved to make this easy and scrumptious French onion soup. There is something quite romantic about eating this under the palm trees on my back deck wearing cutoffs, flip-flops, and a sweater, truly savoring a moment of joie de vivre!

1. In a large heavy skillet (10 to 12 inches), melt the butter over medium heat. Add the onion, salt, and sugar and cook, stirring, while the onion cooks down and caramelizes, about 20 minutes. You may have to reduce the heat to keep the onion from burning and keep scraping the bottom of the pan to loosen all the gooey residue.

2. When the onion is dark brown, add the garlic and cook for 2 minutes more. Stir in the flour, making sure the onion is well coated. Cook for 1 to 2 minutes more, being careful not to burn the mixture.

3. Add the wine to deglaze the pan, stirring continuously and scraping up the browned bits from the bottom of the pan. Remove from the heat and transfer the onion mixture to a medium stockpot.

4. Add the broth, bay leaves, rosemary, pepper, and Worcestershire and bring to a boil over medium-high heat.

5. Let the soup boil for 2 minutes, then cover, reduce the heat to low, and simmer for 45 minutes.

To make the toasted garlic bread rounds:

6. Preheat the broiler.

7. In a small saucepan, melt the butter over medium-low heat. Use a garlic press to press the garlic cloves and stir them into the butter. (If you do not have a garlic press, you can smash the peeled cloves with the flat side of a knife so they are mushy, then stir them into the butter.) Place the bread slices on a baking sheet. Brush the garlic butter over the top of the bread slices. Broil the bread for about 1½ minutes, or until it is beautifully browned. Remove the pan and turn the slices over. Broil on the second side for about 1 minute, keeping a close watch to make sure it browns but doesn't burn. Leave the oven on broil.

To assemble:

8. Remove and discard the bay leaves. Taste the soup and adjust the seasonings with salt and pepper.

9. Place eight ovenproof soup bowls in a sturdy baking dish (or two). Ladle the soup into the bowls. Top each bowl with a toasted garlic bread round and shredded cheese and broil until the cheese is browned and bubbling. Serve immediately.

CUBAN
BLACK BEAN
SOUP

SERVES 6

1 pound dried black beans

3 tablespoons extra-virgin olive oil

4 bacon slices, chopped

2 onions, chopped

1 green bell pepper, chopped

3 celery stalks, chopped

¼ bunch cilantro, finely chopped,
plus sprigs for garnish

4 garlic cloves, finely chopped

1 jalapeño, seeded and finely chopped

7 cups low-sodium chicken broth

2 fresh oregano sprigs

2 tablespoons ground cumin

3 bay leaves

1 smoked ham hock

¼ cup distilled white vinegar or
pepper vinegar

Sea salt and freshly ground
black pepper

1 cup sour cream

2 teaspoons lime zest

Lime wedges, for garnish

WHEN I LIVED in the eclectic Los Angeles community of Venice, one of my neighbors was Ren Blanco, a sweet young man and a great artist, who, like all of us in those days, was struggling to break into the entertainment business. Our little neighborhood band of transplants would get homesick on occasion, so we'd get together and cook the foods from "back home." Ren would often tell us stories about his lively childhood in South Florida with his Cuban immigrant parents. One day I was cooking a pot of black beans, adding my Southern twist of a ham hock and Creole seasoning, when Ren told me they reminded him of his mother's black beans—with one striking difference. "She always adds a little vinegar," he said. Well, I was all for trying something new and authentic, and *wow*—that little something different gave the beans such a brightness. I've heard Ren is now an exceptionally successful production designer still living in Venice, and whenever I cook up a pot of black beans or drive through Miami on the way to Key West, I think of him and his sweet mama and how he taught me how to make my beans truly Cuban!

1. Pick through the black beans to remove rocks or odd beans. Wash them under cold water and set aside.

2. In a medium stockpot, heat the olive oil over medium heat. Add the bacon and cook until it starts to get crispy.

3. Add the onion and sauté for 2 to 3 minutes.

4. Add the bell pepper and sauté for 2 to 3 minutes.

5. Add the celery and cilantro and sauté for 2 to 3 minutes.

6. Add the garlic and jalapeño and sauté for 2 to 3 minutes.

7. Add the broth, oregano, cumin, and bay leaves. Add the black beans and ham hock. Cover slightly and simmer for 2 hours, stirring every 20 minutes, until the beans are tender.

8. Remove and discard the bay leaves. Remove the ham hock. Remove and discard the skin, fat, and bone. Cut the ham meat into pieces and set aside.

CONT.

9. *Very carefully* transfer 3 cups, or about a third, of the soup to a blender and puree until smooth. Return the pureed soup to the pot and stir it in to combine. (Alternatively, you can puree the soup directly in the pot using an immersion blender. If using an immersion blender, try not to overpuree—you want to leave some of the beans whole to create a somewhat chunky texture.) Simmer until the soup is slightly thickened, about 15 minutes.

10. Fold the ham meat back into the soup and add the vinegar. Taste and season with salt and black pepper.

11. In a small bowl, combine the sour cream, lime zest, and 1 teaspoon salt.

12. Spoon the soup into individual bowls. On top of each, spoon a dollop of the sour cream topping, squeeze a wedge of lime, and sprinkle a few sprigs of cilantro.

CHICKEN APPLE SAUSAGE, BUTTERNUT SQUASH, AND TURNIP GREEN SOUP

SERVES 4 TO 6

1 large butternut squash, peeled, seeded, and chopped into 1-inch chunks

2 turnip roots, peeled and chopped into 1-inch chunks (or 2 medium potatoes, peeled and chopped into 1-inch chunks, if using kale instead of turnip greens; see Note)

2 medium carrots, chopped into small chunks

1 teaspoon sea salt

3 tablespoons extra-virgin olive oil

4 or 5 fresh rosemary sprigs

1 pound chicken and apple sausage, cut into half-moons

1 medium onion, chopped

3 celery stalks, chopped

4 garlic cloves, finely chopped

8 cups chicken broth

½ teaspoon freshly ground black pepper

2 bay leaves

½ teaspoon LuLu's Crazy Creola Seasoning (page xxviii) or other Creole seasoning

4 cups chopped turnip green leaves, cleaned, with all spines removed (or 4 cups kale; see Note)

1 tablespoon chopped fresh thyme

Grated Parmesan cheese, for garnish

1. Preheat the oven to 350°F.

2. In a medium baking pan, combine the butternut squash, turnip roots, and carrots. Sprinkle with ½ teaspoon of the salt and 1 tablespoon of the olive oil, and place the rosemary sprigs on top. Roast for 45 minutes to 1 hour, or until the vegetables start to soften and caramelize.

3. Meanwhile, in a medium stockpot, heat 1 tablespoon of the olive oil over medium-high heat. Add the sausage and cook for 5 minutes, or until browned.

4. Add the remaining 1 tablespoon olive oil and the onion. Cook for 3 minutes.

5. Add the celery, stir, and cover. Simmer for about 5 minutes, or until the vegetables start to soften and caramelize.

6. Add the garlic, broth, roasted vegetables, the remaining ½ teaspoon salt, the pepper, bay leaves, and Creole seasoning. Stir to mix well, cover, and simmer over medium heat for 15 minutes.

7. If the soup is at a boil after 15 minutes, reduce the heat to low so the soup is at a nice simmer and cook, uncovered, for 30 minutes.

8. Stir in the turnip greens and simmer for 10 minutes.

9. Add the thyme and simmer for 5 minutes more.

10. Remove and discard the bay leaves. Serve the soup in large soup bowls, garnished with Parmesan.

NOTE: *You can substitute 4 cups kale and 2 medium potatoes for the turnip greens and roots.*

CHAPTER 4

MAIN DISHES

WHEN I'M choosing my main dish for a meal, I want it to be the star of the show. I'm always going to reach first for something in season and local for inspiration. When the trout are running, for example, I'm going for a classic Trout Amandine. Then I'll choose the accompaniments, starters, and side dishes accordingly. All the flavors need to complement one another. I'm all about taste first, followed closely by the colors and textures of a dish. They need to look pretty on a plate—even if it's only a breakfast of an English muffin with hard-boiled egg and sliced mango on the side. Planning, fixing, and serving food is a work of art for me. I'm blessed that it also became my occupation. But at the heart of the matter, it's the way that I love and nurture my family. It matters.

I am nontraditional in almost every aspect of my life, except for sitting down together for a meal, a ritual imprinted on me by my family's Sunday dinners. I consider gathering around a table, whether it's fancy mahogany or a weath-ered pine picnic table, the apex of Southern food culture and a noble tradition I want to pass down to my grandchildren.

Having lived on all three coasts of the United States, I know many Southerners who have left the South and moved away, but very few of them have abandoned their passion for Southern food culture—they take it with them wherever they go. That's not to say every Sunday dinner in the South is an example of family harmony (good-ness knows not every Buffett family dinner was!), but there is something special in this chaotic, speed-obsessed world about sitting down to eat at a table with plates, cloth napkins, forks and knives, and food that someone has thought about, prepared, and presented. It takes a long time and a lot of work to cook! Making a presentation of it shows an appreciation for the effort. It sends the message that food and family are indeed a big deal—and worth celebrating every chance we get. Appreciating our food and each other is always in season.

HONEY-GLAZED
STICKY RIBS

MAKES 20 RIBLETS

2 pounds baby back pork ribs
(your butcher can saw the entire rack
horizontally to make riblets)

½ teaspoon sea salt

½ teaspoon freshly ground
black pepper

½ cup beef broth

1 cup Allegro Original Marinade

Cooking Sauce

¼ cup soy sauce

¼ cup good-quality sake

¼ cup hoisin sauce

½ cup honey

½ cup beef broth

2 tablespoons barbecue sauce
(I like to use Dreamland from
Tuscaloosa, Alabama)

½ teaspoon toasted sesame oil

2 tablespoons vegetable oil

2 tablespoons finely
chopped garlic

2 tablespoons finely chopped
fresh ginger

CONT.

A MILLION YEARS ago, when I was a young cook and read any recipe book I could afford, I purchased a paperback Sunset cookbook on Chinese cooking. I was fascinated by learning this new cuisine, and luckily there was an Asian grocery store in the boondocks in Mobile, Alabama, where I could purchase what were then quite exotic ingredients. One such ingredient was fermented black beans. They had a salty, pungent flavor I had never tasted before and that I found absolutely alluring. In that little cookbook, there was a recipe for cocktail black bean spareribs, and every time I cooked the dish, the compliments were overflowing. Recently, when I was creating some new recipes, I decided to rework that black bean rib recipe with some Gulf Coast attitude, and this was the end result. Full of flavor that's a mix of both the traditional and the unusual, this rib dish has quickly become a stand-up favorite!

1. Preheat the oven to 325°F.

2. Place the rib racks in a roasting pan and sprinkle with the salt and pepper. Add the broth and marinade. Cover with aluminum foil and bake for 1 hour and 45 minutes.

3. When the ribs have completely cooled, remove them from the cooking liquid. Cut in between the bones of the rack so they are cut into individual rib pieces and set aside.

4. Combine all the ingredients for the cooking sauce and set aside.

5. In a large wok or large heavy skillet (10 to 12 inches), heat the vegetable oil over medium heat. When the oil is just about to sizzle, add the garlic, ginger, black beans, and red pepper flakes. Stir for 1 minute.

6. Add the ribs to the wok or skillet, continuously lifting them to make sure they get covered with the garlic mixture. Stir-fry for 5 minutes, or until the ribs are heated through, scraping the bottom of the wok or skillet to make sure there's no burning.

CONT.

2 tablespoons Chinese fermented black beans, if available, or salted black bean paste or sauce (optional)

¼ teaspoon red pepper flakes

½ cup finely chopped green onions

¼ cup finely chopped fresh cilantro

Honey, for drizzling

7. Add the cooking sauce and continue to stir the ribs for 2 minutes. Cover the wok or skillet, reduce the heat to low, and cook the ribs for 10 minutes.

8. Add the green onion and stir well. Cover the wok or skillet and remove it from the heat. Let it sit for 5 minutes.

9. Place the ribs on a large platter or divide among individual serving bowls. Sprinkle them with cilantro and drizzle with honey. Get ready to get sticky!

PORK ROAST
— WITH —
APPLES AND ONIONS

SERVES 8

Marinade

2 teaspoons sea salt

½ teaspoon freshly ground
black pepper

1 teaspoon LuLu's Crazy Creola
Seasoning (page xxviii) or other
Creole seasoning

1 teaspoon apple pie seasoning
or ground cinnamon

1 teaspoon ground cumin

2 tablespoons soy sauce

1 tablespoon balsamic vinegar

2 tablespoons honey

1 tablespoon extra-virgin
olive oil

Pork

1 (3-pound) Boston butt pork roast

8 garlic cloves

2 large sweet onions, coarsely
chopped

3 large, sweet, firm apples, peeled,
cored, and cut into large slices

½ cup beef or chicken broth

½ cup apple juice

To make the marinade:

1. In a large shallow dish, whisk together all the marinade ingredients and set aside.

To make the pork:

2. Preheat the oven to 350°F.

3. With a paring knife, make eight small slits in the pork roast and insert a whole garlic clove into each.

4. Slather the marinade over the roast and set aside.

5. In the bottom of a metal roasting pan, scatter the onion and apple slices. Place the roast on top of the bed of onion and apples, scraping all the marinade into the pan.

6. Add the broth and the apple juice and cover with aluminum foil. Bake for 2½ hours, or 45 minutes per pound, or until the internal temperature of the roast reaches 145 to 165°F. Spoon the onions and apples over the pork to serve.

SPICY COFFEE-RUBBED
BEEF TENDERLOIN

SERVES 8 TO 10

Coffee Rub

2 tablespoons sea salt

2 tablespoons packed dark brown sugar

2 tablespoons freshly ground black pepper

1 teaspoon red pepper flakes

3 tablespoons finely ground dark-roast coffee or espresso

2 tablespoons garlic powder

2 tablespoons onion powder

Tenderloin

1 (4- to 5-pound) beef tenderloin

¼ cup extra-virgin olive oil

Nonstick cooking spray for high temperatures, if grilling, or additional 2 tablespoons extra-virgin olive oil, if roasting

To make the rub:

1. In a small bowl, combine all the coffee rub ingredients and mix well.

To make the tenderloin:

2. In a baking pan, rub the tenderloin with the olive oil. Pour the coffee rub into the baking pan and roll the tenderloin through the coffee rub to coat it on all sides. Use your hands to rub the coffee rub into the tenderloin so it is fully coated on all sides, both ends, and in all crevices.

3. Cover or wrap the tenderloin in plastic and let it come to room temperature, 30 minutes to 1 hour.

To grill:

4. Heat a clean grill to medium-high. Coat the grates with cooking spray. (When spraying an especially hot grill, be careful of flame flare-up.) Place the tenderloin on the grill over direct heat to sear and caramelize the outside of the tenderloin, 4 to 5 minutes per side. Move the tenderloin to indirect heat and cover with aluminum foil or close the lid of the grill. Grill until the internal temperature of the tenderloin reaches 125 to 130°F, 20 to 30 minutes, turning a couple of times. Use a meat thermometer for accuracy. The center will be medium-rare, and the ends will be medium. For a medium middle, cook to an internal temperature of 130 to 140°F, but be sure not to overcook this precious piece of meat! Remove the tenderloin from the grill and let it rest for 10 to 15 minutes before slicing.

To oven-roast:

4. Preheat the oven to 500°F. In a large heavy skillet (10 to 12 inches), heat 2 tablespoons olive oil over medium-high heat. Once the oil is hot, place the tenderloin in the skillet to sear it, 1½ to 2 minutes per side, to seal in the juices and give the meat a nice caramelized coating. Transfer the tenderloin to a roasting pan or baking dish (or you can keep it in the skillet if the skillet is ovenproof). Roast for 10 minutes, then reduce the oven temperature to 375°F and cook for 20 minutes more, or until the internal temperature of the tenderloin reaches 125 to 130°F. Use a meat thermometer for accuracy. The center will be medium-rare, and the ends will be medium. For a medium middle, cook to an internal temperature of 130 to 140°F, but be sure not to overcook this precious piece of meat! Remove the tenderloin from the oven and let it rest for 10 to 15 minutes before slicing.

5. Slice the grilled or roasted meat into 1-inch-thick pieces and arrange on a serving platter or cutting board.

BEER-BRAISED BEEF BRISKET
WITH CUMIN AND GARLIC

SERVES 12 TO 15

1 (8- to 10-pound) beef brisket, untrimmed

6 garlic cloves, finely chopped

2 tablespoons packed brown sugar

2 tablespoons Creole mustard

2 tablespoons sea salt

1 tablespoon freshly ground black pepper

1 teaspoon cayenne pepper

2 tablespoons ground cumin

1 tablespoon ground coriander

1 tablespoon paprika

1 teaspoon dried oregano

3 tablespoons extra-virgin olive oil

2 large sweet yellow onions, sliced vertically

1 (12-ounce) bottle beer or honey ale

I WAS READING one of my cooking magazines on a plane to Key West to give a big sixtieth birthday party for my favorite friend, Bobbo, and I had still not figured out what I was going to serve. There was a photo of a delicious-looking brisket in the magazine, and I thought, *What a great idea to go with my usual seafood entrées.* Of course, I don't think I'd ever cooked brisket for a crowd, but no worries, that is my MO—entertain a bunch of guests I don't know all that well and cook something I've never cooked before! Lucky for me, the brisket was beyond delicious and the favorite of the young fellows. I served it with King's Hawaiian rolls and let the guests make their own little brisket sliders with white horseradish sauce. This brisket keeps beautifully and rewarms easily.

1. Rinse the brisket and pat it dry. If it is extra fatty, trim off a little of the fat, but not too much. With this brisket, you want the fat to make the delicious cooking juice.

2. In a medium bowl, combine the garlic, brown sugar, mustard, salt, black pepper, cayenne, cumin, coriander, paprika, oregano, and olive oil, mixing well until it has the consistency of a wet paste.

3. Slather the paste over the brisket so that it is fully coated on all sides, both ends, and in all crevices. Wrap the brisket in plastic wrap and refrigerate for 24 hours. When you are ready to cook it, pull it out of the refrigerator and let it sit until it reaches room temperature, about 1 hour.

4. Preheat the oven to 325°F.

5. Scatter the onion in the bottom of a large roasting pan.

6. Carefully unwrap the brisket and place it on top of the onion. Pour the beer or honey ale into the pan over the onion. Cover the pan tightly with aluminum foil and bake for 5 to 6 hours. I usually check it at 5 hours. The brisket should be juicy and falling apart. At this point, if you'd like it to have a crispy top, turn the oven to broil, remove the foil, and brown the brisket under the broiler. Otherwise, I usually cover the brisket and put it back in the oven for the additional hour, where it will brown but not as crisply as if you'd broiled it.

CONT.

7. Place the brisket on a shallow serving platter and let it cool slightly. Cut it or pull it apart and spoon some of the cooking juices from the pan over the brisket. Serve with the cooking juices in a bowl alongside.

8. To rewarm the brisket later, just put the brisket back in the pan with the cooking juices, cover, and warm it up in a 250 to 300°F oven for about an hour. By that time, it looks pretty much like the famous debris from Mother's in New Orleans and makes a great day-after sandwich (see page 237).

NOTE: *I often use a disposable aluminum turkey roasting pan, especially if I'm taking the brisket as a potluck dish.*

CHIMILULU
HANGER STEAK

SERVES 4 TO 6

ChimiLuLu Sauce

1 cup chopped fresh parsley

1 cup chopped fresh cilantro

2 tablespoons chopped fresh oregano

4 garlic cloves, finely chopped

1 shallot, finely chopped

1 jalapeño, seeded and finely chopped

1 teaspoon sea salt

½ teaspoon freshly ground black pepper

3 tablespoons fresh lemon juice

2 tablespoons white wine vinegar

¾ cup extra-virgin olive oil

Marinade

½ cup teriyaki sauce

2 tablespoons finely chopped garlic

¼ cup red wine

1 teaspoon freshly ground black pepper

2 tablespoons extra-virgin olive oil

2 or 3 dashes of hot sauce

1 (16- to 18-ounce) hanger steak, trimmed and center vein removed

EVERY MAY, the Rotary Club of Fairhope, Alabama, puts on a steak cook-off, and one year the winner was a chimichurri steak. I'd never heard of chimichurri before, but as soon as I saw that bright-green sauce, tasted it, and found out what was in it, I instantly knew it fit my sensibilities. I just had to add it to my own repertoire—the combination of the garden-fresh herbs with the touch of lemon and that little shot of jalapeño makes the perfect accompaniment for a perfectly grilled or seared steak. You can also use it on grilled fish or chicken or even on fish or steak tacos.

To make the sauce:

1. Combine all the sauce ingredients in a medium bowl or airtight container. Cover and refrigerate overnight.

To make the marinade:

2. In a large shallow dish, whisk together the teriyaki sauce, garlic, wine, pepper, olive oil, and hot sauce.

3. Add the steak to the marinade, turning several times to coat well. Cover and refrigerate for a minimum of 2 hours or overnight for best results.

4. Remove the steak from the refrigerator and let it sit until it is at room temperature, about 30 minutes.

5. Remove the steak from the marinade and pat it dry.

6. Heat a grill to medium-high or a large heavy skillet (10 to 12 inches) over medium-high heat. Place the steak on the grill or skillet, cover, and cook for 4 minutes on each side. Cook to an internal temperature of 125 to 130°F for medium-rare or 140°F for medium. Turn the steak as needed to reach your desired temperature, and use a meat thermometer for accuracy.

7. Remove the steak from the heat and let it sit for 5 to 10 minutes before carving. This resting period is essential for holding in all the good juices. Slice the steak on a cutting board on the diagonal. Transfer the steak to a serving platter or leave on the cutting board to serve. Spoon ChimiLuLu Sauce generously over the steak and enjoy!

CLASSIC COASTAL CRAB-STUFFED SHRIMP
—— WITH ——
HONEY-SRIRACHA GLAZE

SERVES 6
(ABOUT 60 SHRIMP TOTAL)

4 pounds jumbo wild-caught Gulf shrimp, peeled and deveined (do not remove the tails)

¾ cup (1½ sticks) unsalted butter

½ cup finely chopped celery

½ cup finely chopped green bell pepper

¾ cup finely chopped sweet yellow onion

3 garlic cloves, finely chopped

½ cup finely chopped tasso (can substitute spicy chorizo or Canadian bacon)

¼ cup white wine

2 tablespoons fresh lemon juice (from 1 lemon)

½ teaspoon LuLu's Crazy Creola Seasoning (page xxviii) or other Creole seasoning

2 teaspoons Old Bay Seasoning

1 pound cooked blue crabmeat, lump or claw, picked through for shells, handled carefully to keep the meat in big chunks (see Notes on Handling Seafood, pages xxx–xxxi)

½ teaspoon sea salt

CONT.

AS CHILDREN, my brother, sister, and I cherished the twice-monthly after-payday Friday nights when our parents would splurge and take us out to supper. Crab-stuffed shrimp was on the menu of almost every old-school seafood restaurant around, and to this day, if I see it on a menu I always order it. It tastes incredible, with its decadent mix of bacon, shrimp, and crabmeat (how could you ever go wrong with that combination?), and besides that, it lets me relive one of my favorite childhood food memories. How sweet it is—especially served with this honey-sriracha glaze, inspired by the Vietnamese shrimpers and crabbers who live along the Mississippi-Alabama Gulf Coast.

1. Preheat the oven to 450°F.

2. Butterfly the shrimp by using a small knife to cut along the inside of the shrimp. Devein and open the shrimp up, still leaving the tail intact. Place the shrimp in the refrigerator while you prepare the other ingredients.

3. In a large heavy skillet (10 to 12 inches), melt the butter over medium-high heat. Add the celery, bell pepper, and onion and sauté until lightly browned. Add the garlic and tasso and sauté for 2 minutes more.

4. Add the wine to deglaze the pan, scraping up any gooey bits stuck to the pan and stirring them into the wine. Add the lemon juice, Creole seasoning, and Old Bay. Cook for 2 minutes more, then remove from the heat. Let cool.

5. In a large bowl, combine the crabmeat, salt, black pepper, Parmesan, parsley, and crushed crackers and mix together. Add the vegetable mixture from the skillet, gently toss together, and set aside.

6. Cut the bacon slices in half, then arrange the bacon on two rimmed baking sheets. Cook the bacon in the oven for 6 to 8 minutes, so the bacon is *not fully cooked* or crisp but just beginning to brown. Remove the bacon from the oven and transfer to a separate baking sheet lined with paper towels to drain excess grease. Set aside to cool.

CONT.

½ teaspoon freshly ground
black pepper

½ cup grated Parmesan cheese

¼ cup finely chopped fresh parsley

1¼ cups crushed Ritz crackers

30 thin bacon slices (1 to 1½ pounds)

Honey-Sriracha Glaze

Juice of 4 lemons (about ½ cup)

1 cup fresh local honey

½ cup sriracha

Dash of sea salt

Dash of freshly ground
black pepper

2 tablespoons unsalted butter

Zest of 5 to 10 lemons, for serving
(optional)

To make the glaze:

7. In a medium saucepan, combine the lemon juice, honey, sriracha, salt, and pepper over medium heat. Stir or whisk for 3 to 4 minutes as the sauce thickens. The sauce can boil up vigorously, so be careful! If this occurs, remove it from the heat, stir, and then place it back on the heat until the desired consistency is reached. Remove the pan from the heat and add the butter a little at a time, swirling the pan until all the butter is incorporated and the sauce is smooth.

8. To stuff the shrimp, mold 1½ teaspoons of the crabmeat stuffing to the inside of each butterflied shrimp. Wrap each shrimp with half a slice of bacon, starting at the tail and wrapping it to the larger end.

9. Place the wrapped shrimp on two grill pans and bake for 15 minutes. Switch the grill pans halfway through cooking time, with the pan on the top rack moving to the bottom rack and the pan that was on the bottom rack moving to the top rack.

10. Serve the shrimp on individual plates or on a large serving platter and drizzle with the honey-sriracha glaze. If using the lemons, zest them over the plates or serving platter for a bright yellow pop.

GUMBO QUESADILLAS
WITH SHRIMP AND ANDOUILLE

MAKES 4 QUESADILLAS

1 pound medium wild-caught Gulf shrimp, peeled and deveined

8 tablespoons extra-virgin olive oil

2 tablespoons LuLu's Crazy Creola Seasoning (page xxviii) or other Creole seasoning

2 links andouille sausage, chopped

¼ cup chopped tasso (can substitute spicy chorizo or Canadian bacon)

1 green bell pepper, chopped

4 green onions, finely chopped

1 yellow onion, chopped

Pinch of sea salt

Pinch of freshly ground black pepper

2 teaspoons hot sauce

4 (12-inch) flour tortillas

4 cups shredded Monterey Jack cheese

Tomato salsa (pages 71–72), for serving (optional)

Sour cream, for serving

AS STRANGE AS IT MAY SEEM at first glance, a gumbo quesadilla is quite a natural transition between two very popular cuisines. Cajun gumbo with a little Tex-Mex flair? That's such a Gulf Coast thing to do—mix the traditions from different cultures and styles to create something that brings out the best in both. And in this case, you get the taste of a complicated gumbo with the ease of a quesadilla!

1. Toss the shrimp in 1 tablespoon of the olive oil and the Creole seasoning. Set aside.

2. In a large heavy skillet (10 to 12 inches), heat 2 tablespoons of the olive oil over medium heat and sauté the andouille sausage and tasso for about 10 minutes. Remove the sausage and tasso from the skillet, transfer to a plate covered with paper towels, and set aside.

3. Add 2 tablespoons of the olive oil to the same skillet and add the shrimp. Sauté for 3 to 4 minutes, or until the shrimp are pink and tender, being careful not to overcook them.

4. Remove the shrimp from the skillet and transfer to a plate. Add 2 table-spoons of the olive oil to the skillet. Add the bell pepper, green onion, yellow onion, salt, and black pepper to the skillet and sauté until the vegetables are soft and slightly browned on the edges, about 15 minutes.

5. Remove the skillet from the heat and stir in the hot sauce.

6. Heat another large heavy skillet over medium-high heat. Brush one side of a tortilla with a little of the remaining 1 tablespoon olive oil. Place the tortilla oil-side down in the hot skillet.

7. Layer one-quarter of the cheese, one-quarter of the vegetables, one-quarter of the andouille sausage, one-quarter of the tasso, and one-quarter of the shrimp on half of the tortilla. Fold the tortilla in half and cook until the bottom is a nice golden brown. Flip to the other side and cook until it's browned and a little crisp. Repeat with the other three tortillas and remaining filling ingredients.

8. Slice the quesadillas into wedges and serve with salsa, if desired, and sour cream.

SHRIMP SCAMPI

3 tablespoons extra-virgin
olive oil

1½ pounds large wild-caught
Gulf shrimp, peeled and deveined

1 teaspoon sea salt

½ teaspoon freshly ground
black pepper

½ cup (1 stick) unsalted butter

½ cup finely chopped shallots

1 tablespoon finely chopped garlic

½ cup white wine

Juice of 1 lemon
(about 2 tablespoons)

¼ teaspoon red pepper flakes

2 tablespoons chopped
fresh parsley

2 cups cooked white rice,
for serving

THIS IS SO SIMPLE. Anybody can do it! It is a classic dish on every Gulf Coast seafood menu. If you're looking for the easiest way to impress and delight, this is it.

1. In a large heavy skillet (10 to 12 inches), heat the olive oil over medium-high heat.

2. While the oil is heating, season the shrimp with just a little of the salt and black pepper.

3. Add the shrimp to the skillet and sauté for 3 minutes.

4. Remove the shrimp from the skillet and set aside.

5. Add the butter to the skillet and allow it to melt, but be careful not to let it burn. Add the shallot and garlic and sauté until they start to caramelize.

6. Add the wine to deglaze the pan, scraping up any gooey bits stuck to the pan and stirring them into the wine. Add the lemon juice, red pepper flakes, and the remaining salt and black pepper.

7. Cook for about a minute, or until the liquid has reduced by a third.

8. Return the shrimp to the pan and cook for about 1 minute, or just until the shrimp is cooked through.

9. Turn off the heat, add 1 tablespoon of the parsley, and stir well.

10. Place ½ cup of the rice into each of four shallow bowls. Spoon the shrimp and juices over the rice and garnish with the remaining parsley.

EASY-BREEZY ISLAND
SHRIMP CURRY

SERVES 8

2 tablespoons unsalted butter

1 tablespoon finely chopped garlic

1 tablespoon finely chopped
fresh ginger

2 teaspoons finely chopped seeded
jalapeño (or leave the seeds in for
more heat)

1 tablespoon red or green curry paste

2 teaspoons fish sauce

1 cup chicken broth

1 (13.5-ounce) can coconut milk

2½ pounds medium wild-caught Gulf
shrimp, peeled and deveined

3 tablespoons finely chopped
fresh cilantro

½ teaspoon sea salt

Freshly ground black pepper

2 limes, halved or cut into wedges,
for serving

Cuban Yellow Rice (page 181) or
spinach, for serving (optional)

Crusty bread, for serving

1. In a small stockpot, melt the butter over medium heat. Add the garlic, ginger, and jalapeño and cook until fragrant, about 2 minutes.

2. Stir in the curry paste and fish sauce.

3. Add the broth and coconut milk. Stir to combine and bring the ingredients to a simmer.

4. Add the shrimp to the stockpot. Reduce the heat to medium-low and simmer, stirring frequently, for 5 minutes.

5. Once the shrimp are cooked through, remove the pot from the heat. Add the cilantro, salt, and pepper to taste. Squeeze the juice from the limes over the shrimp.

6. Serve over yellow rice or spinach, if desired, with a side of crusty bread to soak up the yummy curry sauce.

129

MAIN DISHES

CAMARONES A LA CRIOLLA

(CUBAN-STYLE SHRIMP CREOLE)

SERVES 6 TO 8

1 tablespoon unsalted butter

3 tablespoons extra-virgin olive oil

2 medium yellow onions, chopped

1 green bell pepper, chopped

6 garlic cloves, finely chopped

2 (15-ounce) cans crushed tomatoes

2 tablespoons tomato paste

2 bay leaves

2 teaspoons dried thyme

2 teaspoons dried oregano

2 teaspoons LuLu's Crazy Creola Seasoning (page xxviii) or other Creole seasoning

1 teaspoon dried basil

½ teaspoon ground cumin

2 tablespoons sugar

2 tablespoons Worcestershire sauce

1 teaspoon hot sauce

1 cup pimento-stuffed green Spanish olives, drained

1½ teaspoons sea salt

½ teaspoon freshly ground black pepper

½ cup white wine

2 pounds medium wild-caught Gulf shrimp, peeled and deveined

¼ cup chopped fresh parsley

Cuban Yellow Rice (page 181)

SHRIMP CREOLE SERVED over rice, a classic Gulf Coast dish with New Orleans roots, was one of the dishes my grandmother would make on no-meat Fridays. When I got older and traveled around the Gulf and the Caribbean, I found that there are so many different versions of shrimp Creole! Living part-time in Key West, however, with its abundant Cuban influence, I've found this version to be one of my favorites—I just love the addition of the cumin and olives.

1. In a large heavy skillet (10 to 12 inches), melt the butter with the olive oil over medium heat. Add the onion and sauté until it is translucent. Add the bell pepper and garlic. Sauté for a few minutes, making sure not to burn the garlic.

2. Add the crushed tomatoes and stir. Add the tomato paste and stir. Add the bay leaves, thyme, oregano, Creole seasoning, basil, cumin, sugar, Worcestershire, and hot sauce. Stir until well combined and simmering.

3. Add the olives, salt, and black pepper. Add the wine, stir, cover, and let it simmer for 30 minutes to let the flavors meld. Add water if the sauce starts to get too thick.

4. About 5 minutes before serving, add the shrimp, stirring to incorporate them into the sauce. Cook for 5 minutes, or until the shrimp turn pink—being careful not to overcook them!

5. Remove from the heat and add the parsley. Remove and discard the bay leaves. Serve over yellow rice.

GROUPER
WITH
BALSAMIC BUTTER GLAZE

SERVES 4

4 grouper fillets, 6 to 8 ounces each

2½ teaspoons sea salt

2½ teaspoons freshly ground
black pepper

6 tablespoons extra-virgin olive oil,
plus more if needed

½ cup (1 stick) unsalted butter

2 tablespoons finely chopped shallot

1 teaspoon finely chopped
fresh thyme

4 tablespoons balsamic vinegar

GROUPER IS ONE of my hands-down favorite Gulf fish—a light, white meat that is so sweet and delicious. The way I usually prepare it is to panfry it in a little butter and olive oil. There are countless ways to finish it by whipping up a savory sauce from the pan drippings. One of the South's best young chefs, Randall Baldwin, once cooked for me a finishing sauce using balsamic vinegar and butter, and his delicious method inspired my own rendition. Ever since balsamic vinegar landed on the culinary scene, it has become one of the top ten ingredients that I use almost daily!

1. Preheat the oven to 250°F.

2. Season the fish with 2 teaspoons of the salt and 2 teaspoons of the pepper.

3. In a large heavy skillet (10 to 12 inches), heat the olive oil over medium-high heat.

4. Add the fillets to the skillet and cook until slightly browned, 2 to 3 minutes, then flip to cook the other side until lightly browned. (Cook in two batches if the skillet isn't large enough; just add more olive oil if needed before starting the second batch.)

5. Remove the fillets from the skillet and place them on a baking pan uncovered. Place in the oven to keep warm.

6. Remove the skillet from the heat and drain off the oil. Put the skillet back on the heat and add the butter to the pan. Once the butter starts to brown, add the shallot and thyme. Cook 1 to 2 minutes. Stir in the vinegar and the remaining ½ teaspoon salt and ½ teaspoon pepper.

7. To serve, place the fish on a serving platter or on individual plates. Generously spoon the sauce from the skillet over the fish, making sure not only to coat the fish but also to have some extra glaze on the platter or plate as well. This is a "broken sauce," meaning it's not completely emulsified, so don't worry when the butter separates a little as you're spooning the sauce over the fish.

RED SNAPPER VERACRUZ

SERVES 4 TO 6

4 red snapper fillets,
6 to 8 ounces each

1 teaspoon sea salt

½ teaspoon freshly ground
black pepper

¼ cup extra-virgin olive oil

2 yellow onions, cut into
¼-inch-thick slices

6 garlic cloves, sliced

1 teaspoon finely chopped
seeded jalapeño

4 ripe tomatoes, peeled and
chopped, or 1 (28-ounce) can
whole tomatoes, drained and
coarsely chopped

1 teaspoon orange zest

¼ cup fresh orange juice

2 bay leaves

¼ cup sliced pitted Spanish olives

¼ cup sliced pitted Kalamata olives

3 tablespoons capers, drained

3 tablespoons golden raisins

1 teaspoon dried oregano

¼ cup white wine

¼ cup finely chopped fresh parsley

2 lemons, cut into wedges,
for garnish

IF YOU FOLLOW the coastline of the Gulf of Mexico from South Padre Island in Texas south, you will find yourself in the port city of Veracruz. The region is renowned for its cuisine, especially its sensational seafood. This recipe has migrated across the Gulf of Mexico from its original roots and found its way into the Southern repertoire. It celebrates the beautiful red snapper, although you can use any variety of white flaky fish. I love to make it for a small dinner party using tomatoes from my garden. It's an easy baked dish using only one pan, and it is light and healthy while still boasting the beautiful flavor of Mexican fresco cuisine.

1. Preheat the oven to 425°F.

2. Season the fillets with ½ teaspoon of the salt and ¼ teaspoon of the pepper. Set aside.

3. In a large heavy skillet (10 to 12 inches), heat the olive oil over medium heat. Add the onion and sauté for 5 minutes, or until it is translucent and soft.

4. Add the garlic and jalapeño. Cook for 2 minutes.

5. Add the tomatoes, orange zest, orange juice, bay leaves, olives, capers, raisins, oregano, the remaining ½ teaspoon salt, and the remaining ¼ teaspoon pepper. Cover and cook for 10 minutes. Remove and discard the bay leaves.

6. Add the wine and cook for 5 minutes more, or until the onion is soft.

7. Ladle a cup of the sauce into the bottom of a 9 x 13-inch baking dish. Place the fish fillets in the dish on top of the sauce. Ladle the remaining sauce over the fish. Sprinkle with the parsley and bake for 15 minutes.

8. Remove from the oven and serve immediately. Garnish with the lemon wedges.

Bronzed Fish Seasoning

1 tablespoon white pepper

1 tablespoon freshly ground black pepper

1 tablespoon granulated onion

1 tablespoon granulated garlic

1 tablespoon dry mustard

½ teaspoon cayenne pepper

2 tablespoons paprika

1 tablespoon smoked paprika

2 teaspoons dried thyme

3 tablespoons sea salt

Citrus Beurre Blanc Sauce

2 tablespoons finely chopped shallots

1 garlic clove, finely chopped

½ cup champagne or dry white wine

½ cup fresh orange juice

¼ cup fresh lime juice

¼ cup fresh lemon juice

⅓ cup heavy cream

1 cup (2 sticks) unsalted butter, chopped into cubes

½ teaspoon sea salt

½ teaspoon white pepper

½ teaspoon sugar

⅛ teaspoon lemon zest

⅛ teaspoon lime zest

⅛ teaspoon orange zest

½ cup extra-virgin olive oil

6 yellowtail snapper fillets, 6 to 8 ounces each

BRONZED
YELLOWTAIL SNAPPER
WITH CITRUS BEURRE BLANC SAUCE

MY SISTER, LAURIE, who has lived in Montana for most of her adult life, finds refuge from the coldest three months of winter with her husband and her four enormous dogs on Boca Grande, an exquisitely beautiful barrier island between Fort Myers and Sarasota, Florida. Known for its tarpon fishing, Boca Grande's Gulf waters are turquoise, with pristine white beaches stretching for miles. The quaint coastal town sports the demeanor of what I call "Old Florida," with mom-and-pop stores lining the quaint streets as well as one of my favorite restaurants, the Temptation. Bronzed Fish with a Citrus Beurre Blanc is a Temptation specialty and one of the tastiest ways to enjoy Gulf fish. This is my humble homage to the Temptation and all the wonderful Old Florida restaurants along the Florida Gulf Coast!

To make the seasoning:

1. In a small bowl, combine all the seasoning ingredients together and set aside.

To make the sauce:

2. In a saucepan, combine the shallots, garlic, champagne, orange juice, lime juice, and lemon juice. Cook over medium-high heat until the liquid has reduced to an almost syrupy consistency. Add the cream and cook until it has reduced some more and is slightly thickened, then reduce the heat to low.

3. Add the butter a few cubes at a time, whisking first on the heat and then off the heat. Continue whisking the butter into the sauce until the mixture is fully emulsified and has reached the consistency of a rich sauce.

4. Season with the salt, white pepper, sugar, and zests and stir together. Keep the sauce warm by leaving it in the saucepan on the back of the stove until ready to use.

5. In a large heavy skillet (10 to 12 inches), heat the olive oil over medium-low heat.

6. Season the fish with the bronzed fish seasoning until lightly coated all over.

7. Cook the fillets in the skillet until lightly browned on the first side, 2 to 3 minutes, then flip to cook the other side until lightly brown.

8. To serve the fish, place all the fillets on a serving platter and generously top with the sauce, or plate each fillet individually and top with sauce.

GULF CLASSIC SCAMP
OR
TROUT AMANDINE

SERVES 4

4 scamp or trout fillets,
6 to 8 ounces each

2 teaspoons sea salt

2 teaspoons freshly ground
black pepper

2 cups all-purpose flour

2 tablespoons extra-virgin olive oil,
plus more if needed

1 cup (2 sticks) plus 2 tablespoons
(chopped into cubes) cold unsalted
butter

1 cup white wine

⅓ cup fresh lemon juice

¼ cup Worcestershire sauce

1 cup sliced almonds, toasted

1 tablespoon chopped
fresh parsley

ONE OF THE places that my folks would take us to dinner was a beloved Mobile restaurant called Constantine's. My father loved to order the Scamp Amandine (or Almondine, as some folks call it). It's a beautifully panfried fish topped with plenty of almonds browned in a lemon-butter sauce. Simply sublime! The scamp is a small Gulf Coast grouper that is supremely tasty. Feel free to substitute another grouper or some delicious seasonal trout for this treasured old-school recipe.

1. Preheat the oven to 250°F.

2. Season the fish fillets with the salt and pepper and dredge them in the flour.

3. In a large heavy skillet (10 to 12 inches), heat the olive oil and 2 sticks of the butter over medium-high heat.

4. When the oil and butter begin to sizzle, add the fish fillets. Don't let the butter begin to brown; reduce the heat if necessary. You don't want to overcrowd the skillet. Cook the fillets in two batches if the skillet isn't large enough; just add more olive oil and butter before starting the second batch. Cook the fillets in the skillet until the first side is a nice golden brown, then flip them and cook the other side until golden brown—the fish should be turned only once, so let it cook thoroughly before flipping.

5. Once golden brown, remove the fish fillets from the skillet and place them on a baking sheet uncovered. Keep warm in the oven.

6. Add the wine to the drippings in the hot skillet. Deglaze the pan, scraping up any gooey bits stuck to the pan and stirring them into the wine. Cook until the liquid has reduced by half.

7. Add the lemon juice, Worcestershire, and almonds. Cook for about a minute.

8. Remove the skillet from the heat and, a little at a time, slowly swirl in the remaining 2 tablespoons butter cubes, then add the parsley and fold it in gently.

9. To serve, place all the fillets on a large platter and top generously with the sauce, or plate each fillet individually and top with sauce.

CLASSIC COASTAL
CRABMEAT AU GRATIN

SERVES 8 TO 10

Organic olive oil cooking spray

½ cup sliced almonds

½ cup (1 stick) unsalted butter

1 teaspoon finely chopped garlic

1 bunch green onions, chopped
(about ½ cup)

½ cup all-purpose flour

1 (12-ounce) can evaporated milk

2 cups whole milk

½ teaspoon sea salt

¼ teaspoon white pepper

¼ teaspoon dry mustard

¼ teaspoon LuLu's Crazy Creola
Seasoning (page xxviii) or other
Creole seasoning

½ teaspoon dried thyme

3 cups grated white cheddar cheese

¼ teaspoon almond extract

¼ teaspoon hot sauce

2 tablespoons finely chopped
fresh parsley

2 pounds cooked jumbo lump blue
crabmeat, picked through carefully for
shells, handled carefully to keep the
meat in big chunks (see Notes on
Handling Seafood, pages xxx–xxxi)

4 cups grated sharp cheddar cheese

BÉCHAMEL WAS THE first fancy sauce I taught myself to make; adding cheese was the next step, and this particular cheese sauce just makes everything absolutely wonderful. Normally I wouldn't use such a heavy sauce with such a precious ingredient as crab—you want to be able to taste the crab and let that flavor be the star of the show. However, this recipe started not as a showcase for the crab but, in the days of my grandmother Bessie Peets, as a way to stretch leftover crab that might spoil if you didn't use it up soon. She'd make a cheesy crab au gratin over rice. This dish is simply delicious, going to show that sometimes the very best dishes are born out of necessity—and the resourcefulness of a wise woman in the kitchen.

1. Preheat the oven to 350°F. Grease a 9 x 13-inch baking dish with olive oil spray.

2. Spread the almonds on a baking sheet and spray with olive oil spray. Place in the oven for 5 minutes, then remove and set aside to cool.

3. In a large saucepan, melt the butter over medium-low heat.

4. Add the garlic and green onion and sauté for about 2 minutes.

5. Add the flour and stir to combine. Cook for 2 minutes, continuing to stir.

6. Stir in the evaporated milk and whole milk. Continue to stir until the sauce thickens.

7. Add the salt, white pepper, dry mustard, Creole seasoning, and thyme and stir together.

8. Add the white cheddar, almond extract, hot sauce, and parsley and stir together.

9. Spread half the crabmeat over the prepared baking dish. Spoon the cheese sauce over the meat until all is covered. Sprinkle about half of the sharp cheddar on top.

10. Repeat and add the remaining sharp cheddar on top.

11. Bake for 30 minutes.

12. Turn the oven to broil and, watching closely, broil for about 2 minutes, or until the cheese starts to brown.

13. Remove the dish from the oven and sprinkle the toasted almonds on top. Let cool for 3 to 5 minutes before serving.

MS. MARGARET'S NOT CUMIN ROASTED CHICKEN THIGHS

SERVES 6 TO 8

Organic olive oil cooking spray

10 large boneless, skinless chicken thighs

½ cup teriyaki sauce

1 tablespoon Worcestershire sauce

1 heaping teaspoon finely chopped garlic

¼ cup finely chopped green onions

¼ cup finely chopped fresh cilantro

2 teaspoons Lawry's Seasoned Salt

3 teaspoons lemon pepper

MARGARET IS MY right-hand woman, and this is one of her staples. She uses it for salads, sandwiches, and as a main dish—anything that needs chicken in it. It is incredibly versatile, and a tasty and moist way to prepare chicken. The recipe originated from my friend Esme in Key West, who made some delicious chicken thighs for Margaret and me one day using a lot of cumin and other spices. When we got back to Alabama, Margaret started cooking the dish for us regularly, and doing what most cooks do, she started to add her own little flair. A few years later, I decided I wanted to include the recipe in the cookbook. Testing recipes in Key West, I tried cooking the dish the way I remembered it. But it just wasn't as good as the version from Margaret that I'd become accustomed to. I tried it with more cumin, then less cumin, every which way I could think of, but I could never come close to Margaret's.

When I got back to Alabama, I asked Margaret to cook the chicken thighs while I watched. She started seasoning the chicken, adding a little of this and a little of that as I recorded every ingredient and action. When she started to put the baking dish in the oven, I hollered out, "Wait! When do you add the cumin?" She just shrugged and said, "I don't use any cumin." Well, we all died laughing, and that's how the Not Cumin Roasted Chicken Thighs got their name.

1. Preheat the oven to 400°F. Coat a 9 x 13-inch baking pan or dish with olive oil spray.

2. Place the chicken thighs in a large bowl. Add the teriyaki sauce, Worcestershire, garlic, green onion, cilantro, seasoned salt, and 2 teaspoons of the lemon pepper to the bowl. Using your hands, combine all the ingredients, making sure all the thighs are well coated.

3. Roll each thigh before placing it in the baking pan. The rolled thighs will be snug and close together. Pour all the excess juice from the bowl on top of the thighs. Sprinkle the remaining 1 teaspoon lemon pepper on top of the thighs.

4. Bake for 30 minutes, then remove the pan from the oven. Flip the thighs, and bake for 30 minutes or so more. As Ms. Margaret says, "The thicker the thighs, the longer they take."

DADDY'S FRIED CHICKEN

Sunday family meals were a must-attend in our home as kids and sometimes a painful ordeal, especially when we wanted to be at our friends' houses or simply playing outside. But after I grew up and became a young adult with children of my own, that mandate became a sweet salvation and a delightful way to spend a Sunday with my family. By this time, my folks had moved into their "dream home" on Mobile Bay, a gift from my brother. My parents named their home Homeport. It represented so many things to them—the American Dream, a long-deserved retirement, devotion from a beloved child—but mainly it became a gathering place for friends and family to enjoy the delights of waterfront living on the Gulf Coast.

Homeport was a home away from home for my children and me. A modest two-bedroom ranch-style house situated upon a high bluff with a long-ass walkway to a pier and boat lift and featuring a rustic cook's kitchen and iron bunk beds pilfered from the shipyard where my parents worked, it was a haven of weekend recreation for young and old alike, especially on Sunday, because Daddy would cook one of his fabulous meals.

By this time, my father would joke that he "might as well sell the stove" because my mother had finally been able to retire not only from work but, as she liked to say, "from all things I don't like to do," and at the top of that list was cooking. So it was my dad who picked up the baton, or more accurately the spatula, although he had always been the Sunday cook in our home. He had about ten great dishes in his cooking repertoire, but our favorite was his famous fried chicken. When Daddy fried chicken, it became a special occasion. It was a lot of work, but that never stopped a

Buffett! I think the pure delight of the anticipation of biting into a perfect piece of fried chicken is what created the celebratory atmosphere.

The way Daddy fried, like everything cooking related, he'd learned from his own mama. He'd fill a paper bag half full with flour and season it with plain ol' salt and pepper. Heat up a cast-iron skillet full of grease on the stove. Put those chicken pieces in that bag of flour and shake till kingdom come. Then plop those babies in the hot grease, and when they were done, with a beautiful golden brown crust, snatch them out of the skillet and drain them on another paper bag.

There was something magical in that bag of flour, and anytime I've tried to improve this dish by using a batter or increasing the seasoning or double dipping, nothing seems to work as well as shaking the chicken in the bag of flour to obtain the perfect crust for traditional Southern fried chicken. Daddy would serve it with potato salad, an arduous task since his method included making sure each vegetable was chopped in pieces precisely the same size. Or, if we were lucky, he would do mashed potatoes with gravy made from the leftover grease and crispy crumbs left in the skillet.

As my sister, brother, and I left home for all our adventures, we had two important requests every time we called our parents to tell them we were coming home for a visit: "Will Mama make West Indies salad?" and "Will Daddy do his fried chicken?" Food and family, even with my mother, who could cook only a few dishes, have always been tied up together for me. That is not a connection I'm willing to sever—at least not when it comes to Daddy's fried chicken. I have never been able to replicate it exactly, but I keep trying, and this is how I do it.

DADDY'S
FRIED CHICKEN

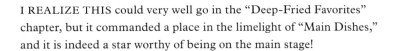

SERVES 6

1 whole chicken, cut up

5½ tablespoons LuLu's Crazy Creola Seasoning (page xxviii) or other Creole seasoning

6 cups all-purpose flour

About 2 cups vegetable oil, for frying, or enough to fill the skillet halfway (Daddy always used Crisco brand)

I REALIZE THIS could very well go in the "Deep-Fried Favorites" chapter, but it commanded a place in the limelight of "Main Dishes," and it is indeed a star worthy of being on the main stage!

1. Season the chicken pieces generously with 1½ tablespoons of the Creole seasoning.

2. In a paper bag, combine the remaining 4 tablespoons Creole seasoning and the flour. Shake and lightly turn the bag to distribute the spices in the flour.

3. Put the chicken pieces in the bag. Shake and turn the bag to evenly coat each piece of chicken.

4. In a large heavy skillet (10 to 12 inches, preferably cast iron), heat the oil over medium-high heat until it registers 355°F on a candy/deep-fry thermometer, or until a little flour flicked into the oil sizzles.

5. Place the white meat pieces in the skillet and fry for 8 to 10 minutes, then flip and cook for 5 minutes or so more, making sure the thickest part of the thickest chicken pieces reaches at least 165°F. Daddy never used a thermometer on his chicken, but not all of us have his magic touch—so do use a thermometer if you're worried about pulling the chicken out before it's finished cooking all the way through. Your touch and your eye will get better with practice, though.

6. Once all the white meat is finished cooking, repeat with the dark meat pieces. Cooking the dark meat will take 3 to 4 minutes more.

7. Place the chicken on a baking sheet lined with paper towels until ready to serve. Try not to steal a wing when nobody's looking.

NOTE: *You will need a heavy-duty paper bag.*

GARLICKY GOOD-WOMAN CHICKEN

(CHICKEN BONNE FEMME)

SERVES 4

6 bacon slices, chopped into
1-inch squares

1 whole chicken, cut up

4 tablespoons sea salt

3 tablespoons freshly ground
black pepper

4 cups all-purpose flour

3 tablespoons extra-virgin olive oil

1 cup finely chopped tasso
(can substitute spicy chorizo or
Canadian bacon)

1 cup plus 2 tablespoons sliced
green onions, green part only

1 cup chopped yellow onion

2 cups sliced mushrooms

1 cup dry white wine

1 tablespoon Worcestershire sauce

1 teaspoon hot sauce

About 2 cups vegetable oil, for frying

1 pound russet potatoes, unpeeled,
chopped into ½-inch cubes

½ cup (1 stick) unsalted butter

2 tablespoons finely chopped garlic

THIS DISH IS inspired by the chicken bonne femme at the legendary Tujague's restaurant in New Orleans and is part of a much-beloved Jazz Fest tradition for me. After two weeks of music, food, and flat-out nonstop fun, that last Sunday night is the end of a very long, wonderful road, with the real world still in hiding but ready in the wings to tap you on the shoulder and usher you back to work and other obligations. That last night we always order takeout from Tujague's, and it's always the chicken bonne femme. For me, it is almost a sad ritual, mourning the end of Jazz Fest, knowing it's over, but also knowing it will be back the next year. There is hope! This version is my humble attempt at creating some solace food of my own, a dish I can cook when something fabulous is ending—with the promise that it will come back again one day. It's panfried chicken with a ton of garlic and smothered with fried potatoes. If you want to try the original, reserve it when you call Tujague's for a reservation because the best dish at Tujague's is not on the menu!

1. Preheat the oven to 400°F.

2. In a large heavy skillet (10 to 12 inches), fry the bacon until crisp. Remove it with a slotted spoon, place it on a plate covered with paper towels, and set aside. Leave the bacon fat in the skillet.

3. Season the chicken with 2 tablespoons of the salt and 1 tablespoon of the pepper. In a large bowl, combine the remaining 2 tablespoons salt and 2 tablespoons pepper with the flour and mix together.

4. Add the olive oil to the skillet with the bacon fat and heat over medium to medium-high heat. Lightly dust and pat the chicken with the flour mixture. In batches, place the chicken pieces in the skillet and cook until they've browned on both sides (the chicken only needs to brown, not be cooked all the way through). After they've browned, place the chicken pieces in a baking dish large enough to hold them all and cover to keep warm.

5. Once all the chicken is out of the skillet and in the baking dish, add the tasso, 1 cup of the green onion, and the yellow onion to the same skillet.

CONT.

Sauté until the onion turns translucent. Add the mushrooms, wine, Worcestershire, and hot sauce. Bring to a boil, then reduce the heat to maintain a low simmer.

6. While the tasso mixture is simmering, in another large heavy skillet that's at least 2 inches deep, heat 1 inch of frying oil over medium-high heat until it registers 375°F on a candy/deep-fry thermometer, or until a little flour flicked into the oil sizzles. Add the potatoes and fry until lightly browned. Drain them well, then add them to the skillet with the tasso and onions.

7. Simmer the tasso mixture until all the liquid has been absorbed. Lightly stir to distribute the ingredients, then remove the skillet from the heat.

8. In a small saucepan, melt the butter and heat until it starts bubbling. Reduce the heat, skim the foam off the top, and add the garlic. Cook the garlic in the hot butter for about 1 minute.

9. Coat each piece of chicken in the baking dish with the garlic butter. It may seem like a lot of garlic and butter, but don't be shy—it comes together perfectly in the end.

10. Smother the chicken with the tasso mixture.

11. Bake for about 20 minutes, or until the thickest part of the thickest piece of chicken reaches an internal temperature of 165°F.

12. Garnish with the remaining 2 tablespoons green onion and serve.

CASSEROLES, ONE-POTS, AND PASTAS

HEAVENLY (OR *DIVINE*) CASSEROLE

SERVES 10

Butter, for the baking dish

1 bunch green onions (about 6)

1 (8-ounce) package cream cheese, at room temperature

1 cup cottage cheese

2 teaspoons finely chopped fresh rosemary

1 cup sour cream

2 pounds ground beef

3 garlic cloves, finely chopped

1 teaspoon dried Italian seasoning

1 teaspoon sea salt

¼ teaspoon freshly ground black pepper

1 teaspoon dried basil

½ to 1 teaspoon LuLu's Crazy Creola Seasoning (page xxviii) or other Creole seasoning

2 (15-ounce) cans tomato sauce (3⅓ cups)

1 tablespoon Worcestershire sauce

2 teaspoons hot sauce

CONT.

I DON'T KNOW what I would have done without *Jubilee!*, the Mobile Junior League cookbook. I still have my original copy, and because they are out of print, I now buy more whenever I spot them in used bookstores. There I was, not yet twenty and already a wife and mother. Where to turn but to the eminent league of Mrs. Somebodies whose tables I emulated with Divine Casserole, Chicken Divan, and other elegant one-dish wonders. Though I am not and never was Junior League material, nothing so far, including marriages and many miles, has come between me and *Jubilee!*—or my love for casseroles. The original version of this casserole from *Jubilee!* was truly the first recipe I ever learned to cook, and it was one of the few dishes my two young children would eat. Ground beef, buttery noodles, and a savory cream cheese filling—this is comfort food at its very best. It is also a great dish to serve a crowd.

1. Preheat the oven to 350°F. Lightly butter a 9 x 13-inch baking dish.

2. In a food processor, process the green onions until finely chopped.

3. Add the cream cheese (you may want to cut it into quarters before adding), cottage cheese, rosemary, and sour cream to the food processor and pulse until thoroughly combined. Set aside at room temperature.

4. In a large heavy skillet (10 to 12 inches), brown the beef, using a fork to break it up into small chunks. Once browned, drain any excess grease from the beef.

5. Add the garlic, Italian seasoning, salt, pepper, basil, Creole seasoning, and tomato sauce to the beef in the skillet. Stir well.

6. Add the Worcestershire, hot sauce, and sugar and simmer over low heat for 20 minutes.

CONT.

1 teaspoon sugar

1 (16-ounce) package penne pasta

½ cup (1 stick) unsalted butter, melted

1 cup shredded mozzarella cheese

1 cup shredded cheddar cheese

7. Prepare the pasta according to the shortest time on the package directions—you'll want it al dente, with a little bit of firmness—stirring occasionally.

8. Drain the pasta and place half into the prepared baking dish.

9. Pour half of the melted butter over the top of the pasta and then add half the cream cheese mixture, spreading the mixture over the top in an even layer.

10. Spoon half the meat mixture over the cream cheese layer, and then sprinkle the mozzarella on top.

11. Repeat the layers, beginning with the remaining half of the melted butter, and sprinkling the cheddar on top as the last layer.

12. Bake for 55 minutes to 1 hour, or until bubbling and heated through in the middle. You might want to place a baking sheet underneath the baking dish in case the casserole bubbles over.

PICADILLO

SERVES 6 TO 8

4 tablespoons extra-virgin olive oil

1½ pounds lean ground beef

2 yellow onions, chopped

½ teaspoon sea salt

1 green bell pepper, chopped

6 garlic cloves, finely chopped

4 ripe tomatoes, peeled and chopped, or 1 (28-ounce) can whole tomatoes, drained and coarsely chopped

3 tablespoons tomato paste

¾ cup red wine

½ cup chopped pitted green olives

¼ cup small capers, drained

½ cup coarsely chopped golden raisins

½ teaspoon freshly ground black pepper

1 bunch green onions, chopped (about 1 cup)

2 tablespoons Worcestershire sauce

½ teaspoon ground cinnamon

Cuban Yellow Rice (page 181), for serving

WHEN I FIRST moved to Key West and began to experience new cuisines, I fell in love with Cuban food. Picadillo, often called "Cuban Hamburger Helper," was my first taste of having sweet and savory flavors together in one dish, and it immediately had my heart. There are so many different flavors in this very simple dish, and, like Hamburger Helper, it's a great meal to fix on a busy weeknight or for last-minute dinner guests.

1. In a large heavy skillet (10 to 12 inches), heat 2 tablespoons of the olive oil over medium heat.

2. Add the beef and brown, using a fork to break it up into small chunks. Once browned, drain any excess grease from the beef. Transfer to a bowl and set aside.

3. In the same skillet, heat the remaining 2 tablespoons olive oil over medium-high heat.

4. Add the onion and salt and sauté until the onion is slightly brown and beginning to caramelize.

5. Add the bell pepper and sauté for 2 minutes.

6. Stir in the garlic and sauté for 1 minute.

7. Return the beef to the pan, add the tomatoes and tomato paste, and stir together.

8. Stir in the wine, olives, capers, raisins, black pepper, and green onion.

9. Stir in the Worcestershire and cinnamon. Cover and simmer for 30 minutes.

10. Serve over yellow rice.

MONDAY MAKIN'
RED BEANS & RICE

SERVES 6

1 pound dried red kidney beans

2 tablespoons unsalted butter

1 pound smoked or andouille sausage, chopped into ⅛-inch-thick rounds or half-moons

1 pound tasso, chopped (can substitute spicy chorizo or Canadian bacon; optional)

1 yellow onion, chopped

1 green bell pepper, chopped

2 celery stalks, chopped

3 garlic cloves, finely chopped

6 cups chicken broth

1 smoked ham hock

2 bay leaves

1 teaspoon LuLu's Crazy Creola Seasoning (page xxviii) or other Creole seasoning

1 teaspoon hot sauce, or more to taste

Sea salt and freshly ground black pepper

Cooked white rice, for serving

IN NEW ORLEANS, the traditional lunch or dinner served in homes and restaurants every Monday is red beans and rice. The legend goes that before there were electric washers, homemakers doing their laundry on Mondays planned for an easy-to-prepare meal—thus was born the Monday red beans and rice tradition in New Orleans. It's not surprising that this dish made its way east along the Gulf Coast to my grandmother's kitchen and became one of the big ten dishes that my daddy regularly cooked for us. Some recipes use sausage and some use a ham hock, but this is also a great vegetarian dish without adding the meat.

1. Pick through the beans to remove rocks or odd beans. Rinse the beans under cold water, then put them in a large bowl. Cover the beans with 3 inches of water and set them aside on the counter for 6 to 8 hours or overnight.

2. Drain and rinse the beans.

3. In a Dutch oven or small stockpot, melt the butter over medium-high heat. Add the sausage and tasso (if using) and sauté until brown, about 5 minutes. Transfer the sausage and tasso to a plate covered with paper towels and set aside.

4. Reduce the heat to medium. Add the onion, bell pepper, and celery. Cook until soft, about 5 minutes. Add the garlic and sauté for 1 minute more.

5. Pour the broth into the pot with the sautéed vegetables. Add the beans, ham hock, bay leaves, Creole seasoning, and hot sauce. Bring to a boil, skimming off any foam that forms on the surface.

6. Reduce the heat to low and simmer, uncovered, for 1 hour, stirring occasionally so it doesn't stick to the bottom of the pot.

7. Return the sausage and tasso to the pot and cook for 1½ to 2½ hours more, or until the beans are soft and the texture is to your liking. Remove and discard the bay leaves. Season with salt and black pepper. Serve over white rice.

CREOLE SHRIMP
AND
EGGPLANT CASSEROLE

SERVES 6 TO 8

Organic olive oil cooking spray

5 tablespoons extra-virgin olive oil

2 medium eggplants, peeled and chopped into 1-inch cubes

½ cup chicken broth, plus more if needed

½ (8-ounce) package cream cheese

¾ cup chopped yellow onion

¼ cup chopped yellow bell pepper (about ½ pepper)

¼ cup chopped red bell pepper (about ½ pepper)

¼ cup chopped green bell pepper (about ½ pepper)

½ cup chopped celery

2 tablespoons finely chopped garlic

1 cup chopped tasso (can substitute spicy chorizo or Canadian bacon)

1 pound medium wild-caught Gulf shrimp, peeled and deveined

1 cup white wine

½ teaspoon dried basil

½ teaspoon dried oregano

¼ teaspoon dried thyme

2 cups panko breadcrumbs

LuLu's Crazy Creola Seasoning (page xxviii) or other Creole seasoning

Freshly ground black pepper

1 cup shredded mozzarella cheese

½ cup shredded Parmesan cheese

1. Preheat the oven to 350°F. Lightly grease a 9-inch square baking dish with olive oil spray.

2. In a large heavy skillet (10 to 12 inches), heat 2 tablespoons of the olive oil over medium-high heat. Working in batches if necessary, add the eggplant and cook for 4 to 5 minutes. Transfer the eggplant to a bowl and set aside.

3. In a small skillet, bring the broth to a simmer over medium heat. Add the cream cheese and stir until blended. Remove from the heat and set aside.

4. In a large heavy skillet (10 to 12 inches), heat the remaining 3 tablespoons olive oil over medium heat. Add the onion, bell peppers, celery, and garlic. Sauté for 4 to 5 minutes.

5. As the onion becomes translucent, add the tasso and sauté for 1 to 2 minutes.

6. Add the shrimp and sauté for 1 to 2 minutes, or until the shrimp are slightly pink.

7. Add the wine and the broth–cream cheese mixture. Cook for 2 minutes.

8. Fold in the eggplant, basil, oregano, and thyme. Stir in the breadcrumbs slowly, allowing them to absorb the broth. Season with Creole seasoning and black pepper. If the overall mixture seems too dry, add a little more broth to moisten it.

9. Spread the mixture into the prepared baking dish. Cover the top with the mozzarella and Parmesan.

10. Bake for 15 to 20 minutes or longer, until golden brown and bubbling.

2 pounds ground turkey

4 tablespoons extra-virgin olive oil

3 cups chopped onion

2 teaspoons sea salt

1 red bell pepper, chopped

1 green bell pepper, chopped

6 garlic cloves, finely chopped

1 teaspoon finely chopped
seeded jalapeño

1 (4-ounce) can chopped green chilies

3 (15.5-ounce) cans white beans,
drained and rinsed

1 cup fresh or frozen corn kernels
(optional)

4 cups chicken broth

½ teaspoon white pepper

½ teaspoon freshly ground
black pepper

2 bay leaves

2 teaspoons ground cumin

1 teaspoon ground coriander

2 teaspoons chili powder

½ teaspoon smoked paprika

2 teaspoons dried oregano

1 teaspoon dried Italian seasoning

2 tablespoons finely chopped
fresh cilantro

2 tablespoons cornmeal

Garnishes

Sour cream

Shredded cheddar cheese

Sliced avocado

Cilantro leaves

Sliced green onions

Chopped jalapeños

WHITE BEAN
TURKEY CHILI

1. In a medium stockpot, brown the turkey in 2 tablespoons of the olive oil. Once browned, remove the turkey from the pot, drain, and set aside.

2. To the same pot, add the remaining 2 tablespoons olive oil. Add the onion and ½ teaspoon of the salt. Sauté for 3 to 4 minutes.

3. Add the red and green bell pepper to the pot and sauté for 2 to 3 minutes.

4. Add the garlic, jalapeño, and green chilies. Sauté for 1 minute.

5. Return the turkey to the pot with the sautéed vegetables.

6. Add the beans, corn (if using), and broth to the pot. Stir well.

7. Add the remaining 1½ teaspoons salt, the white pepper, black pepper, bay leaves, cumin, coriander, chili powder, paprika, oregano, Italian seasoning, and 1 tablespoon of the cilantro.

8. Cover the pot and bring to a boil. Reduce the heat and simmer, uncovered, for 45 minutes, stirring occasionally.

9. In a small bowl, combine some of the broth from the chili with the cornmeal. Stir and then add it to the chili pot. Cook for 3 minutes.

10. Add the remaining 1 tablespoon cilantro. Remove and discard the bay leaves. Taste, adjust the seasonings, and serve with the garnishes set out in small bowls for everyone to top their chili as they choose.

RUSTIC CHICKEN POTPIE

SERVES 6

Organic olive oil cooking spray

3 boneless, skinless chicken breasts

4 boneless, skin-on chicken thighs

Seasoned salt

Lemon pepper

4 cups chicken broth

1 package small pearl onions (about 2 cups)

1 cup frozen peas

½ cup white wine or sake

3 tablespoons extra-virgin olive oil

2 cups coarsely chopped sweet onion

1 teaspoon sea salt

2 cups coarsely chopped celery

2 cups coarsely chopped carrots

3 tablespoons unsalted butter

½ cup all-purpose flour

1 cup heavy cream

½ teaspoon dried oregano

½ teaspoon dried thyme

2 teaspoons dried tarragon

¼ teaspoon white pepper

¼ teaspoon ground turmeric

1 cup loosely packed coarsely chopped fresh parsley

1 Pillsbury refrigerated piecrust (see Note)

1 egg white, slightly beaten

MY NON-COOKING MOTHER fed my siblings and me a lot of fish sticks, TV dinners, and chicken potpies. Those convenience foods were lifesavers for her, as she was a working mom who went back to work when I was six weeks old, which was unusual for a mother in Mobile, Alabama, in those days. Of the three frozen meals, it was the chicken potpie that I always looked forward to. When I started to cook, I wanted to know how to make that dish on my own. I've perfected the filling over the years, and I like it seasoned with fresh tarragon. Some days I will make my own dough for the crust, but most of the time I'm happy to use a good frozen pastry, because I'm all about easy and good.

1. Preheat the oven to 350°F. Grease a 9 x 13-inch baking dish with olive oil spray and set aside.

2. Place all the chicken pieces in a metal baking pan. Generously season the chicken with seasoned salt and lemon pepper. Add 1 cup of the broth. Bake for 1 hour, basting and turning the chicken every 20 minutes, until most of the broth and the chicken juices have reduced to golden brown drippings.

3. While the chicken is baking, in a medium saucepan, bring 2 to 3 cups water to a boil. Add the pearl onions and boil for 3 to 4 minutes. Remove from the heat and let cool. Remove and discard the onion skins and set the onions aside.

4. Run hot water over the peas in a strainer until they are thawed. Drain completely. Place in a bowl and set aside.

5. Once the chicken is done baking, remove it from the pan to cool (keep the oven on). While the pan is still hot, add the wine to deglaze the baking pan, whisking and scraping all the chicken bits from the bottom of the pan and stirring them into the wine. Pour the drippings into a measuring cup and set aside.

6. Chop the chicken into bite-size pieces (do not shred). Set aside.

CONT.

7. In a medium stockpot, heat the olive oil over medium-high heat. Add the chopped sweet onion and ½ teaspoon of the salt and sauté until the onion just begins to caramelize, about 5 minutes.

8. Add the celery and carrots. Sauté until the vegetables are soft and lightly browned, about 10 minutes.

9. Add the butter and stir until it's melted. Add the flour and stir to combine. Cook, stirring continuously, for 2 to 3 minutes, or until the flour begins to brown slightly.

10. Add the remaining 3 cups broth and the cream. Cook over low heat until the mixture thickens, then add the reserved liquid from the chicken drippings.

11. Add the oregano, thyme, tarragon, white pepper, turmeric, and the remaining ½ teaspoon salt. Stir together.

12. Add the pearl onions and thawed peas and gently stir.

13. Gently stir in the chicken and parsley.

14. Sprinkle flour over the counter or a marble pastry slab and roll out the piecrust dough to fit the 9 x 13-inch baking dish.

15. Transfer the chicken mixture to the prepared baking dish. Drape the piecrust over the dish, crimping the sides—I like mine very rough and rustic.

16. Brush the top of the piecrust with the beaten egg white. Use a knife to make a few thin slits in the crust to release the steam as it cooks.

17. Place the potpie in the oven on a low rack and bake for 30 minutes.

18. Move the potpie to a top rack and bake for 30 minutes more, or until the pastry is golden brown.

NOTE: *I'm not a very good baker, which is why I usually use a ready-made pastry. I've found Pillsbury to be the closest to homemade. If you're an avid baker or proficient pastry chef, by all means use your favorite piecrust recipe or the one on page 13.*

LUCY B. GOODE'S
FAMOUS-FOR-FIFTEEN-MINUTES MAC AND CHEESE

SERVES 8

Organic olive oil cooking spray

1 pound elbow macaroni

2 tablespoons extra-virgin olive oil

4 tablespoons (½ stick) unsalted butter

2 ounces all-purpose flour

3 cups whole milk

1 cup heavy cream

1 pound extra-sharp cheddar cheese, shredded

½ cup shredded Gouda cheese

½ cup shredded Parmesan cheese

1 teaspoon sea salt

1 teaspoon freshly ground black pepper

1 pound medium wild-caught Gulf shrimp, peeled and deveined (optional)

THIS MAC AND CHEESE with its cooked sauce is truly hearty enough to serve as a main dish—with a salad on the side to make up for the cheese, butter, and cream! But if you really want to launch it to the next level as a scrumptious all-in-one casserole, make it a shrimp mac and cheese.

1. Grease a 9 x 13-inch baking dish with olive oil spray.

2. Prepare the pasta according to the shortest time on the package directions—you'll want it al dente, with a little bit of firmness—stirring occasionally. Drain the pasta, reserving ¼ to ½ cup of the cooking liquid. Return the pasta to the pot and toss with the olive oil and reserved cooking liquid. Cover to keep warm.

3. In a medium saucepan, melt the butter over medium heat. Add the flour and cook, stirring continuously, for 3 to 4 minutes, to make a blond roux. Add the milk, then the cream a little at a time, stirring to prevent lumps. Reduce the heat to low and simmer, stirring occasionally, for about 6 minutes.

4. Stir in 2 cups of the cheddar a little at a time, followed by the Gouda and Parmesan. Once the cheeses are fully melted, season with the salt and pepper.

5. Preheat the oven to broil.

6. Mix together the cooked pasta, cheese sauce, and shrimp (if using) and pour into the prepared baking dish. Top with the remaining cheddar and broil for 10 to 12 minutes, or until the top is lightly browned.

LOUISIANA-STYLE CRAWFISH CREAM SAUCE
OVER PASTA

SERVES 6

4 cups baby spinach

1 pound bow-tie or penne pasta

2 tablespoons extra-virgin olive oil

½ cup (1 stick) unsalted butter

6 shallots, finely chopped (about 2 cups)

1 cup finely chopped tasso (can substitute spicy chorizo or Canadian bacon)

2 tablespoons crushed and finely chopped garlic

2 teaspoons LuLu's Crazy Creola Seasoning (page xxviii) or other Creole seasoning

½ teaspoon sea salt

¼ teaspoon cayenne pepper

¼ cup dry white wine

2 cups heavy cream

Juice of ½ lemon

1 pound crawfish tails, boiled and shells removed (see Note)

½ cup finely chopped green onions

¼ cup plus 2 tablespoons finely chopped fresh parsley

1 cup grated Parmesan cheese

THIS IS ANOTHER one of my favorite Jazz Fest traditions! I attended the Jazz and Heritage Fest in New Orleans for twenty-six years in a row, if you can believe it, and I still go back when I can. The year Crawfish Monica hit the concession scene, it exploded with popularity, with multiple lines of people backing up for what seemed like miles to purchase a bowl. There are so many fantastic dishes and food vendors at Jazz Fest that you can imagine how tasty something must be to become a stand-out star, and Crawfish Monica continues to be a must-have on people-in-the-know's Jazz Fest food map. The secret ingredient that keeps people lining up for hours for a taste of the original? I don't have any clue as to what exactly it is, but here is my humble attempt at bringing a little Jazz Fest and Crawfish Monica home with me.

1. Bring a large saucepan of water to a boil. Add the spinach and push it down to submerge it in the water. Blanch it for about 40 seconds, then drain the spinach well and set aside.

2. Prepare the pasta according to the shortest time on the package directions—you'll want it al dente, with a little bit of firmness—stirring occasionally. Drain the pasta, reserving ¼ to ½ cup of the cooking liquid. Return the pasta to the pot and toss with the olive oil and reserved cooking liquid. Cover to keep warm.

3. In a large heavy skillet (10 to 12 inches), melt the butter over medium-high heat. Add the shallot and sauté until soft, about 5 minutes. Add the tasso, garlic, Creole seasoning, salt, and cayenne pepper. Add the wine and cook over medium-high heat until all the wine has evaporated.

4. Add the cream and lemon juice and cook, stirring occasionally, until slightly reduced.

5. Add the crawfish tails and cook, stirring, to warm through. Add the green onion and ¼ cup of the parsley and cook for 1 minute. Add the blanched spinach and cooked pasta and toss to coat with the sauce.

6. Remove from the heat and stir in ½ cup of the Parmesan. Sprinkle the remaining ½ cup Parmesan and the remaining 2 tablespoons parsley over the top. Serve immediately.

NOTE: *Crawfish that have already been boiled are readily available for purchase, including online.*

CRAWFISH CORNBREAD

CASSEROLE

SERVES 6 TO 8

Organic olive oil cooking spray

¾ cup finely chopped Conecuh sausage or other Cajun-style smoked pork sausage

1 cup finely chopped yellow onion

⅔ cup finely chopped celery

⅔ cup finely chopped red bell pepper

¼ cup finely chopped seeded jalapeño

2 teaspoons finely chopped garlic

1 teaspoon dried thyme

1 pound crawfish tails, boiled and shells removed (see Note)

1 cup self-rising flour

2 cups self-rising yellow cornmeal mix

1 teaspoon sea salt

1 teaspoon freshly ground black pepper

1 teaspoon LuLu's Crazy Creola Seasoning (page xxviii) or other Creole seasoning

1 tablespoon sugar

7 large eggs

⅔ cup vegetable oil

1 cup buttermilk

1 cup shredded sharp cheddar cheese

1 cup Southern Fried Creamed Corn (page 171) or canned creamed corn

CRAWFISH CORNBREAD is a Louisiana dish resembling a Southern spoon bread, but features that exotic New Orleans ingredient, crawfish. Freshwater shellfish born in the bayous of Louisiana, crawfish were, until recently, impossible to enjoy unless you traveled there. These days, crawfish meat exported from Louisiana is available frozen in markets around the country. Probably most famously featured in the Cajun dish crawfish étouffée, crawfish can be used in any gumbo or seafood cream sauce. This recipe takes the little "bugs" and adds them to a very moist, almost pudding-textured cornbread featuring all the flavors of an étouffée, along with the knockout combination of cheese and creamed corn. This recipe makes for a great one-dish main course or a hearty side dish.

1. Preheat the oven to 400°F. Grease a 9 x 13-inch baking dish with olive oil spray.

2. Heat a large heavy skillet (10 to 12 inches) over medium-high heat. Add the sausage and cook until browned. Transfer the sausage to a plate covered in paper towels.

3. In the same skillet, sauté the onion, celery, bell pepper, and jalapeño in the leftover grease from the sausage until tender, adding a little vegetable oil if needed. Add the garlic and sauté for 1 minute more. Turn the heat off and add the thyme and crawfish tails. Return the sausage to the pan. Set aside to cool slightly to room temperature.

4. In a medium bowl, combine the flour, cornmeal mix, salt, black pepper, Creole seasoning, and sugar.

5. In a large bowl, whisk together the eggs, oil, and buttermilk until blended. Fold the cheese and creamed corn into the egg mixture until just combined. Fold the dry flour mixture into the creamed corn mixture until just combined, making sure not to overmix. Stir the crawfish mixture into the batter just to combine, again making sure not to overmix.

6. Pour the batter into the prepared baking dish and bake for 55 to 60 minutes, or until a toothpick inserted into the center comes out clean.

NOTE: *Crawfish that have already been boiled are readily available for purchase, including online.*

VEGETABLES AND SIDES

IN MY part of the world, as soon as Mardi Gras rolls around, it's time to start dreaming of tomatoes. Six weeks later, just after Easter, it's planting time, and that chore is at the top of my spring to-do list. The homegrown tomato is the crown jewel of the Deep South and the key ingredient in so many of my favorite recipes. At LuLu's in Gulf Shores, we even have our very own *superwoman tomato farmer*! Christen Ordonez grows the tomatoes for the restaurant and has a roadside sign on her tomato field that reads *WE'RE GROWIN' FOR LULU'S!*

When the tomatoes are at their peak, my right-hand lady and earth angel, Margaret, picks up several cases from Christen and we spend a whole day in the kitchen putting them up in hallowed mason jars. I give the put-up homegrown tomatoes to my brother and sister every Christmas as a little bit of home. My sister especially would rather have home-canned tomatoes than caviar any day.

Throughout the Gulf Coast, fresh produce plays a treasured role in local cuisine. As Easter brings planting season, summertime brings pop-up vegetable stands and acres of planted fields with new potatoes, soybeans, and all kinds of peas and beans, along with the royal darling of the bunch, fresh Silver Queen corn. I cherish my daily drive along the country highways of my coastal home and seeing those beautiful green rows of regal cornstalks, standing proud, ready for harvest—and for my next seafood boil.

Watermelon from a cooler with the juice dribbling down your arm is a hot-weather must. As are baskets of fragrant peaches, just sitting pretty and getting sweeter by the day, waiting Zen-like to turn into a scrumptious cobbler.

And you're missing out if you haven't learned to love okra! (If you're an okra skeptic, turn over to the fried chapter and try it that way. You'll never go back to a life without it!) We are truly blessed along the Gulf with a bounty of produce and Southern traditions handed down for years with so many tasty ways to enjoy it. That being said, sometimes a simple homegrown tomato from my garden, all juicy, naked, and humble, is about as tasty as it gets.

ROASTED TOMATOES
WITH GARLIC, BASIL, BALSAMIC, AND BLACK OLIVES

SERVES 6 TO 8

3 pounds pretty tomatoes (homegrown, heirloom, or Roma), unpeeled, cored, and sliced into quarters (removing seeds is optional)

2 (or more) garlic cloves, sliced lengthwise

1 cup oil-cured black olives, pitted and halved

¼ cup extra-virgin olive oil

1½ teaspoons sea salt

½ teaspoon freshly ground black pepper

2 teaspoons sugar

¼ cup good balsamic vinegar

3 tablespoons thinly sliced fresh basil

THIS IS ONE of those recipes that I made up one summer day when I had a crate of extra tomatoes and needed to do something different with them. I like them juicy so that I can either serve them with a slotted spoon as a veggie side or pour the whole baking dish over a bowl of pasta. The sugar cuts the acid and the oil-cured olives are my all-time favorite olive to lend a mild yet pungent flavor. I've been conservative here with the amount of garlic, so garlic lovers, you can use as many cloves as you like! And I use an aged balsamic glaze, but any decent balsamic vinegar will do.

1. Preheat the oven to 350°F.

2. Place the tomatoes in a large glass bowl. Add the garlic, olives, olive oil, salt, pepper, and sugar. Toss together well, making sure to thoroughly coat the tomatoes. Transfer to a baking dish.

3. Bake for 15 minutes, then drizzle with the vinegar and bake for 15 minutes more.

4. Add the basil to the tomatoes, stirring it in to combine, then bake for 5 minutes more.

5. Remove from the oven and serve immediately.

WHOLE ROASTED OKRA
— WITH —
PARMESAN CRUNCH

SERVES 4

2 tablespoons extra-virgin
olive oil

1 teaspoon sea salt

1 teaspoon freshly ground
black pepper

1¼ pounds fresh whole okra,
washed and patted dry

½ cup shredded Parmesan cheese

OKRA IS A strange vegetable that is misunderstood and under-appreciated. An essential ingredient for summer gumbos, any cook will tell you, however, that it is a fright to cut and prepare, as it gets weirdly slimy. But when you take the whole pod and roast it and add some Parmesan cheese, the result is amazingly sweet and salty. Plus, this recipe is so darn easy, it can be done at a moment's notice.

1. Preheat the oven to 400°F.

2. In a medium bowl, combine the olive oil, salt, and pepper and mix well. Add the okra and toss well to coat each piece.

3. Place the okra on a baking sheet, keeping the pieces close together but in a single layer. Top with the Parmesan and bake for 20 minutes, or until the Parmesan is golden brown. Remove from the oven and serve as a side dish.

SOUTHERN FRIED
CREAMED CORN

SERVES 8

8 thick-cut bacon slices

½ cup (1 stick) unsalted butter

10 cups fresh corn kernels, cut off the cob (see Note)

4 teaspoons sea salt

1 tablespoon freshly ground black pepper

1 cup heavy cream

IN OUR NECK of the woods, when we say "fried corn," what we mean is creamed corn that has been cooked in a skillet with butter, bacon, and cream. It's a "save up the calories" dish for sure! Use only fresh corn so you can scrape the sweet, milky juices from the cob. For me, it's got to be from Baldwin County, but if you're not in Sweet Home Alabama, choose some sweet local corn from *your* neck of the woods.

1. In a large heavy skillet (10 to 12 inches), cook the bacon until crisp. Remove it from the skillet and set it aside on a plate covered with paper towels, leaving the bacon grease in the skillet. When the bacon is cool, chop it into bite-size pieces.

2. Add the butter to the skillet with the bacon grease and melt over medium heat. Add the corn and sauté for 10 to 12 minutes, stirring frequently to keep the corn from sticking.

3. Season with the salt and pepper, return the bacon to the skillet, and sauté for 2 minutes.

4. Add the cream and stir. Bring it to a simmer, then remove from the heat and serve.

NOTE: *Fresh corn varies in size, and it could take 14 to 24 fresh corncobs to make the 10 cups of kernels you'll need. Scrape down the sides of the cobs with a knife after removing the kernels to release the remaining sweet juices and include those juices with the kernels in the skillet.*

BEST SUMMER SQUASH
CASEROLE

SERVES 6 TO 8

Organic olive oil cooking spray

1 sleeve Ritz crackers

1½ cups shredded cheddar cheese

½ cup heavy cream

2 large eggs

2 teaspoons sea salt

4 large yellow squash, halved
lengthwise and cut into half-moons
(about 6 cups)

4 tablespoons (½ stick)
unsalted butter

1 large yellow onion, chopped

½ cup chopped red bell pepper

3 garlic cloves, finely chopped

Freshly ground black pepper

1. Preheat the oven to 350°F. Grease a 9 x 13-inch baking dish with olive oil spray.

2. Crush the crackers into fine to medium pieces and place them in a small bowl. Add the cheddar and mix well. Set aside.

3. In a small bowl, mix together the cream and eggs and set aside.

4. In a medium saucepan, combine 8 cups water and 1 teaspoon of the salt and bring to a boil over high heat.

5. Add the squash, reduce the heat to medium, cover, and cook the squash for 10 minutes, or until just barely tender. Drain well and place the squash in a large bowl.

6. While the squash is cooking, in a large heavy skillet (10 to 12 inches), melt the butter over medium heat. Add the onion and ½ teaspoon of the salt and sauté until the onion is tender, 8 to 10 minutes. Add the bell pepper and garlic and cook for about 5 minutes.

7. Add the onion mixture to the squash and stir well. Add three-quarters of the cheese mixture to the squash mixture and stir well.

8. Fold in the cream mixture, the remaining ½ teaspoon salt, and black pepper to taste. Gently stir until well combined. Pour into the baking dish. Top with the remaining cheese mixture.

9. Bake for 30 minutes, or until the mixture is bubbling and the top is brown.

SHAVED BRUSSELS SPROUTS
WITH
SHALLOTS AND COUNTRY HAM

SERVES 4

1 tablespoon extra-virgin olive oil

½ cup coarsely chopped country ham

2 tablespoons unsalted butter

2 large shallots, thinly sliced lengthwise

¼ cup large pecan pieces

1 pound Brussels sprouts, ends trimmed, thinly sliced

1 cup chicken broth

3 tablespoons balsamic or red wine vinegar

¼ teaspoon freshly ground black pepper

¼ cup dried cranberries

I WAS NEVER a big fan of Brussels sprouts, but I changed my mind when I had them at the Temptation restaurant in Boca Grande, Florida, and now every time I go I always order grilled fish with Brussels sprouts. In this recipe they have an almost slaw-like texture, and if you'd like to channel the Temptation, make a beautiful bed out of the sprouts on each plate and then perch a fillet of Bronzed Yellow-tail Snapper with Citrus Beurre Blanc Sauce (page 135) right on top.

1. In a large heavy skillet (10 to 12 inches), heat the olive oil over medium heat.

2. Add the country ham and sauté for 5 minutes.

3. Add the butter. Once the butter has melted, add the shallots and pecans. Reduce the heat to medium-low and sauté until the shallots are soft, 2 to 3 minutes.

4. Add the Brussels sprouts and stir, making sure all the sprouts are coated.

5. Add the broth, vinegar, pepper, and cranberries. Stir together, reduce the heat to low, and cover. Simmer for 20 minutes, stirring occasionally.

6. Remove from the heat, stir, and serve.

FRESH BUTTER BEANS

SERVES 4 TO 6

1 (1-ounce) piece fatback, or
2 tablespoons unsalted butter

1 Vidalia onion or other sweet onion,
finely chopped

4 cups freshly shelled butter beans
(about 3 pounds in the shell)

Sea salt and freshly ground
black pepper

6 cups chicken broth, plus more
as needed

1 jalapeño

FRESH BUTTER BEANS are one of my favorite roadside produce stand purchases. I have memories of my grandmother sitting on the porch with a bowl of beans and shelling them for hours, but these days the farmers have figured out they can get a lot more money for their beans if they go ahead and shell them for you and sell them in handy resealable plastic bags. This is good news indeed because not only can you get the freshest beans possible without time spent shelling, but you can buy up a whole bunch and store them in your freezer so you have fresh beans all year long. That being said, if you miss the season and don't stock up, frozen butter beans from the grocery store (labeled lima beans) are one produce item that translates well to the fresh version.

1. In a medium saucepan, melt the fatback over medium-high heat.

2. Add the onion and sauté until translucent.

3. Stir in the butter beans and season with salt and pepper. Sauté for 5 minutes.

4. Pour in the broth to cover the beans, adding more as needed. Add the whole jalapeño to the pot and bring the broth to a boil. Reduce the heat to low and simmer, uncovered, for 30 to 45 minutes, or until the beans are tender.

5. Taste and adjust the seasonings. Remove the jalapeño and serve.

BRAISED COLLARDS
WITH TURKEY BACON, PECANS, AND BALSAMIC

SERVES 6 TO 8

3 tablespoons extra-virgin olive oil

3 turkey bacon or pork belly slices, chopped into 1-inch pieces

2 tablespoons unsalted butter

1 cup thinly sliced shallots

½ cup large pecan pieces

1 pound collards, washed, ribs removed, and leaves torn into pieces

2 cups chicken broth

1 teaspoon sea salt

½ teaspoon freshly ground black pepper

¼ cup balsamic vinegar

1 tablespoon packed brown sugar or honey

1. In a large heavy skillet (10 to 12 inches), heat 1 tablespoon of the olive oil over medium heat. Add the bacon and fry until crisp. Remove the bacon from the skillet and set aside on a plate covered with paper towels.

2. Add the remaining 2 tablespoons olive oil and the butter to the hot pan. When the butter has melted, add the shallots. Sauté until softened, about 2 minutes.

3. Add the pecans and sauté for 2 minutes more.

4. Add the collards, broth, salt, and pepper. Return the bacon to the pan. Stir well and cover. Cook for 10 minutes, or until the collards are wilted.

5. Stir and cook, uncovered, until half the liquid has evaporated, about another 10 minutes.

6. Add the vinegar and brown sugar. Stir well. Cover and reduce the heat to low. Cook, stirring occasionally, for 20 minutes, as the collards slowly caramelize. Remove from the heat and serve.

CREAMED SPINACH

SERVES 6 TO 8

¾ cup (1½ sticks) unsalted butter,
plus more for the baking dish

1 cup all-purpose flour

¾ cup finely chopped yellow onion

4 garlic cloves, finely chopped

1 cup whole milk

1 cup heavy cream

1 to 1½ cups chicken broth

1½ teaspoons sea salt

1½ teaspoons freshly ground
black pepper

⅛ teaspoon ground nutmeg

3 pounds fresh spinach, chopped

¾ cup grated Parmesan cheese

½ cup fresh breadcrumbs

GROWING UP, we considered a steak house the epitome of a "fancy restaurant." Creamed spinach was their classic accompaniment for all the steaks. Spinach was one of those vegetables I tended to turn my nose up at, but as I got older I got wiser. And what doesn't taste delicious with a buttery cream sauce? People love this recipe, and it really is pretty on a plate next to a gorgeous medium-rare steak.

1. In a large saucepan, melt ½ cup (1 stick) of the butter over medium heat. Sprinkle in the flour and whisk together. Cook, stirring, for 5 minutes, or until light golden brown.

2. Add the onion and garlic, stir, and cook for 1 to 2 minutes more. Add the milk, cream, and 1 cup of the broth, whisking constantly. Cook for 5 minutes more and season with the salt, pepper, and nutmeg.

3. To sauté the spinach, in a large heavy skillet (10 to 12 inches), melt the remaining ¼ cup (½ stick) butter over medium heat. Add the spinach a handful at a time and sauté until barely wilted—dark green, but not soggy.

4. Drain the sautéed spinach and add to the cream sauce. Stir gently to combine. If the sauce is too thick, you can add a little more broth to get it to the consistency you like.

5. Preheat the oven to broil on high. Butter a 2-quart baking or gratin dish.

6. Transfer the spinach mixture to the prepared dish. Top with the Parmesan and breadcrumbs. Place the dish under the broiler on the top rack and broil for 3 minutes, or until the top is golden and crunchy. Serve immediately.

2 tablespoons extra-virgin olive oil

1 sweet onion, finely chopped

1 green bell pepper, finely chopped

6 garlic cloves, finely chopped

1 cup fresh corn off the cob, or you can use frozen

1 (28-ounce) can whole tomatoes, drained and coarsely chopped

1 (4.5-ounce) can chopped green chilies, with their juice

2 cups uncooked basmati rice

2 (15-ounce) cans black beans, drained and thoroughly rinsed

4 cups chicken broth

½ teaspoon sea salt

½ teaspoon LuLu's Crazy Creola Seasoning (page xxviii) or other Creole seasoning

1 teaspoon chili powder

1 teaspoon ground cumin

½ teaspoon ground turmeric

½ teaspoon hot sauce

2 tablespoons finely chopped fresh cilantro

2 handfuls fresh baby spinach

4 cups shredded sharp cheddar cheese

Cilantro-Lime Sour Cream

1 cup sour cream

2 teaspoons lime zest

½ cup finely chopped fresh cilantro

1 teaspoon sea salt

½ cup finely chopped green onions, for garnish

2 tablespoons finely chopped fresh cilantro, for garnish

MEXICAN RICE
AND
BLACK BEAN CASSEROLE

1. Preheat the oven to 350°F.

2. In a deep, ovenproof skillet or Dutch oven, heat the olive oil over medium heat. Add the sweet onion and sauté until it begins to turn translucent.

3. Add the bell pepper, garlic, corn, tomatoes, and green chilies (including the juice from the can). Sauté for 2 to 3 minutes, stirring occasionally.

4. Stir in the rice, making sure it gets coated with the vegetable mixture. Add the black beans and broth.

5. Stir in the salt, Creole seasoning, chili powder, cumin, turmeric, hot sauce, and cilantro. Bring the mixture to a boil, then reduce the heat to low. Cover and simmer for 15 minutes, or until most of the liquid has been absorbed by the rice.

6. Add the spinach and mix well. Cover and cook for 5 minutes. Remove from the heat.

7. Stir in 2 cups of the cheese, then place the remainder of the cheese on top of the rice. Place the skillet in the oven and cook for 12 minutes. Then switch the oven to broil and broil for 3 minutes so the cheesy top turns golden brown.

To make the cilantro-lime sour cream:

8. While the casserole is baking, in a small bowl, combine all the ingredients and mix well.

9. When the casserole is finished baking, sprinkle the green onion and cilantro on the top to garnish and serve with the cilantro-lime sour cream on the side.

CUBAN
YELLOW RICE

SERVES 6

1½ teaspoons extra-virgin olive oil

1 small onion, finely chopped

1 red bell pepper, finely chopped

2 cups jasmine rice

3 cups chicken broth

1 teaspoon ground turmeric

½ teaspoon sea salt

YOU CAN CERTAINLY buy yellow rice, but it is so easy to make your own using turmeric. Turmeric is a super spice with a long list of anti-inflammatory healing properties. My mother always hated rice because she said it had no flavor, but she loved mine because I gave it life! This yellow rice will bring a punch of life to any main dish and maybe even give a little lift to your health.

1. In a large heavy skillet (10 to 12 inches), heat the olive oil over medium heat. Add the onion and pepper and sauté 2 minutes.

2. Add the rice. Stir so that the rice is coated with the oil and the rice grains turn white in color.

3. Add the broth, turmeric, and salt. Bring to a boil, cover, and reduce the heat to low. Simmer, covered, for 20 minutes.

BROWN RICE MUSHROOM RISOTTO

SERVES 6

4 tablespoons extra-virgin olive oil

1 cup chopped green onions

1 teaspoon finely chopped garlic

½ cup shredded carrots

2 cups coarsely chopped assorted mushrooms (I use button, shiitake, baby bella, and oyster mushrooms)

6 cups chicken broth

½ cup white wine

3 tablespoons unsalted butter

1½ cups short-grain brown rice or a rice blend

½ teaspoon sea salt

¼ teaspoon freshly ground black pepper

1 teaspoon dried thyme

¼ cup plus 2 tablespoons finely chopped fresh parsley

½ cup frozen peas, thawed

½ heaping cup shredded Parmesan cheese

1. In a large heavy skillet (10 to 12 inches), heat 2 tablespoons of the olive oil over medium heat. Add the green onion and sauté for 3 minutes. Add the garlic and carrots. Sauté for 1 minute.

2. Add the remaining 2 tablespoons olive oil and the mushrooms. Once the mushrooms are heated through, cover and reduce the heat to low. Cook for 3 minutes, stirring occasionally. Remove from the heat and set aside.

3. While the mushroom mixture is cooking, heat the broth and wine in a medium saucepan until just simmering—try not to let it boil.

4. In a Dutch oven or small stockpot, melt the butter over medium-low heat. Add the rice and stir, coating the rice completely. Cook for 2 minutes.

5. Add 1 cup of the warm broth mixture to the rice, stirring until the rice has absorbed all the liquid. Add the remaining broth mixture, 1 cup at a time, continuing to stir.

6. Add the mushroom mixture, salt, pepper, thyme, and ¼ cup of the parsley. Cook until almost all the broth has been absorbed.

7. Add the peas and Parmesan. Cook until all the liquid has been absorbed and the risotto is moist and creamy.

8. Remove from the heat and sprinkle the remaining 2 tablespoons parsley over the top. Serve immediately.

ROSEMARY ROASTED
GARLIC POTATOES

SERVES 2 TO 4

Organic olive oil cooking spray

1 pound assorted small potatoes or red new potatoes, quartered

2 teaspoons sea salt

2 tablespoons extra-virgin olive oil

1 tablespoon unsalted butter

1 large red onion, chopped

1 teaspoon sugar

6 garlic cloves, sliced

2 tablespoons finely chopped fresh rosemary

¼ teaspoon freshly ground black pepper

¼ teaspoon LuLu's Crazy Creola Seasoning (page xxviii) or other Creole seasoning

1. Preheat the oven to 350°F. Grease a 9 x 13-inch baking dish with olive oil spray.

2. Place the potatoes in a large saucepan and add enough water to cover them. Add 1 teaspoon of the salt. Bring to a boil and cook for 5 minutes. Immediately drain the potatoes and set aside.

3. In a large heavy skillet (10 to 12 inches), heat 1 tablespoon of the olive oil and the butter over medium heat. Add the onion, ½ teaspoon of the salt, and the sugar. Sauté until the onion begins to caramelize, about 5 minutes. Add the garlic and sauté for 2 to 3 minutes more, or until the garlic is soft. Remove from the heat.

4. In a large bowl, combine the potatoes and the onion mixture. Add the rosemary, the remaining ½ teaspoon salt, the pepper, Creole seasoning, and the remaining 1 tablespoon olive oil. Mix together gently, making sure to coat the potatoes.

5. Transfer the potatoes to the prepared baking dish and bake for 45 minutes, or until the potatoes are soft and tender. Turn the oven to broil and broil for a few minutes to brown the tops. Serve immediately.

NOTE: *If you are adventurous, try using Irish butter and truffle salt. It makes the flavor pop a bit.*

THYME-SCENTED
SCALLOPED POTATOES
WITH CARAMELIZED ONIONS

SERVES 8 TO 10

Organic olive oil cooking spray

3 pounds large red potatoes

4 tablespoons unsalted butter

1 tablespoon extra-virgin olive oil

2 large onions, sliced into
¼-inch-thick rounds

1 teaspoon sea salt

2 teaspoons sugar

6 large garlic cloves, finely chopped

3 tablespoons all-purpose flour

2 cups whole milk

2 cups grated Gruyère or
Swiss cheese

1½ cups grated Parmesan cheese

½ cup chicken broth

¼ teaspoon white pepper

¼ teaspoon ground nutmeg

4 teaspoons finely chopped
fresh thyme, or 1 teaspoon
dried thyme

1. Preheat the oven to 350°F. Grease a 9 x 13-inch baking dish with olive oil spray.

2. Peel the potatoes and slice them into ¼-inch-thick rounds. Place them in a bowl of water until ready to use.

3. In a heavy skillet, heat 1 tablespoon of the butter and the olive oil over medium heat until it starts to sizzle.

4. Add the onion, the teaspoon of salt, and 1 teaspoon of the sugar. Sauté over medium heat, stirring frequently as the onions begin to caramelize. Turn the onion rounds and scrape the pan as they cook and turn brown, about 10 minutes.

5. Add the garlic and the remaining 1 teaspoon sugar and sauté until the onions are completely dark brown and caramelized. Remove the onions and garlic from the heat and let them cool.

6. In a medium saucepan, melt 3 tablespoons of the butter. When the butter sizzles, add the flour and whisk until smooth. Cook, whisking continuously, for 2 to 3 minutes. You *don't* want this roux to brown!

7. Add the milk and whisk continuously as the mixture thickens.

8. Add the Gruyère, 1 cup of the Parmesan, and the broth and whisk continuously until the cheese has melted.

9. Add the white pepper, nutmeg, and 3 teaspoons of the thyme to the sauce. Stir well and remove from the heat.

10. Rinse and drain the potato slices, and then dry them on paper towels.

11. Spread the caramelized onions over the bottom of the prepared baking dish.

12. Layer half the potato slices over the onions. Pour half the cheese sauce over the potatoes. Layer the remaining potato slices and cover with the remaining sauce.

13. Sprinkle the top with the remaining ½ cup Parmesan and the remaining 1 teaspoon thyme.

14. Bake for 40 minutes, or until the potatoes are heated through and the top is golden brown.

ANDOUILLE BAKED GRITS

SERVES 8 TO 10

Organic olive oil cooking spray

1 pound andouille sausage, quartered, then chopped crosswise into rounds (about 1½ cups)

½ cup hot coffee

4 garlic cloves, finely chopped

½ cup finely chopped yellow onion

¾ cup very thinly sliced mushrooms

1 jalapeño, seeded and finely chopped

3 fresh tomatoes, peeled and coarsely chopped (see Note)

2 teaspoons sea salt

1 teaspoon white pepper

½ teaspoon sugar

1 teaspoon LuLu's Crazy Creola Seasoning (page xxviii) or other Creole seasoning

2 cups heavy cream

4 cups water

1 cup grits

2 cups grated Gruyère cheese

THIS RECIPE IS one of those happy accidents that happened when I was looking in the fridge, knowing that I had to use what I had on hand at that moment. The result was amazing, and it became one of my go-to dishes. Louisiana-style andouille is a key ingredient in Cajun gumbos, and thankfully it's now widely available in grocery stores nationwide. It is fragrant, garlicky, and tasty, and I highly recommend it, but any smoked country-type link sausage will do here—including whatever you happen to have on hand in your fridge at the moment!

1. Preheat the oven to 350°F. Coat a 2-quart baking dish with olive oil spray.

2. Lightly coat a large heavy skillet (10 to 12 inches) with the olive oil spray. Add the sausage and cook over medium-high heat until very browned. You want pieces of it to stick to the pan.

3. Add the coffee to deglaze the pan, scraping up the bits stuck to the pan and stirring them into the coffee. Cook until the liquid has reduced by half.

4. Add the garlic, onion, mushrooms, and jalapeño. Cover and cook for 1 minute. Uncover and simmer for a few minutes.

5. Add the tomatoes and cook, covered, for 1 to 2 minutes. Uncover and simmer for a few minutes more to reduce the liquid.

6. Add 1½ teaspoons of the salt, the white pepper, sugar, and Creole seasoning. Cook for 1 to 2 minutes more, then turn off the heat.

7. In a medium saucepan, combine the cream, the remaining ½ teaspoon salt, and the water and bring to a boil over medium-high heat.

8. Whisk the grits into the boiling liquid, then reduce the heat to low. Cook, whisking often, until the grits thicken.

9. Once the grits are thickened, add the sausage and vegetable mixture and mix well.

10. Pour the grits mixture into the prepared baking dish.

11. Top with the Gruyère and bake for 30 minutes.

12. Switch the oven to broil and broil for 3 minutes so the cheesy top turns golden brown. Let cool slightly before serving—when you first remove it from the oven, it'll be as hot as a heat tile on the space shuttle, and unless you really want to injure your guests, it's best to wait a few minutes.

NOTE: *To ease the tomato peeling process, drop the tomatoes into boiling water for 1 minute. Let them cool for a minute, and the skins will peel right off.*

GREENS AND GRITS

I KNOW WHY some folks turn their noses up at grits. Like rice, cooked without seasoning and special ingredients, grits are bland and unappetizing. But cooked with cheese and garlic like my grandmother taught me, grits turn into a gourmet meal. Honestly, from fancy Gruyère to red-rind cheddar, from smoked Gouda to Velveeta, any kind of cheese will do. Pair these gussied-up grits with any seasonal green (collards, mustard greens, or turnip greens), and these two humble Southern ingredients become a masterpiece.

SERVES 8

Organic olive oil cooking spray

6 bacon slices

2 tablespoons unsalted butter

1 onion, halved and sliced lengthwise

1 tablespoon sugar

1 pound collards or other seasonal greens, washed, ribs removed, and leaves torn into pieces

1½ teaspoons sea salt

6½ cups chicken broth

2 cups heavy cream

½ teaspoon white pepper

2 cups yellow grits

1 tablespoon finely chopped garlic

4 cups shredded cheese

2 tablespoons hot sauce

2 large eggs

1. Preheat the oven to 350°F. Grease a 9 x 13-inch baking dish with olive oil spray.

2. Slice the bacon into small to medium pieces and fry in a large heavy skillet (10 to 12 inches) until crisp. Transfer to a plate covered with paper towels and set aside.

3. In the same skillet used for the bacon, melt the butter over medium heat. Add the onion and sugar and sauté until the onion is caramelized and dark brown.

4. Add the collards, ½ teaspoon of the salt, and ½ cup of the broth. Mix well using tongs. Cover and cook for 5 minutes.

5. Uncover and cook, stirring occasionally, until all the liquid has been absorbed. Remove from the heat and set aside.

6. To make the grits, in a Dutch oven or small stockpot, combine the remaining 6 cups broth, the cream, pepper, and the remaining 1 teaspoon salt and bring to a boil over medium heat. Reduce the heat to low and whisk in the grits. Cover and cook for 5 minutes, whisking occasionally.

7. Add the garlic, 2 cups of the cheese, and the hot sauce. Stir until well combined and creamy.

8. Beat the eggs in a medium bowl. Add 1 cup of the hot grits to the eggs, ½ cup at a time, whisking well, to temper the eggs. Transfer the egg mixture back into the pot of grits and whisk until combined. Cover and turn off the heat, but keep the pot on the burner to keep the grits warm.

9. Pour half the grits into the prepared baking dish. Spoon the collards on top of the grits. Pour the remaining grits over the collards. Top with the remaining 2 cups cheese and the bacon pieces.

10. Bake for 15 minutes, or until the grits are bubbling. Turn the oven to broil and broil until the cheese is browned.

DEEP-FRIED FAVORITES: A SOUTHERN MUST

IN THE coastal South, learning to fry is a rite of passage, like learning to swim or picking blackberries or playing with tadpoles in the watershed red-clay gullies of my youth. As little barefoot bay kids, the exquisite bounty from our warm Gulf waters—shrimp, crab, and oysters—seemed ridiculously weird to us as something to eat and became palatable only when we discovered the hidden lusciousness disguised within a scalding-hot, deep-fried crispy nugget.

There is nothing as inviting as the aroma of something frying in the kitchen or as tantalizing to the taste buds as a delicately fried morsel of your favorite food. Having gotten a bad rap in the modern days of clean eating, fried food is one of the most delicious and classic ways to prepare beautiful, fresh food. Now, know this: I am a passionate advocate of the healthy eating and clean cooking movement and a firm believer in the popular anthem of "everything in moderation." I've been able to follow that sage advice for short periods of time, and it works for those

folks who are what I call "normal eaters." But I didn't get that particular moderation brain chip on the assembly line of creation! Instead, I got the full-throttle, all-or-nothing chip—especially when it comes to eating.

I remember one of my first visits to a nutritionist who told me all the foods that were "bad" for me. I was heartbroken, crestfallen, you-name-it disappointed! And being a rebel and someone who doesn't like to be told what to do, I'm hard-wired to do the exact opposite, so in that moment I was crystal clear that I was *never* going to give up fried chicken like my daddy used to make. Or stop celebrating the fine food that has been my passion and later became my occupation and livelihood.

I don't believe in "good food" and "bad food." I believe in celebrating food, and where there is love, mindfulness, and gratitude, all food is a gift. Sure, some foods support the body more than others, and science updates and contradicts itself frequently. But the attitude a person has about what they eat is equally as important as the food they eat. Approaching any food that we eat or cook with love and gratitude positively charges that food to best support our bodies and minds. It's time to take the taboo off fried food in all forms—one quality fried-food meal a week eaten with total love and appreciation isn't a mortal sin.

One of my sweetest pleasures in life is to gather beautiful food ingredients and, using any and all cooking methods, including frying, to transform them into delicious, aromatic, colorful meals. I'll admit it: I'm a downright overindulger in all things wonderful. It's that all-or-nothing gene that seems to run in my adventurous family, and eating great food is a meaningful part of my life. So I've had to come up with what I call the "save-up" method of eating.

In my youth, I could eat anything I wanted, but the older I've gotten, like most of us baby boomers, I've spent more time on the heavier end of my weight spectrum. Now I choose lighter fare for most days and "save up" for the days when I can splurge. Fridays have become my "Fry-days," when I usually find myself at LuLu's for lunch indulging in one of our specialty dishes like our fried green tomatoes.

Cooking up a mess of fried shrimp or Daddy's fried chicken has become a hallowed family tradition, like making gumbo. It's not necessarily difficult, but it requires time, preparation, and patience—the last being for the cleanup. But like all good things, it's worth the effort, especially when you receive so much love in return with the *oooh*s, *aaaah*s, and groans of delight from your guests.

So if you're gonna fry, fry happy. Make it a family gathering. Make it a party. Make the save-up worth it and enjoy every step, even the messy ones. Let go of the worry and fear of doing it right, the guilt of it being fattening, and the anguish of making a mess, and make every Fry-day a celebration.

FRY MAMA LULU'S TIPS FOR EASY FRYING

Okay, friends, there is panfrying, stir-frying, and sautéing—all cooking methods using oil or fat to cook food. But when I'm talking about frying here, I'm talking about the honored Southern culinary tradition of *deep-frying*. The big kahuna of frying, deep-frying is the grand marshal at Carnival. There's a holy-moly pleasure and sense of accomplishment in mastering the fear of frying, and the rewards are nothing short of deliciously sublime. So roll up your sleeves, put on your marching flip-flops, and join the parade with the following helpful fry hints.

CHOOSE YOUR DISH WITH CARE. Frying is an adventure, so make sure you are preparing something that you absolutely love and make sure it is the best quality you can find. Sometimes that will be the fish your husband or you just cleaned and brought home, and other times it may be flash-frozen shrimp from the supermarket or mail-order oysters from Louisiana. I will let you in on a little secret, folks: shoe leather would taste decent if it was fried. Still, similar to my anthem of "Do the best you can," find the best ingredients that you can afford.

TO BREAD OR TO BATTER—THAT IS THE QUESTION. Most fried-food dishes are going to use one or the other. Breading uses dry ingredients like flour, cornmeal, or cracker meal and a liquid like buttermilk, milk, or beaten eggs. You dip the ingredient into the liquid, then dredge it through the dry ingredient before you put it in the hot oil. Some recipes even call for double dipping, like we do at my restaurants. This simply means you perform the process twice, enhancing the crustiness of the end result. Creating a batter, on the other hand, simply means you combine the dry and the wet ingredients together rather than dipping and dredging separately. There are several types of batter for frying, such as a beer batter (used often for onion rings) or a tempura batter using cornstarch and water to create a super-light batter (used often for Asian-style fried seafood and vegetables).

The dish and ingredient you choose usually determine which method you use. For instance, I like my oysters breaded using a seasoned cornmeal mixture, but I like my shrimp double-dipped into seasoned flour and buttermilk. There are no rules—or if there are, break 'em. It's simply your preference in my world of LuLuFrying.

CHOOSE YOUR OIL WISELY. Traditionally,

peanut oil was always the best option for frying because of its high smoke point, which simply means it doesn't start to burn at a low heat like butter or olive oil. You need your oil at a high heat for deep-frying, anywhere from 325 to 375°F, depending on what you are cooking. In recent times, however, peanut oil has become a problem because of the growing number of people with peanut allergies. That's why we now use canola oil in the restaurant, which also has a high smoke point, as does straight-up vegetable oil. I don't advise using any "manufactured for high heat" oils because I think a whole food is always better than one that has been meddled with by scientists or marketers.

THE FRYING VESSEL MATTERS—OR DOES IT?

Any pan that is going to be used for frying has to be heavy, but the key word is *any*. Don't be deterred or intimidated because you don't have

a fancy FryDaddy machine. There are lots of options for the right pan or pot, and any of them are fine as long as they are heavy-duty. A skillet, sauté pan, Dutch oven, or wok will do. Whatever you choose, just be sure it is large enough to hold the quantity of oil needed for the food you're frying to be totally submerged, with little room to spare. I typically use hand-me-down cast-iron pots and skillets, but sometimes I use my stainless steel sauté pan or my ancient enameled cast-iron Dutch oven. And when cooking for a crowd, I will often move my frying outdoors and use a large stockpot over a propane burner or my old trusty electric skillet because you can rely on its temperature remaining consistent.

PREP FOR SUCCESS. Set up your "fry station"

before you start the cooking process. Have all your ingredients laid out in the order that you will use them and close to the stovetop where you will be frying. I always give my seafood a good rinse, then pat it dry with a paper towel. If I'm frying fish, I soak it in milk for about half an hour because I think it diminishes that strong "fishy" taste and smell. That may be an old wives' tale, but it makes me feel better to do it.

READY, SET, FRY. If you're using a skillet, fill it

with oil to about 2 inches from the top edge of the pan. If you're using a Dutch oven or larger pot, make sure there is enough oil to thoroughly cover the ingredients. When you place your breaded or battered food in the hot oil, it's going to bubble and rise up, so you want to make sure that the oil level is not near the top of the pan or it could bubble over, and that is the dangerous part of frying.

Heat the oil to the desired temperature between 325 and 375°F. Doughnuts or fritters, for instance, may not require as high a temperature as a piece of chicken, and different chefs recommend differing frying temperatures, which can be confusing. *I have found that a temperature of 355°F works for me on most anything I fry.* If you are a novice fryer not using an electric skillet, I highly recommend using a candy/deep-fry thermometer for temperature accuracy. If you are an adventurous sort, the gauge I use to determine if the oil is hot enough is flicking a little flour into the hot oil and seeing how fast it sizzles and turns brown. If it browns too quickly, lower the temperature. It's one of those things that just takes practice. Most times, I have the oil a little too high, and part of the whole process is throwing away the first couple of pieces before I get the oil adjusted to the right temperature.

FRY A LITTLE TENDERNESS. Frying in batches is simply part of the frying process. Gently drop or slide your food into the hot oil from a short distance above the oil to minimize any back splash. You don't want to crowd the food in the hot oil, so fry only a few pieces at a time. When frying small pieces of food, you don't need to turn it because the food is submerged in the oil and it will float to the top when it is done; you can keep it frying for a little longer to get to the desired golden color. I like to use tongs or a slotted spoon to fetch the fried food out of the oil onto a baking pan lined with plenty of paper towels so the oil can thoroughly drain from the food. Then I pop the pan into a 200°F oven to keep the food warm and to keep it from getting soggy until I'm ready to serve. Never, ever cover fried food that has just come out of the fryer. It will create steam and turn your beautiful fried food into a soggy mess.

In between batches, spoon out any fragments of breading or batter that have fallen off while frying and throw them away before you put in another batch. Sometimes at a party I will set up a fry station outside and folks will stand around

with their drinks snatching up the piping-hot delicacies as soon as they come out of the fryer. It's a fun way to start a gathering.

THE DREADED CLEANUP. Yep, I'm going to be straight up: frying is a messy process, but that's also part of the fun. It is so tactile, like finger painting. You have to dive in with your hands first, and your fingers get caked with the repetitive dipping, dredging, and dropping. You will end up washing your hands a lot during the process. The flour will rise up in clouds and inevitably find its way along the counter, floor, and on some part of your body, even your face. But think of it all as a work of art and make it fun. After all the accolades and the stuffed tummies, the final step of a successful fried-food event is the dreaded cleanup. For me, though, I actually get great satisfaction in cleaning a kitchen and getting it back to "shipshape" condition after a marathon meal prep. But with frying, there is the last pesky piece—what do you do with the oil? Folks, this is an age-old question, so don't let it deter you from frying.

First of all, you can drain and reuse frying oil a couple of times, depending on how clean it is. If you made homemade French fries, the oil stays pretty clean. But when you're cooking battered or breaded seafood, it can get funky with all the residue that falls from the food in the cooking process and settles at the bottom of the pan. When the oil starts to turn dark, it's time to change it. At home, I let the oil cool completely, then drain it well and store it in either mason jars or old quart mayonnaise jars. Never attempt to pour even warm oil into a container, especially a plastic one. Some folks use the bottle it came in, and my grandmother used coffee cans. Never pour it down the drain.

In the "olden" days, there wasn't much envi-

ronmental consciousness. But these days, the question looms of what to do with the oil that needs to be discarded. Some progressive communities have facilities and services that dispose of the oil in a kind-to-the-planet way, but those are few and far between.

You may find a restaurant that is kindly willing to take the oil, as they are required to hire professionals to dispose of their used cooking oil. At LuLu's, our fry oil is literally delivered by tanker truck. We have an automated system that pumps the new oil into our eight commercial fryers with the capability to pump our used oil into a holding tank. But we have also developed a program to recycle some of our oil into usable biodiesel fuel with the intention to use it in converted diesel engines powering shrimp boats.

As in all things, I say, "Do your best." Since I'm a believer that Mother Nature can take care of recycling any material that is natural, I'm okay with pouring it back into the earth. I find a place

in the corner of the yard or under some bushes and pour it out. But if that is not an option and the old oil is ready to be discarded, place it in sealed containers or jars and put them in the trash. Bless it and be grateful.

THE JOY IS IN THE JOURNEY NOT THE DESTINATION. Last but certainly not least is my mandate in all things, especially the difficult or challenging ones, to find the bright spot and enjoy the process. Growing up, I was always focused on the end result and just getting to where I needed to be. It's taken years of introspection and work on my inner self to embrace the idea that every step along the way on any journey is vital and meaningful, and has purpose. I apply this in many areas of my life, but it is so beautifully apparent in my cooking, especially when I attempt to put together a large meal for my family consisting of the heartfelt recipes of my family tradition, including the "fried, died, and gone to heaven" ones.

STEP-BY-STEP

1. Mix together the fry mix in a large bowl or dish.

2. In a large bowl or dish, mix together the milk/liquids to make the dipping mix.

3. Heat the oil (peanut, vegetable, or canola) in a cast-iron Dutch oven, large heavy skillet (10 to 12 inches, preferably cast iron), or electric skillet until it registers 355°F (or the temperature indicated in the recipe) on a candy/deep-fry thermometer, or until a little flour flicked into the oil sizzles.

4. Dredge the food through the fry mix.

5. Dip it into the dipping mix.

6. Dredge again through the fry mix.

7. Drop it into the hot oil without crowding.

8. Adjust the temperature/heat as needed to maintain 355°F (or the temperature indicated in the recipe).

9. When the fried food is golden brown or floating to the top, remove with a slotted or mesh utensil and place on a baking sheet lined with paper towels or a wire rack.

10. Keep warm in a 200°F oven until ready to serve.

FLOUR POWER FRY MIX

MAKES 2 CUPS

2 cups all-purpose flour

2 tablespoons LuLu's Crazy Creola Seasoning (page xxviii) or other Creole seasoning

1½ teaspoons sea salt (see Note)

1 tablespoon freshly ground black pepper

Combine all the ingredients and mix well.

NOTE: *If using other Creole seasoning, reduce the salt to 1 teaspoon.*

CORNMEAL FRY MIX
MAKES 2 CUPS

2 cups white all-purpose cornmeal

2 tablespoons LuLu's Crazy Creola Seasoning (page xxviii) or other Creole seasoning

1½ teapoons sea salt (see Note)

1 tablespoon freshly ground black pepper

Combine all the ingredients and mix well.

NOTE: *If using other Creole seasoning, reduce the salt to 1 teaspoon.*

FRIED SHRIMP

SERVES 6

2 pounds large wild-caught Gulf shrimp, peeled, with tails on or off according to your preference

Flour Power Fry Mix (page 196)

2 cups whole milk

6 cups peanut, vegetable, or canola oil

1. Cut the back of the shrimp halfway to butterfly and remove the vein. Place the shrimp in a bowl with a little ice and set aside.

2. Put the fry mix in a medium bowl.

3. Put the milk in another medium bowl.

4. In a large heavy skillet (10 to 12 inches, preferably cast iron), heat the oil over medium-high heat until it registers 355°F on a candy/deep-fry thermometer, or until a little flour flicked into the oil sizzles.

5. Working with a few shrimp at a time, dredge them through the fry mix, then dip them into the milk, and then dredge them through the fry mix again.

6. Working in batches, gently drop the shrimp into the hot oil. Fry them until golden brown or until they float to the top, 3 to 4 minutes. Adjust the heat as necessary to keep the oil temperature around 355°F. Drain on a baking sheet lined with paper towels or on a wire rack and serve immediately.

FRIED GREEN TOMATOES

SERVES 4

2 cups Flour Power Fry Mix
(page 196)

2 cups buttermilk

1 tablespoon hot sauce

4 green tomatoes, sliced
¼ inch thick

6 cups peanut, vegetable, or
canola oil, or enough to fill the
skillet about 2 inches deep

LuLu's Famous WOW Sauce
(page 279)

1. Preheat the oven to 200°F. Line a baking sheet with paper towels or set a wire rack over the top.

2. Put the fry mix in a medium bowl. In another medium bowl, combine the buttermilk and the hot sauce.

3. Dip the tomato slices into the buttermilk mixture, then dredge them through the fry mix. Repeat once more, coating the slices thoroughly.

4. In a large heavy skillet (10 to 12 inches, preferably cast iron), heat the oil over medium-high heat until it registers 355°F on a candy/deep-fry thermometer, or until a little flour flicked into the oil sizzles.

5. Fry the tomatoes in the hot oil in small batches (about 4 slices at a time) until golden brown, about 2 minutes on each side, turning once during cooking. Carefully remove the fried tomatoes with a slotted spatula and transfer to the prepared baking sheet to drain. Keep warm in the oven while you finish frying the remaining tomatoes.

6. Serve immediately with WOW Sauce alongside.

FRIED GULF OYSTERS

SERVES 4

Cornmeal Fry Mix
(page 196)

6 cups peanut, vegetable,
or canola oil, or enough to fill a skillet
about 2 inches deep

1 quart Gulf oysters, drained

1. Put the fry mix in a medium bowl.

2. In a large heavy skillet (10 to 12 inches, preferably cast iron), heat the oil over medium-high heat until it registers 355°F on a candy/deep-fry thermometer, or until a little flour flicked into the oil sizzles.

3. Taking a few oysters at a time, dredge them through the fry mix, coating them thoroughly.

4. Working in batches, gently drop the oysters into the hot oil. Fry until golden brown, turning once, or until they float to the top. Drain on a baking sheet lined with paper towels or on a wire rack and serve immediately.

FRIED FISH

SERVES 6
(8 OUNCES EACH)

About 6 cups peanut, vegetable,
or canola oil, for frying

1½ cups cornmeal

½ cup all-purpose flour

1 tablespoon LuLu's Crazy Creola
Seasoning (page xxviii) or other
Creole seasoning

½ teaspoon sea salt

1 tablespoon freshly ground
black pepper

2 cups whole milk

6 Gulf or Southern flounder,
snapper, or grouper fillets,
6 to 8 ounces each

1. In a large heavy skillet (10 to 12 inches, preferably cast iron), heat the oil over medium-high heat until it registers 355°F on a candy/deep-fry thermometer, or until a little flour flicked into the oil sizzles.

2. Combine the cornmeal, flour, Creole seasoning, salt, and pepper in a shallow dish and mix well. Pour the milk into a separate shallow dish.

3. Dip each fillet into the milk, allowing any excess to drain off, and gently dredge the fillet through the cornmeal mixture.

4. Working in small batches, place the fillets in the hot oil and fry, keeping an eye on the temperature and adjusting as needed to stay at 355°F. Remove the fillets when they turn golden brown and begin to float to the surface, 4 to 5 minutes. Drain the fillets on a baking sheet lined with paper towels or on a wire rack. Serve immediately.

HEART'S DESIRE

Growing up, my brother and sister and I would wake up Sunday mornings wondering, *Is it roast beef Sunday or fried chicken Sunday?* And you know which one we were rooting for! So Sunday is my "heart's desire day"—there are no restrictions, and I cook an old family favorite or try some new recipe. About once a month or so my own children and grandchildren come to join us for Sunday lunch and I'm amazed, but not surprised, by how my wild and crazy life has come full circle and now I'm living much like my parents even though in my youth I declared I'd never do so. I call that the Divine Ha-Ha, the joke being on me, and I'm grateful for it.

On those family Sundays, the menu is often going to include something fried. Yes, the house will smell like fried food for twenty-four hours and yes, it's a mess, but there is a sublime experience of drooling over a plate of fresh grouper fingers sitting regally on a paper towel–lined plate waiting for the perfect moment when they're cool enough to pop into your mouth. For me, folks, that's a piece of heaven on earth that I love sharing with my family.

HEAVENLY
FRIED CRAB CLAWS

SERVES 4

2 cups Flour Power Fry Mix
(page 196)

2 cups whole milk

1 tablespoon hot sauce

6 cups peanut, vegetable, or
canola oil, or enough to fill your
skillet about 2 inches deep

1 pound fresh blue crab claws,
not frozen, shells removed

Lemon wedges, for garnish

1. Put the fry mix in a medium bowl.

2. In another medium bowl, combine the milk and the hot sauce.

3. In a large heavy skillet (10 to 12 inches, preferably cast iron), heat the oil over medium-high heat until it registers 355°F on a candy/deep-fry thermometer, or until a little flour flicked into the oil sizzles.

4. Take a few crab claws at a time and dredge them through the fry mix. Dip them into the milk mixture and then dredge them through the fry mix again.

5. Working in batches, gently drop them into the hot oil. Fry the crab claws until golden brown, turning once during cooking, until they float to the top, about 2 minutes on each side. Keep an eye on the temperature and adjust as necessary to keep the oil temperature around 355°F. Drain on a baking sheet lined with paper towels or on a wire rack and serve immediately with lemon wedges.

FRITTERS 2 WAYS

CRAB AND CORN FRITTERS

SERVES 6
(5 TO 6 FRITTERS
PER SERVING)

½ cup self-rising yellow cornmeal

½ cup self-rising flour

1 teaspoon baking powder

½ teaspoon sea salt

½ teaspoon freshly ground
black pepper

1 tablespoon sugar

1 large egg

½ cup buttermilk

½ cup finely chopped yellow onion

½ cup finely chopped
red bell pepper

2 tablespoons finely chopped
fresh parsley

1 cup Southern Fried Creamed
Corn (page 171) or canned
creamed corn

1 cup cooked lump blue crabmeat
(about ½ pound), picked through
for shells, handled carefully
to keep the meat in big chunks
(see Notes on Handling Seafood,
pages xxx–xxxi)

About 6 cups vegetable oil,
for frying

1. Preheat the oven to 250°F.

2. In a large bowl, combine the cornmeal, flour, baking powder, salt, black pepper, and sugar and set aside.

3. In another large bowl, whisk together the egg and buttermilk. Fold the onion, bell pepper, parsley, and creamed corn into the egg mixture.

4. Fold the cornmeal mixture into the egg mixture until just combined, making sure not to overmix, which could make the fritters too dense.

5. Gently fold in the crabmeat until just combined.

6. In a large heavy Dutch oven or deep cast-iron skillet, heat the oil over medium-high heat until it registers 355°F on a candy/deep-fry thermometer, or until a little flour flicked into the oil sizzles. Be careful not to fill the pot more than halfway with oil.

7. Working in batches of 6 to 8 fritters, use a small rounded spoon to scoop up about 1 tablespoon of the batter, and use another spoon to carefully scrape the mixture from the rounded spoon into the hot oil.

8. As the fritters float to the top, roll them over in the oil to brown evenly on all sides, 3 to 4 minutes per batch. Remove the fritters with tongs or a slotted spoon and transfer to a baking sheet lined with paper towels; keep warm in the oven uncovered. As you continue with the batches, adjust the heat if necessary, not letting the oil get too hot or "smoke," but also not letting the temperature drop below 300 to 325°F. You don't want the fritters to brown too quickly or be raw in the middle.

SHRIMP FRITTERS

**SERVES 6
(5 TO 6 FRITTERS
PER SERVING)**

½ cup self-rising yellow cornmeal

½ cup self-rising flour

1 teaspoon baking powder

½ teaspoon sea salt

½ teaspoon freshly ground
black pepper

½ teaspoon LuLu's Crazy
Creola Seasoning (page xxviii) or
other Creole seasoning

1 large egg

½ cup buttermilk

½ teaspoon hot sauce

1 teaspoon finely chopped garlic

½ cup finely chopped yellow onion

½ cup finely chopped red bell pepper

2 tablespoons finely chopped
fresh parsley

1 pound peeled and deveined shrimp,
chopped into ¼-inch pieces

About 6 cups vegetable oil,
for frying

1. Preheat the oven to 250°F.

2. In a large bowl, combine the cornmeal, flour, baking powder, salt, black pepper, and Creole seasoning and set aside.

3. In another large bowl, whisk together the egg and the buttermilk. Fold the hot sauce, garlic, onion, bell pepper, and parsley into the egg mixture.

4. Fold the cornmeal mixture into the egg mixture until just combined, making sure not to overmix, which could make the fritters too dense.

5. Gently fold in the shrimp, again until just combined.

6. In a large heavy Dutch oven or deep cast-iron skillet, heat the oil over medium-high heat until it registers 355°F on a candy/deep-fry thermometer, or until a little flour flicked into the oil sizzles. Be careful not to fill the pot more than halfway with oil.

7. Working in batches of 6 to 8 fritters, use a small rounded spoon to scoop up about 1 tablespoon of the batter, and use another spoon to carefully scrape the mixture from the rounded spoon into the hot oil.

8. As the fritters float to the top, roll them over in the oil to brown evenly on all sides, 3 to 4 minutes per batch. Remove the fritters with tongs or a slotted spoon and transfer to a baking sheet lined with paper towels; keep warm in the oven uncovered. As you continue with the batches, adjust the heat if necessary, not letting the oil get too hot or "smoke," but also not letting the temperature drop below 300 to 325°F. You don't want the fritters to brown too quickly or be raw in the middle.

DEEP-FRIED OKRA
(OR ZUCCHINI OR GREEN BEANS OR WHATEVER VEGGIE YOU'D LIKE)

SERVES 4 TO 6

2 cups Flour Power Fry Mix
(page 196)

2 cups whole milk

1 tablespoon hot sauce
(optional)

6 cups peanut, vegetable, or
canola oil, or enough to fill the
skillet about 2 inches deep

4 cups fresh okra, whole pods
or chopped into ¼-inch pieces
(see Note)

LuLu's Famous WOW Sauce
(page 279), for serving

1. Put the fry mix in a medium bowl.

2. In another medium bowl, combine the milk and the hot sauce (if using).

3. In a large heavy skillet (10 to 12 inches, preferably cast iron), heat the oil over medium-high heat until it registers 355°F on a candy/deep-fry thermometer, or until a little flour flicked into the oil sizzles.

4. Dredge the okra through the fry mix, dip it into the milk, and then dredge it again in the fry mix, coating the okra thoroughly.

5. Working in small batches, gently drop a handful of okra into the hot oil and fry until golden brown.

6. Drain on a baking sheet lined with paper towels or a wire rack and serve immediately with WOW Sauce.

NOTE: *Sometimes I fry the whole pods, and sometimes I chop the okra into pieces first. Try it both ways!*

HUSHPUPPIES

6 cups vegetable oil, for frying

1 cup yellow cornmeal

½ cup all-purpose flour

1½ tablespoons sugar

1 teaspoon baking powder

1 teaspoon baking soda

1 teaspoon sea salt

1 teaspoon freshly ground
black pepper

1 large egg

1 cup buttermilk

¼ cup finely chopped onion

¼ cup seeded and finely chopped
jalapeño

¼ cup Southern Fried Creamed Corn
(page 171) or canned creamed corn

⅔ cup shredded sharp
cheddar cheese

1. In a large heavy Dutch oven or pot, heat the oil over medium-high heat until it registers 355°F on a candy/deep-fry thermometer, or until a little flour flicked into the oil sizzles.

2. In a small bowl, combine the cornmeal, flour, sugar, baking powder, baking soda, salt, and pepper and set aside.

3. In a large bowl, combine the egg and the buttermilk and whisk together until blended. Fold the onion, jalapeño, creamed corn, and cheese into the egg mixture.

4. Fold the dry ingredients into the egg mixture until all is incorporated, making sure not to overmix.

5. Using a rounded tablespoon, or your hands, form the dough into small balls, using about 1 tablespoon of the hushpuppy mixture for each.

6. Working in batches of 6 to 8, carefully place the dough balls in the hot oil and fry until golden brown, 1 to 1½ minutes, rolling them over in the oil to brown evenly on all sides. Remove the hushpuppies and place them on a baking sheet lined with paper towels or a wire rack.

CHAPTER 7

SALADS

SOME days, I've just gotta have some greens. I truly love the variety of lettuces now easily available, especially the tender sweet baby varieties of romaine, red leaf, and mâche mixed with the spicy, peppered, and bitter-in-a-good-way ones like arugula, dandelion, watercress, and kale. A salad always accompanies my casual home dinners, and if I add a little piece of grilled fish or some boiled shrimp, I've got a light supper. In the Deep Coastal South, where the summer temperatures soar into the eighties and nineties, it's custom to throw together some meals that don't require the heat of cooking, so cold salads become main players on menus.

These days I turn more to salad as my mainstay and my mea culpa when I've been indulging in my favorite guilty food pleasures like fried chicken, mashed potatoes, and blueberry cobbler. I won't ever give up the food of my youth, but these days I balance my eating with lots of salad, something I learned to do when I was a chef for private clients.

Years and years ago, a lovely New Orleans gentleman hired me as a private chef to make healthy food for his absolutely beautiful and adorable wife. Both of them were probably in their late sixties or early seventies, and like many of us gals, the wife loved to eat and sported a little more weight than either she or her husband wanted. Mainly that was because they had a whole staff of people, including their precious cook, who had worked for them for forty-two years and who every day made the most delicious New Orleans meals for the family and staff. When I was hired, she kept on cooking her meals, because after forty-two years, she did pretty much whatever she wanted to do, and I was grateful because she always left a plate for me on the stove before she left each day. I would come in at three p.m. and eat a delicious late lunch, then begin preparing the slim pickin's for the couple's "healthy" dinner: a piece of grilled salmon, steamed vegetables, sliced Creole tomatoes, and stewed apples, all of it strictly portion controlled.

It was a good plan, and it would have worked. But not too long after we'd started this system, the couple would finish eating and go upstairs... and then the wife would come back down to the kitchen to supposedly say good night to me. "Is there any pecan pie left?" she would ask with a twinkle in her laughing eyes. Before you knew it, she would be digging into the cook's leftovers, something like shrimp Creole with fried okra and a little café au lait to go with the pie, while I did the dishes.

The following day, I'd always make up for it with a big salad for supper, which was a win-win for all of us—and which remained the boss lady's and my little secret. The husband thought I was doing a great job providing healthy, tasty fare, the wife was delighted to have what we in the South call a "do-over," and I was grateful to still have a job and be able to make everyone happy!

OLD-FASHIONED
SHRIMP SALAD

SERVES 6 TO 8

3 pounds Easy Boiled Shrimp (page 39), peeled and chopped into medium to large pieces

1 cup chopped celery

½ cup finely chopped red onion

½ cup finely chopped green onion

3 hard-boiled eggs, chopped

2 tablespoons finely chopped fresh parsley

1 teaspoon sea salt

1 teaspoon white pepper

1 teaspoon LuLu's Crazy Creola Seasoning (page xxviii) or other Creole seasoning

2 tablespoons Dijon mustard

½ cup mayonnaise

1 tablespoon fresh lemon juice (from ½ lemon)

IN OUR WORLD, when we talk about "shrimp salad," we do not mean a few pitiful-looking shrimp served over a bed of wilted lettuce. What we mean when we say shrimp salad is a mayonnaise-based deli salad with cut-up Gulf shrimp mixed with celery, onion, chopped-up egg, and Creole seasoning. It tastes delicious on its own, with crackers, with sliced tomatoes, on a toasted croissant, in a wrap, *even on a bed of wilted lettuce*! This recipe is not an original—it is a very good version of an old classic.

In a large bowl, combine all the ingredients and stir gently. Cover and refrigerate for 2 hours or overnight before serving.

NOTE: *To make a fantastic shrimp salad wrap, pile shrimp salad, lettuce, and two slices of Fried Green Tomatoes (page 199) on a flour tortilla, roll it all up, and enjoy!*

WEST INDIES SALAD

SERVES 4 TO 6

1 pound cooked fresh jumbo lump blue crabmeat, picked through for shells, handled carefully to keep the meat in big chunks (see Notes on Handling Seafood, pages xxx–xxxi)

Sea salt and freshly ground black pepper

½ medium Vidalia or other sweet onion, sliced into paper-thin half-moons

⅓ cup vegetable oil

⅓ cup distilled white vinegar

4 or 5 ice cubes

WEST INDIES SALAD has been a mainstay dish in my family since I was a child. My mother's claim to fame is that she could make an impeccable West Indies. This crab salad originated decades ago at Bayley's Steak House in Mobile, Alabama. No one is quite certain how the dish got its name, but what is certain is that it had nothing to do with the down-island region in the Caribbean. Using the delicate white meat from the beautiful blue crab that inhabits the warm, brackish water of Mobile Bay, this salad basically combines the crab with sweet onion and a simple vinaigrette. But the water *with ice cubes* is the secret ingredient of this Alabama Gulf Coast classic.

1. Place half the crabmeat on the bottom of a glass bowl or airtight plastic container. Sprinkle with just a smidgen of salt and pepper.

2. Cover the crab with a thin layer of the onion.

3. Repeat these steps with the remaining crab, salt, pepper, and onion.

4. Pour the oil and vinegar over the layers.

5. Place the ice cubes in a liquid measuring cup. Fill the cup with water until the volume reaches ⅓ cup and pour it over the crab. (The ice cubes are crucial! Don't ask me why, but when I haven't included them, it just doesn't taste the same.)

6. Cover and marinate in the refrigerator for at least 2 hours before serving.

7. When ready to serve, shake the bowl gently, or if using an airtight plastic container, turn it upside down and then back upright to gently mix the salad.

8. Serve in a shallow bowl.

Crab Salad

1 cup mayonnaise

¼ cup white wine vinegar

¼ cup Creole mustard

1 tablespoon extra-virgin olive oil

1 tablespoon fresh lemon juice
(from ½ lemon)

1 teaspoon Worcestershire sauce

1 teaspoon hot sauce

3 tablespoons chopped green onion

3 tablespoons capers

½ teaspoon prepared or freshly
grated horseradish

1 garlic clove, pressed

2 tablespoons chopped fresh parsley

½ teaspoon LuLu's Crazy Creola
Seasoning (page xxviii) or other
Creole seasoning

½ teaspoon sea salt

¼ teaspoon white pepper

Pinch of sugar

1 pound cooked lump blue crabmeat,
picked through for shells, handled
carefully to keep the meat in
big chunks (see Notes on Handling
Seafood, pages xxx–xxxi)

Toasted Garlic French Bread Rounds

4 tablespoons (½ stick)
unsalted butter

2 garlic cloves

1 loaf French bread, cut into
1-inch-thick slices

LUCIA ANNA'S CASA CRAB SALAD
WITH
TOASTED GARLIC FRENCH BREAD ROUNDS

GALATOIRE'S RESTAURANT IN New Orleans is one of the sexiest restaurants I've ever been to. There is a series of mirrors that line the back wall, and honestly, you can sit anywhere and catch the eye of another diner across the room or down the wall, which just begs for a little anonymous flirting adventure! But even more enticing than the décor is the classic Creole food, elegantly presented and served with old-style flair. One of the dishes they are famous for is their Crabmeat Maison, meaning their "house" crab salad. They use a variation of the old French recipe for ravigote sauce, a classic French dressing of herbs, mustard, and capers.

Although my original "house" salad that I typically use when entertaining is West Indies Salad (page 217), I had to find an alternative when I knew a guest I'd invited had a particular aversion to onions. So I created my version of Crabmeat Maison. It was a hit, and now it is a regular on my entertaining menu. The name of the salad comes from another one of my brother's nicknames for me, Lucia Anna, and since I first made this salad in my Key West casa, Lucia Anna's Casa Crab Salad just seemed to fit!

To make the crab salad:

1. In a medium bowl, mix together all the crab salad ingredients *except the crabmeat*. Refrigerate for 2 hours or overnight.

To make the toasted garlic French bread rounds:

2. Preheat the broiler.

3. In a small saucepan, melt the butter over medium-low heat. Use a garlic press to press the garlic cloves and then stir them into the butter. (If you do not have a garlic press, you can smash the peeled cloves with the flat side of a knife so they are mushy, then stir them into the butter.) Place the bread slices on a baking sheet. Brush the melted garlic butter over the bread slices and broil for about 1½ minutes, or until the bread is beautifully browned. Turn the slices over and brush them with the melted garlic butter. Broil on the second side for about a minute, keeping a close watch to make sure it browns but doesn't burn.

4. To serve, gently fold the crabmeat into the chilled salad ingredients and serve with the toasted garlic French bread rounds.

FLORIDA LOBSTER SALAD
WITH GRAPEFRUIT AND AVOCADO

SERVES 4

4 Florida lobster tails, or
2 cups lobster meat

1 lemon, thinly sliced

½ cup white wine

1 teaspoon sea salt

1 tablespoon whole black
peppercorns

½ cup thinly sliced celery

2 grapefruits, peeled, sliced, and
chopped into chunks

⅛ cup thinly sliced red onion
(see Note)

1 (1-pound) bag fresh salad greens

Citrus-Tarragon Dressing
(page 287)

1 avocado, pitted, peeled, and
thinly sliced

1 teaspoon finely chopped fresh
tarragon, for garnish

WHEN THE TWO-DAY mini season for Florida lobster comes around—always the last Wednesday and Thursday in July—a mad rush takes place, with lobster lovers from all over Florida descending on the Keys to "dive for some bugs." Everybody has their secret spot that they rush to get to before anyone else, where they free dive for these spiny creatures that taste so good it's always worth the effort. Lucky for the rest of us, there are plenty of places that sell fresh Florida lobster, including shipping it right to your door. You can also substitute Maine lobster anytime a recipe calls for Florida lobster—or, by all means, you can even use shrimp.

1. Cut the lobster tails (if using) in half lengthwise, making sure to cut through both sides.

2. Fill a large heavy skillet (10 to 12 inches) with water to about an inch from the top. Add the lemon, wine, salt, and peppercorns and bring to a boil.

3. Add the lobster tails, reduce the heat to medium, and cover. Poach the tails for 7 minutes, or until cooked through. Transfer the tails to a plate and let cool completely.

4. Remove the lobster meat from the shells, chop the meat into bite-size chunks, and refrigerate until well chilled.

5. In a large bowl, combine the chilled lobster, celery, grapefruit, and onion. Mix together using your hands.

6. Place the salad greens in a separate bowl right before serving. Pour a small amount of the dressing over the greens and toss together to mix.

7. Pour the remaining dressing over the lobster mixture and toss to coat.

8. To serve, put some greens on each plate, top with the lobster mixture, and add slices of avocado. Garnish with the chopped tarragon.

NOTE: *In a salad, always keep onion in large enough pieces that if someone doesn't want onion, they can move it to the side.*

MANGO, AVOCADO, AND
ARUGULA SALAD
WITH SOUR ORANGE VINAIGRETTE

SERVES 4 TO 6

½ red onion, sliced

Sea salt

1 tablespoon fresh lime juice
(from ½ lime)

3 cups arugula

3 cups red romaine lettuce

Sour Orange Vinaigrette
(page 289)

1 avocado, pitted, peeled, and
sliced lengthwise

1 mango, pitted, peeled, and
sliced lengthwise

1. Soak the onion slices in a small bowl of warm water with a dash of salt and the lime juice for about 10 minutes.

2. Rinse and drain the onion slices, discarding the liquid.

3. In a large bowl, toss the arugula and romaine leaves with half the vinaigrette.

4. Add the avocado slices, mango slices, and onion slices to the greens. Drizzle the remaining vinaigrette on top.

5. Serve immediately.

MUFFULETTA SALAD

SERVES 6 TO 8

½ pound hard salami, chopped into bite-size pieces

½ pound ham, chopped into bite-size pieces

1 (7-ounce) dry Italian sausage, chopped into bite-size pieces

½ pound provolone cheese, chopped into bite-size pieces

1 cup coarsely chopped pitted Spanish olives

1 cup coarsely chopped pitted Kalamata olives

¼ cup capers, drained

½ cup julienned sun-dried tomatoes

1 (16-ounce) jar giardiniera mix, drained and coarsely chopped

4 celery stalks, with leaves, chopped

1 red bell pepper, chopped

¼ cup chopped red onion

1 heaping tablespoon finely chopped garlic

1 heaping tablespoon finely chopped fresh basil

1 tablespoon finely chopped fresh oregano

1 tablespoon finely chopped fresh parsley

¼ cup white balsamic vinegar

½ cup extra-virgin olive oil

1 teaspoon freshly ground black pepper

A MUFFULETTA is a classic New Orleans sandwich of Italian meats and a savory olive salad served on a huge round of sesame seed bread. I decided one day that I wanted to try the ingredients without the bread, and the results were amazing—and so colorful! This salad makes for a beautiful presentation.

Combine all the ingredients and refrigerate for 2 hours before serving.

GRILLED VEGGIE SALAD
WITH CREOLE
MUSTARD VINAIGRETTE

SERVES 8

2 zucchini

2 yellow squash

1 red bell pepper

1 orange bell pepper

1 green bell pepper

1 yellow bell pepper

1 red onion

½ cup extra-virgin olive oil

1 tablespoon finely chopped
fresh rosemary

1 tablespoon sea salt

2 tablespoons freshly ground
black pepper

4 cups delicate leafy greens or
lettuce (such as red-leaf lettuce,
arugula, or butter lettuce)

Creole Mustard Vinaigrette
(page 289)

1. Heat a grill to 375°F.

2. Chop the zucchini and squash in half lengthwise, then again in half lengthwise to make 4 thick wedges.

3. Chop the bell peppers in half lengthwise, then in thirds lengthwise.

4. Chop the onion into 3 big fat slices.

5. In a large bowl, toss the vegetables with the olive oil, rosemary, salt, and black pepper, coating the vegetables well.

6. Place the vegetables on the hot grill, skin-side down, and grill for 10 minutes. Turn the vegetables and grill on the second side for 7 minutes more.

7. Remove the vegetables from the grill and let cool to room temperature. Chop them into 2- to 3-inch pieces.

8. In the bottom of a large glass bowl, place the greens, followed by the vegetables.

9. Just before serving, toss with your desired amount of Creole mustard vinaigrette dressing.

NOTE: *Cook the vegetables directly on the grill to achieve the proper markings and slight caramelization. If you prefer, you can use a grill basket, but the vegetables won't have as strong a grilled flavor. You want vegetables that are flavorful but not overcooked. Grill the vegetables until just al dente; otherwise, you'll end up with chargrilled mush. Be sure to adjust the grilling time if necessary based on the "personality" and tendencies of your grill.*

WATERMELON
— AND —
FETA CHEESE
SALAD

SERVES 6 TO 10

¼ cup white wine vinegar

2 tablespoons sugar

2 teaspoons sea salt

1 teaspoon freshly ground
black pepper

Pinch of red pepper flakes

1 red onion, halved and sliced
lengthwise

1 cucumber, halved, seeded,
scored with a zester, and sliced
into half-moons

1 small seedless watermelon
(I like the sugar baby variety),
chopped

4 ounces feta cheese, crumbled

¼ cup extra-virgin olive oil

¼ cup balsamic vinegar

2 tablespoons chopped fresh mint

1.   In a small bowl, whisk together the white wine vinegar, sugar, 1 teaspoon of the salt, the black pepper, and the red pepper flakes until the sugar has dissolved.

2.   Add the red onion and let the mixture stand for 1 to 2 hours. Drain the red onion, discarding the liquid.

3.   Make one large salad in a salad bowl or make individual salads by gently combining the red onion, cucumber, watermelon, and feta.

4.   Season with the remaining 1 teaspoon salt and lightly drizzle with the olive oil and balsamic vinegar. Garnish with chopped mint.

SILVER QUEEN CORN
SALAD

MAKES 7 CUPS

7 small ears Silver Queen corn

½ cup plus 1 tablespoon extra-virgin olive oil

1 cup finely chopped red bell pepper

1 cup finely chopped green bell pepper

3 green onions, thinly sliced

1 jalapeño, seeded and finely chopped

1 cup finely chopped red onion

½ cup finely chopped fresh cilantro

3 tablespoons fresh lime juice

2 tablespoons honey

2 teaspoons sea salt

2 teaspoons freshly ground black pepper

ALL OF THE fresh local Silver Queen corn comes in at one time during the summer, so you have to get a little inventive in how to use it all. The corn is so sweet, and this recipe brings out its fresh taste with a little zing from the jalapeño, cilantro, and lime juice. This makes a great accompaniment for any summer dish, since it's served cold and you can make it ahead. I always have some of this corn salad on hand in the fridge during the season so I have something yummy to grab between all my busy summer activities.

1. Preheat a grill.

2. Shuck the corn, removing all of the attached silk, then wash and drain the ears.

3. Lightly oil the ears with ½ cup of the olive oil, then place them on the grill. Grill until the corn is tender and lightly charred. Remove the ears from the grill and set aside to cool while you prepare the other ingredients.

4. In a large bowl, combine the bell peppers, green onion, jalapeño, red onion, and cilantro. Using a corn stripper or chef's knife, cut the corn off the cob and add the kernels to the vegetable mixture. Scrape down the sides of the corncobs with a knife to release the remaining sweet juices and add these juices to the bowl of vegetables.

5. In a small bowl, stir together the lime juice, honey, salt, black pepper, and the remaining 1 tablespoon olive oil. Pour the dressing over the vegetable mixture, stir well, cover, and refrigerate overnight. Serve the next day or eat it all yourself (because it's that good!).

RAW BROCCOLI SALAD

MAKES 4 QUARTS

Salad

2 bunches broccoli, or about
8 cups broccoli florets

2 cups finely chopped pimento-stuffed
green olives

1 bunch green onions, finely chopped

Lemon-Garlic Dressing

4 garlic cloves, pressed

1 cup mayonnaise

Juice of ½ lemon
(about 1 tablespoon)

1 teaspoon freshly ground
black pepper, plus more as needed

½ teaspoon sugar

Sea salt

I LEARNED TO make this salad years ago when I worked in a deli in Fairhope, Alabama. I was skeptical when I first saw the recipe; I'm not a big fan of raw broccoli. But this salad surprised me because it is wonderfully tasty; the olives and lemon-garlic dressing give it a delightful zing.

To make the salad:

1. Coarsely chop the broccoli into florets and place them in a large bowl.

2. In a food processor, combine the olives and green onions. Pulse together until finely chopped.

3. Fold the olive mixture into the broccoli.

To make the dressing:

4. In a separate bowl, mix together the garlic, mayonnaise, lemon juice, pepper, and sugar.

5. Combine the broccoli salad and lemon-garlic dressing and mix together well. Season with salt and pepper, then refrigerate for at least 2 hours or overnight before serving.

CHAPTER 8

SANDWICHES

THE Gulf region is a place of humble means and make-do ingenuity. My parents had to scrimp to get by, but anyone who knows our family will tell you that the Buffetts would spend their last five dollars on a shrimp loaf and a cold beer, a priority for the good things in life I'm proud to have inherited. A shrimp loaf, or "po'boy" as they call it in New Orleans, may sound like a simple affair, but what could be more luxurious, more sumptuous than shrimp fresh from the Gulf, curled and crunchy atop tomatoes grown right down the road and tucked inside a buttery, crusty-on-the-outside-but-pillowy-on-the-inside loaf of New Orleans–style French bread? Our humble Gulf roots are rich indeed, and places to indulge abound. It's a family pastime comparing the best places to get the best sandwich all along the Gulf Coast, an activity that started in my youth and goes on to this day. A Buffett will drop everything and travel miles by car, boat, or plane to find the newest, best sandwich.

Mama's idea of a "special" sandwich was stopping by Pollman's Bakery in Mobile on her way home from work on Friday night and picking up their buttery pocketbook rolls and sliced ham. She served them at *every* party she gave because those rolls and ham were the go-to party sandwiches for the society hostesses all around Mobile.

Long before the Eastern Shore of Mobile Bay became the preferred area for swanky year-round residents, it was mostly made up of funky summer cottages. The bar was set pretty high back then, many years ago, for the best shrimp, oyster, or fish "loaf" because the one served at a little dive called Max's in Battles Wharf, Alabama, couldn't be beat. Now long gone, the reputation and memories still abound, maybe because that's all they served. No substitutions. No broiled or blackened. Pure Southern-fried tradition at its best. Max's remains my inspiration today for the fried seafood I serve at home and at LuLu's.

Moving west along the coast to New Orleans, my tribe has been known to have a hankering for a roast beef sandwich and hop in the car for a spontaneous road trip to Mother's just for their famous "debris" po'boy. With two types of roast beef on crusty French bread, served with a silky au jus gravy, this classic sandwich consistently has a line of folks wrapped around the block waiting for hours to bite into one of those babies.

And while you're there, if the line wears you down, wander over to Esplanade for a Port of Call burger, one of the best you'll ever taste. They use shredded instead of sliced cheese and it just melts in your mouth. And I have to say, nothing tastes as good as my specialty "Pa-menna Burger" at

GUMBO LOVE

LuLu's: a half-pound burger with pimento cheese, bacon, and fried green tomatoes.

For a real Cuban, head south to my second home in Key West. Five Brothers is a favorite spot for the fishing guides, locals, and tourists. Of course, there is the famous Sandy's—part classic Cuban, part Mexican, part Laundromat, part sidewalk café, complete with roosters crowing under your stool. They are just around the corner from my house and deliver twenty-four hours a day. A place like Key West needs a heavy-duty, soak-it-up food to gobble before you go to bed after a night of walking Duval Street. There's nothing better than a classic Cuban sandwich or mega burrito delivered to your doorstep at two a.m.

But if you're a water person, a fisherman, a sailor, someone who prefers to sleep with the waves rocking you in a lullaby, then it's all about the fish sandwich. A water person pulls into the marina and the first thing they want to know is, "Where's the best fish sandwich around here?" I'm a huge fan of the fish Reuben and recently had one of the best ever at Sid and Roxie's at the Green Turtle Inn in Islamorada. When I'm in Key West, I go to BO's Fish Wagon at least twice a week. If you want to sound like a local, make sure you pronounce it *bee-ohs*. It's a great dive. I usually start with the conch fritters and then go straight to the yellowtail fish sandwich.

If you go any place along the Gulf Coast and ask where the best fish sandwich is, you won't just find a good sandwich, you'll be speaking the international language of food. You'll be showing a sign of respect: "Thanks for having me. I'm glad to be here. Now show me how y'all do things around here!"

DAY-AFTER
BRISKET PO'BOY

**MAKES 2 TO 4
SANDWICHES**

Day-after (leftover) Beer-Braised
Beef Brisket with Cumin and Garlic
(page 119)

1 cup beef broth

1 or 2 (12-inch) po'boy or French
bread loaves

Mayonnaise

Slices of Swiss cheese or your
favorite cheese (optional)

½ head iceberg lettuce, thinly
shredded

1 tomato, very thinly sliced

Dill pickles, thinly sliced (optional)

Hot sauce (optional)

WHEN I MAKE a brisket, I always cook a big one to make sure we have leftovers to make this New Orleans–style roast beef sandwich. Reminiscent of the famous debris sandwich at Mother's in New Orleans, I shred the remaining meat and heat it up in the cooking juices. Pile that awesomeness on French bread, add your favorite cheese, and dress it Southern-style with shredded lettuce and tomato. This is my family's favorite day-after lunch!

1. Shred the remaining brisket and put it back into a baking pan with its cooking juices, adding beef broth if more liquid is needed. Cover with a lid or aluminum foil, and warm it up in a 250 to 300°F oven for about 1 hour. (Or you can put the shredded brisket and its juices in a pot, adding beef broth if more liquid is needed, and heat it on the stovetop over medium-low heat.)

2. To make the po'boy, cut the bread into the desired lengths according to your preference or how many people you'll be serving. Slice the bread in half lengthwise, leaving one side intact like a hinge. This will help keep the sandwich from falling apart. Spread both sides liberally with mayonnaise. Spoon the moist brisket over the bottom side of each piece of bread, and drizzle extra juices as desired. Top the shredded brisket with slices of cheese, if desired.

3. To dress the po'boy, generously top with shredded lettuce and sliced tomato. Add pickles and a sprinkle of hot sauce, if using. Fold the sandwich sides together and serve immediately. It's a messy sandwich, but well worth it! In my opinion, it should be "paired" with a very cold Barq's root beer for the ultimate po'boy experience!

1/2 SHRIMP AND 1/2 OYSTER LOAF (OR PO' BOY)

MAKES 4 SANDWICHES

24 medium wild-caught Gulf shrimp, peeled and deveined

½ quart Gulf oysters

4 (8-inch) loaves New Orleans–style French bread, or 2 baguettes, each cut in half

2 to 3 tablespoons unsalted butter, at room temperature

Mayonnaise

Creole mustard

½ head iceberg lettuce, shredded

2 medium tomatoes, sliced

Pickle slices, store-bought or Lucy's Sweet and Sassy Icebox Pickles (page 251; optional)

Hot sauce

BECAUSE HOW COULD you ever decide between a fried shrimp and a fried oyster sandwich?

1. Preheat the oven to 250°F.

2. Fry the shrimp and the oysters in batches following the recipes on pages 197 and 201. Place the cooked shrimp and oysters on a baking sheet uncovered in the oven to keep warm.

3. Slice the French bread loaves in half lengthwise, leaving one side intact like a hinge. This will help keep the sandwich from falling apart.

4. Spread a little butter on the inside surface of the French bread and toast. (I like to place mine facedown on a warm skillet or grill.)

5. Spread mayonnaise on one side of the toasted bread and Creole mustard on the other side.

6. Layer lettuce, tomato slices, and pickles (if using) on the bottom side of the bread.

7. Top each sandwich bottom with fried shrimp on one half, using 5 to 6 shrimp per sandwich, and fried oysters on the other half, using about 4 oysters per sandwich.

8. Add a few dashes of hot sauce to taste.

KEY WEST TUNA BURGER

WITH

PICKLED ONION, SOY-SOAKED CUKES, AND WASABI MAYO

MAKES 4 BURGERS

1½ pounds sushi-grade tuna

2 teaspoons finely chopped fresh ginger

2 teaspoons finely chopped garlic

1 tablespoon finely chopped fresh cilantro

¼ teaspoon sea salt

¼ teaspoon freshly ground black pepper

½ egg white, slightly beaten

Organic olive oil cooking spray

4 buns (optional)

Wasabi Mayonnaise (recipe follows), for serving

Pickled Red Onions (recipe follows), for serving

Soy-Soaked Cukes (recipe follows), for serving

FISHING FOR TUNA is a popular pastime along the Gulf Coast. For a foodie, taking a slice of sashimi tuna straight off the fillet knife that just cleaned the fish and popping it into your mouth while you're still cruising back to the dock is a peak taste experience. The freshness of the tuna is indescribable. Later, you hopefully have lots of tuna that needs cooking! Don't miss the chance to grind some up in a food processor for burgers. However, take caution: bacteria can begin to grow in the red meat of the tuna when it gets warm or even room temperature. It is vitally important that you use fresh tuna, that you keep the tuna chilled before you grind it, and that you immediately place the burger patties back into the refrigerator until you are ready to use them.

1. Pulse the tuna in a food processor until it is the consistency of ground beef.

2. Remove any stringy fat or membrane from the meat.

3. In a large bowl, combine the meat, ginger, garlic, cilantro, salt, pepper, and egg white and form the mixture into patties.

4. Place the patties on a sheet of waxed paper and refrigerate for half an hour.

5. Coat a grill pan with olive oil spray. Heat the pan over high heat. Once the pan is hot, cook the patties for 3 to 5 minutes on each side, according to your desired doneness. Serve the burgers on buns—or without buns—spread with wasabi mayo, and top with pickled red onions and soy-soaked cukes.

——— PICKLED RED ONIONS ———

2 red onions

1 cup apple cider vinegar

1 teaspoon sea salt

1 teaspoon sugar

1. Slice the onions very thinly by hand or using a mandoline.

2. Bring a small saucepan of water to a boil. Place the onions in the boiling water for 1 minute, then drain and set aside.

3. In the same saucepan, bring the vinegar to a boil.

4. Add the onion, salt, and sugar and boil for 1 minute.

5. Remove from the heat and let cool. The onion will be a pretty pink color.

6. Pour the onion slices into a jar and refrigerate until ready to use. The onion will keep up to 1 week in the refrigerator.

SOY-SOAKED CUKES

¼ cup rice vinegar

2 tablespoons soy sauce

1 teaspoon sugar

1 teaspoon toasted sesame oil

½ teaspoon chili powder

½ teaspoon finely chopped garlic

1 seedless cucumber,
thinly sliced

1. In a small bowl, whisk together the vinegar, soy sauce, sugar, and sesame oil.

2. Add the chili powder and garlic and whisk to combine. Pour the liquid into a 1-quart jar.

3. Add the cucumber slices to the jar, shake, and let sit for at least 15 minutes before serving.

WASABI MAYONNAISE

MAKES ABOUT 1½ CUPS

3 tablespoons dry wasabi powder

1½ tablespoons cold water

1 cup mayonnaise

1 teaspoon fresh lime juice

1 teaspoon soy sauce

¼ teaspoon sea salt

1 tablespoon chopped fresh cilantro

1. Mix the wasabi powder with just enough of the water to form a paste.

2. In a food processor, combine the wasabi paste, mayonnaise, lime juice, soy sauce, and salt. Pulse together until thoroughly combined.

3. Add the cilantro and continue to pulse until thoroughly combined and light green in color.

4. Refrigerate in an airtight container until ready to serve. Serve chilled.

MAHI REUBEN

MAKES 6 SANDWICHES

6 mahi-mahi fillets, about 8 ounces each, butterflied

2 tablespoons sea salt

2 tablespoons freshly ground black pepper

¼ cup olive oil

4 tablespoons (½ stick) unsalted butter, melted

12 slices marbled rye bread

¾ cup Thousand Island Dressing (recipe follows)

12 slices Swiss cheese

2 cups Crazy Coleslaw (recipe follows)

ANYTIME I SEE this sandwich on a menu I try it, because I always want to know who has the best! You can use any type of fish for the sandwich, and you can certainly use sauerkraut instead of coleslaw if you prefer.

1. Preheat the oven to 250°F.

2. Generously season both sides of each mahi-mahi fillet with the salt and pepper.

3. In a large heavy skillet (10 to 12 inches), heat 2 tablespoons of the olive oil over medium-high heat.

4. Once the oil is hot, place two or three of the fish fillets in the pan, or as many as will fit without overcrowding. Cook in batches, adding more olive oil as needed. Cook the fish until a nice golden brown on the first side, about 4 minutes—the fish should be turned only once, so let it cook thoroughly before flipping to the other side. Flip and cook the second side until golden brown. Once golden brown, remove the fish fillets from the skillet and place them on a baking sheet uncovered. Keep warm in the oven until ready to assemble sandwiches.

5. Heat another large heavy skillet over medium-high heat. Butter one side of each slice of rye bread and place them butter-side down in the skillet. You will need to do this in batches or use more than one skillet. Spread some Thousand Island dressing on the non-buttered side of the bread and layer the Swiss cheese over the dressing. Allow the bread to toast nicely and the cheese to melt. Transfer to plates.

6. On 6 of the bread slices, layer a mahi fillet on top of the melted cheese. Then top each piece of fish with about ⅓ cup of the coleslaw. Top each sandwich with one of the remaining bread slices with dressing and cheese, insert a toothpick through each side of the sandwich, and slice in half to serve.

MAKES 3 CUPS

1 hard-boiled egg, finely chopped

2 cups mayonnaise

2 tablespoons sugar

½ cup finely chopped yellow onion

¼ cup ketchup

2 tablespoons dill relish

2 tablespoons white vinegar

½ teaspoon sea salt

½ teaspoon freshly ground
black pepper

MAKES 8 CUPS

½ head green cabbage,
thinly sliced

½ head purple cabbage,
thinly sliced

1½ cups coarsely grated carrots

2 tablespoons finely grated onion

1 cup mayonnaise

1 tablespoon apple cider vinegar

3 tablespoons sugar

Pinch of sea salt

1 teaspoon freshly ground
black pepper

2 teaspoons prepared or freshly
grated horseradish

—— THOUSAND ISLAND DRESSING ——

Combine all the ingredients in a medium bowl or airtight container. Cover and refrigerate for at least 30 minutes before serving.

—— CRAZY COLESLAW ——

1. In a large bowl, combine the cabbages, carrots, and onion and set aside.

2. In a small bowl, combine the mayonnaise, vinegar, sugar, salt, pepper, and horseradish. Whisk together well, making sure the sugar is dissolved.

3. Add the mayonnaise mixture to the cabbage mixture and mix together well. Cover and refrigerate for 30 minutes, then serve immediately.

MINI MUFFULETTAS

**MAKES 24 MINI
SANDWICHES**

Olive Salad

1 cup chopped pimento-stuffed
green olives

1 cup chopped pitted Kalamata olives

1 cup chopped giardiniera mix

2 tablespoons capers, drained

2 teaspoons finely chopped garlic

3 tablespoons chopped fresh parsley

1 teaspoon dried oregano

1 teaspoon red pepper flakes

3 tablespoons red wine vinegar

1 teaspoon freshly ground
black pepper

1 cup extra-virgin olive oil

Sea salt (optional)

Sandwiches

24 dinner rolls, or 4 tubes refrigerated
Pillsbury French bread dough

1 tablespoon sesame seeds (optional)

Extra-virgin olive oil

¾ pound sliced mozzarella cheese

¾ pound sliced provolone cheese

¾ pound sliced hot capicola

¾ pound sliced mortadella

¾ pound sliced Genoa salami

THESE ARE MY New Orleans sliders! People love having a tiny sandwich, and these taste good and are cute, too. Great for a New Orleans–themed party.

To make the olive salad:

1. In a medium bowl, combine the green olives, Kalamata olives, and giardiniera mix.

2. Add the capers, garlic, parsley, oregano, red pepper flakes, vinegar, black pepper, and olive oil.

3. Stir it all together well, then taste to see if salt is needed.

To assemble the sandwiches:

4. If using Pillsbury French bread dough, cut each tube into 6 equal parts and roll them into balls. Dip each ball into the sesame seeds and bake according to package directions.

5. Slice the rolls. Drizzle olive oil on the inside of the top and bottom rolls.

6. Spread the olive salad on both sides of the rolls. Layer the cheeses and meats on each roll bottom and then add the tops. These little sandwiches are so cute, they win in the taste and presentation categories!

PERFECT BURGER
TWO WAYS

WHEN I WANTED to create two memorable signature burgers for LuLu's, I turned first to my homemade cheese dips that I serve at home when I have company. Pimento cheese is a Southern food staple; I make mine with a touch of honey ale that gives it a little tang. When I paired it with fried green tomatoes, I knew it was good. Then I added a little bacon, and wow! I knew I had a winner. To bring a little class to my next signature burger, I used my fresh herb and garlic cheese spread and added some caramelized onions. Ooh la la! What a great combination—simply scrumptious! I've given you two cooking methods here: on the grill and in a pan. So consider yourself fully equipped to make *your* signature version of the perfect burger.

MAKES 4 (8-OUNCE) BURGERS

2 pounds ground chuck or sirloin

½ tablespoon sea salt

½ tablespoon freshly ground black pepper

Organic olive oil cooking spray (for grilling), or 1½ tablespoons extra-virgin olive oil (for pan cooking)

4 brioche buns or ciabatta rolls

1 tablespoon unsalted butter

Fried Green Tomatoes (page 199)

Honey Ale Pimento Cheese (page 63)

8 bacon slices, cooked

Lettuce of choice for garnish (I prefer the delicate varieties of Bibb, baby romaine, or even spicy arugula)

PIMENTO BURGER
——— WITH ———
FRIED GREEN TOMATOES

1. Divide the ground beef into four equal portions.

2. On a baking sheet or flat surface, gently form each portion into a patty, trying not to overwork the meat. Lightly press your thumb in the center of each patty, making a slight indentation. Season the patties with the salt and pepper.

Make the burgers:

3. *To grill the burgers:* Preheat a grill and lightly coat the grates of the grill with cooking spray. Make sure the grates are nice and hot. Place the burgers on the grill and cook until the first side is lightly charred. Flip and grill the burgers, uncovered, to your desired internal temperature: for medium-rare, about 3 minutes on each side; and for medium, 4 to 5 minutes on each side. If the juices from a burger are dripping fat onto the coals and it starts to flame or the burger is on a hot spot, move the burger while cooking it but don't flip it. I try to flip the burgers only once, and I never press down on the burgers with the spatula because I don't want to release all the good juices!

To cook the burgers in a pan: In a large heavy skillet (10 to 12 inches, preferably cast iron), heat the olive oil over medium heat. Once the oil starts to shimmer, add the burgers to the pan and cook until the first side is lightly charred, 3 to 5 minutes (follow the cooking times for grilling). Flip the burgers and char them on the second side to your desired doneness. Again, try to flip the burgers only once and avoid the temptation to press down on the burgers with your spatula.

4. Slice each bun or roll in half. Place each piece facedown on the grill or skillet to lightly toast. Remove the buns from the grill/skillet, lightly butter them, and arrange them on a serving platter. Remove the burgers from the grill/skillet for a minute or two to let them rest but not cool.

5. Place a thick slice of fried tomato on the bottom half of each bun, then top each tomato slice with a burger. Add a dollop of pimento cheese on top of each burger, followed by two slices of crispy bacon and the top half of the bun. Garnish with lettuce and enjoy!

MAKES 4 (8-OUNCE) BURGERS

2 pounds ground chuck or sirloin

½ tablespoon plus 1 teaspoon sea salt

½ tablespoon freshly ground black pepper

1 tablespoon unsalted butter

1 tablespoon extra-virgin olive oil

2 large onions, sliced into ¼-inch rounds

2 teaspoons sugar

Organic olive oil cooking spray (for grilling), or 1½ tablespoons extra-virgin olive oil (for pan cooking)

4 brioche buns or ciabatta rolls

1 tablespoon unsalted butter

Lettuce of choice for garnish (I prefer the delicate varieties of Bibb, baby romaine, or even spicy arugula)

Fresh Herb and Garlic Cheese Spread (page 60)

GARLIC-HERB CHEESE BURGER
WITH
CARAMELIZED ONIONS

1. Divide the ground beef into four equal portions.

2. On a baking sheet or flat surface, gently form each portion into a patty, trying not to overwork the meat. Lightly press your thumb in the center of each patty, making a slight indentation. Season the patties with ½ tablespoon each of salt and pepper.

Make the caramelized onions:

3. In a heavy medium skillet, heat the butter and olive oil over medium heat until they start to sizzle. Add the onion, the remaining 1 teaspoon of sea salt, and 1 teaspoon of the sugar. Sauté over medium heat, stirring frequently as the onion begins to caramelize. Turn the onion and scrape the pan as it cooks and turns brown, about 10 minutes. Add the remaining 1 teaspoon of sugar and sauté until the onion is completely dark brown and caramelized.

Make the burgers:

4. *To grill the burgers:* Preheat a grill and lightly coat the grates of the grill with cooking spray. Make sure the grates are nice and hot. Place the burgers on the grill and cook until the first side is lightly charred. Flip and grill the burgers, uncovered, to your desired internal temperature: for medium-rare, about 3 minutes on each side; and for medium, 4 to 5 minutes on each side. If the juices from a burger are dripping fat onto the coals and it starts to flame or the burger is on a hot spot, move the burger while cooking it but don't flip it. I try to flip the burgers only once, and I never press down on the burgers with the spatula because I don't want to release all the good juices!

To cook the burgers in a pan: In a large heavy skillet (10 to 12 inches, preferably cast iron), heat the olive oil over medium heat. Once the oil starts to shimmer, add the burgers to the pan and cook until the first side is lightly charred, 3 to 5 minutes (follow the cooking times for grilling). Flip the burgers and char them on the second side to your desired doneness. Again, try to flip the burgers only once and avoid the temptation to press down on the burgers with your spatula.

5. Slice each bun or roll in half. Place each piece facedown on the grill or skillet to lightly toast. Remove the buns from the grill/skillet, lightly butter, and arrange them on a serving platter. Remove the burgers from the grill/skillet for a minute or two to let them rest but not cool.

6. Place lettuce on the bottom of each bun, then top the lettuce with a burger. Add a dollop of the cheese spread to the top of each burger, followed by a smattering of caramelized onions and the top half of the bun. Amazing!

LUCY B. GOODE
CUBAN SANDWICH

MAKES 6 SANDWICHES

2 (18-inch) loaves Cuban bread (can substitute French bread if you can't find Cuban bread), cut into thirds

¾ cup Classic Aioli (recipe follows) or mayonnaise

¾ cup Creole mustard

12 slices Swiss cheese

36 slices Lucy's Sweet and Sassy Icebox Pickles (recipe follows) or other pickles

1½ pounds thinly sliced ham

1½ pounds smoked pulled pork

2 tablespoons extra-virgin olive oil

2 tablespoons unsalted butter

IN KEY WEST you have a Cuban sandwich once a week the way you would have a burger anywhere else. Picking up a sack of Cubans from 5 Brothers is my favorite way to pack a picnic for the boat. There's nothing like being on those turquoise waters and soaking up the Florida sun enjoying a Cuban sandwich and washing it down with a cold, cold beer. It completes the Key West experience.

1. Preheat the oven to 250°F.

2. Slice the bread loaves in half.

3. In a small bowl, mix together the aioli and the mustard.

4. Spread the aioli mixture on the top and bottom bread halves. Layer the Swiss cheese on both halves of bread. Layer the pickles on the top half, then layer the ham and pulled pork on the bottom half. Fold the sandwich together.

5. In a large skillet or a flat-top griddle pan, heat 1 tablespoon of the olive oil and 1 tablespoon of the butter over medium heat.

6. Place three of the sandwiches in the skillet or griddle pan.

7. Place a heavy cast-iron skillet on top of the sandwiches to press them down; press the sandwiches until the bread is toasted and the cheese is melted. Transfer the sandwiches to a baking sheet and place uncovered in the oven to keep warm. Repeat with the three remaining sandwiches.

8. Cut the sandwiches in half to serve.

———— CLASSIC AIOLI ————

MAKES 2 CUPS

3 large *pasteurized* egg yolks (see Note)

¼ cup fresh lemon juice

1 teaspoon sea salt

⅛ teaspoon white pepper

3 large garlic cloves, finely chopped

1½ cups extra-virgin olive oil

1. In a food processor, combine the egg yolks, lemon juice, salt, and pepper and pulse slowly to combine. Add the garlic. Pulse for 10 seconds more.

2. With the food processor running, *slowly* pour the oil in through the feed tube in a thin, steady stream until the mixture is emulsified.

3. Refrigerate in an airtight container until ready to serve. Aioli will keep for 1 week in the refrigerator.

NOTE: *Be sure to use pasteurized eggs as raw eggs can contain bacteria.*

MAKES 1 GALLON

1 (1-gallon) jar whole kosher dill pickles

4 medium onions, thinly sliced

20 garlic cloves, halved lengthwise

⅔ cup thin half-moon slices peeled fresh ginger

¼ cup prepared or freshly grated horseradish

1 tablespoon red pepper flakes

1 tablespoon whole mustard seeds

½ teaspoon ground turmeric

8 cinnamon sticks

4 cups granulated sugar

4 cups packed light brown sugar

1 cup apple cider vinegar

IT MAY SEEM like a lot of trouble to make all these pickles just for a few sandwiches, but they are incredible, and you'll end up enjoying them on other sandwiches, as a tangy side, and on their own, straight out of the "icebox." Plus, they make great host or hostess gifts when you go to someone else's house for dinner.

1. Drain the pickles and chop them into ¼-inch slices. Save the 1-gallon jar for storing the pickles later.

2. Place the pickles and the remaining ingredients in a big stainless steel bowl or a large plastic container with an airtight lid.

3. Using your hands, toss it all together well. Cover and refrigerate overnight. The pickles will reduce in volume, so the next day you can return them to the 1-gallon jar for easier storage.

4. Refrigerate the pickles for at least a week, turning them topsy-turvy every day. The pickles are ready when the sugar has dissolved and all the dill flavor has vanished.

NOTE: *These pickles will keep in the refrigerator indefinitely. I have canned them to make them shelf stable in order to give them as Christmas gifts. When I do, I remove the cinnamon sticks before placing the pickles in canning jars because the heat from the hot water bath releases too much cinnamon flavor.*

251

SANDWICHES

LULU'S AT
HOMEPORT CRAB MELT

MAKES 4 SANDWICHES

1 pound cooked fresh blue crab claw meat, picked through for shells, handled carefully to keep the meat in big chunks (see Notes on Handling Seafood, pages xxx–xxxi)

2 cups shredded Swiss cheese

½ cup finely chopped green onions

½ teaspoon sea salt

½ teaspoon freshly ground black pepper

1½ cups mayonnaise

4 (8-inch) loaves New Orleans–style French bread

I DEVELOPED THIS recipe when I worked as a catering chef aboard the motor yacht *Mariner III* in New York. I originally used the rich, addictive cheesy crab filling in puff pastry hors d'oeuvres. It is such a versatile recipe that can be used as a filling, spread, or a dip—I love it golden, hot, and bubbling in a small baking dish, served with crackers. Here it works beautifully on an open-faced sandwich. My mother loved this sandwich; I put it on the original LuLu's menu for her, and I'm glad I did because it is now one of the best-selling sandwiches at my restaurants.

1. Preheat the oven to 350°F.

2. In a medium bowl, combine the crabmeat, cheese, green onion, salt, and pepper.

3. Add the mayonnaise and mix well.

4. Cut each French loaf in half horizontally.

5. Spread the crabmeat mixture generously over each piece of bread.

6. Place all 8 pieces on a baking sheet and bake for 15 minutes, or until the crabmeat mixture is hot and the cheese starts to bubble.

7. Turn the oven to broil and broil for a few minutes, until the cheese is golden brown.

NOTE: *I serve this "open-faced" on the French bread, but I have also made it as an hors d'oeuvre for parties on toast points or as an individual appetizer wrapped in phyllo dough...There are many ways to serve this rich, addictive dish.*

VACATION LIBATIONS AND MOCKTAILS

WE SEEM to be in the midst of a craft cocktail craze. Bartenders are now "mixologists," and every drink is a work of art. I'm all for this creative movement, as I always serve a specialty cocktail at my dinner parties. Being festive is second nature to us Coastal Southerners, and we've been celebrating our cocktail culture for as long as I can remember. "It's martini time," was the five o'clock daily anthem echoed along the shore of Mobile Bay during our summer vacations. We're glad the rest of the world has caught on!

Coming from a family of sailors, the ritual of the welcome-home celebration or the mournful sendoff is etched in our DNA, and always infused with the appropriate libation at our favorite portside establishments. When it was time for my sea captain grandfather to catch his ship docked at the Governor Nicholls Wharf in New Orleans, he would meet my grandmother at Tujague's in the French Quarter for a drink and then say good-bye. While he was away, sometimes for as long as a year, my grandmother would make bathtub beer for his arrival and then serve him a Café Royale, coffee with a shot of rum, every morning while he was home.

Growing up, ice-cold beer; bottles of gin, rum, and scotch; and mixed drinks on the pier were how our parents celebrated and dealt with life. My mother was the queen of the frozen concoction. She had a first-generation Vitamix, and every weekend the daiquiris and piña coladas flowed for hours for the adults as we floated for hours in our beloved brackish bay.

Things have always been a little looser along the coast, and I think that attitude attracts our tourists almost as much as our beautiful coastline and beaches. Our open outlook combined with our hospitality makes for an experience where people feel free to indulge, to let loose, to daydream, laugh, play, tell stories, and even float for hours without a care in the world. Sometimes a festive drink helps speed this process along, especially when you're trying to make that transition from the real-world doldrums to a sail full of vacation breezes and sunshine. So even if it's thirty degrees outside and the beach is a world away, try making one of these festive drinks and indulge in a little liquid vacation. You'll feel like you've taken a little piece of our coastal paradise home with you.

BAMA BREEZE

1 lime, cut into wedges

½ ounce simple syrup
(recipe follows)

¾ ounce ruby red grapefruit-
flavored vodka

¾ ounce coconut rum

Cranberry juice

THIS DRINK FEATURES all my favorite ingredients. We came up with it after my brother's song by the same name. My one and only acting gig, in fact, came when I got to play the bar owner singing onstage for the "Bama Breeze" music video. It was a whole lot of fun, but the experience made me thankful for my day job!

1. Put 2 lime wedges in the bottom of a metal cocktail shaker. Add the simple syrup, vodka, and rum.

2. Muddle gently, avoiding the lime rinds, which can add a bitter taste.

3. Fill the shaker with ice and cranberry juice. Pour the mixture back and forth between the shaker and a large mixing glass a few times.

4. Pour the drink into a glass, add a straw, garnish with a lime wedge, and enjoy the Breeze!

SIMPLE SYRUP

MAKES ABOUT 8 OUNCES

½ cup sugar

½ cup water

Combine the sugar and water in a small saucepan. Bring to a boil. Remove from the heat and let cool to room temperature. Once cool, pour the syrup into a storage container. It will keep, refrigerated, for a long time.

NOTE: *You can make larger quantities—simply use equal parts water and sugar.*

A GULF COAST RITE OF PASSAGE:
HEADIN' TO SIN CITY

When I was a teenager growing up in Mobile, Alabama, we had a long-standing tradition of "breaking out." The first vital part of this plan was getting a fake ID. Back then, our driver's licenses were printed on small thick paper cards, and there was no such thing as a photo ID. If you didn't have a big sister's or brother's to use, you could craftily use an X-ACTO knife from art class and cut out two digits from your license number, along with the last two digits from your date of birth, and switch them to make you "of age." Then you would go to the office supply store or the local camera shop where they would laminate the license, and you were set. That was how you made a fake ID in the late sixties in Lower Alabama!

After weeks of planning, we'd start our escape with that age-old ruse of "spending the night with a friend." And then we were off! First, a forty-five-minute drive just over the Mississippi state line to a bar called the Red Barn on Old Highway 90 off of the brand-new I-10. It was literally a barn structure painted red and housing a quintessential honky-tonk—a smoky bar with jukebox music. The drinking age in Mississippi was only eighteen, so if you were sixteen or seventeen, you could pull it off.

A round-trip to the Red Barn was where you cut your teeth, but when you really wanted a high adventure, you'd keep driving that extra two hours to the *big city...New Orleans*! Most of us had never been north of Montgomery; Birmingham and Atlanta were wayyyyyy north to us coastlings. New Orleans had a well-deserved mystique and allure for me, especially because we had grown up

with hints of lurid family tales set there, always the topic of whispered conversations in the backyard, away from our big ears. But we kids all knew the "honest truth": New Orleans was where the action happened. It was mysterious, forbidden, wild, loud, and unpredictable, the home of pirates, sailors, Rhett Butler, and the infamous Bourbon Street. It was a rite of passage for Southern teenagers to flock to New Orleans on any given sultry Saturday night. But we also had a secret dedicated mission when we barreled down that black highway traveling due west! We were headed to the notorious Pat O'Brien's bar, and what we wanted there wasn't just any drink but their famous red-fruity Hurricane cocktail, served in their signature curvy tall glass with the hand-painted green logo that you'd get refills in and then take home with you.

If breaking out was our rite of passage, that souvenir glass was our badge of courage. And when we crept back home the next day, trying to act all normal, then darting straight to our rooms for refuge, the first thing we did before crawling into bed was hide that Hurricane glass way back in the closet or in the bottom of our sweater drawer. Inevitably, months later, our parents would be looking for something and find that Pat O'Brien's Hurricane glass and they'd know we'd been to Sin City. We'd get in trouble, but our parents really couldn't say too much...we were only doing what they'd done before us and their parents before them! Pat O'Brien's still sells its famous Hurricanes, and I have a feeling there are plenty of those glasses still hidden to this day in drawers and closets all over the Gulf Coast.

HIGHBROW MARGARITA

MAKES 1 COCKTAIL

Kosher salt, for rimming the glass
(optional)

1 orange, cut into thick wedges

1 lime, cut into wedges

2 ounces Patrón Añejo tequila

½ ounce Patrón Citrónge lime liqueur

5 to 6 ounces soda water

FOR AN HONEST-TO-GOODNESS margarita, you need to use high-quality ingredients without a lot of juice or extra flavors—in other words, get to the heart of the matter.

1. Salt the rim of the glass, if desired.

2. Put 4 orange wedges and 2 lime wedges into a metal cocktail shaker. Add the tequila and lime liqueur.

3. Muddle gently, avoiding the rinds, which can add a bitter taste.

4. Add a small scoop of ice and the soda water to the shaker. Pour back and forth between the shaker and a large mixing glass a few times.

5. Pour the margarita into the salted (if using) serving glass. Garnish with a lime wedge.

HURRICANE

MAKES 1 COCKTAIL

1 ounce Southern Comfort

1 ounce light rum

½ ounce raspberry liqueur

3 ounces fresh orange juice

3 ounces unsweetened pineapple juice

½ ounce grenadine

Splash of high-proof or overproof
white rum

Orange slice, for garnish

Pineapple wedge, for garnish

Maraschino cherry, for garnish

1. Fill a hurricane glass with ice.

2. In a metal cocktail shaker, combine the Southern Comfort, light rum, raspberry liqueur, orange juice, pineapple juice, and grenadine. Shake vigorously ("Shake it like a hurricane!").

3. Pour into the hurricane glass, top with a *splash* of high-proof or overproof white rum, and garnish with the orange slice, pineapple wedge, and cherry.

CUCUMBER MARGARITA

MAKES 1 COCKTAIL

Kosher salt, for rimming the glass
(optional)

1 cucumber, cut into thick slices

1 lime, cut into wedges

Splash of simple syrup
(see page 256)

1½ ounces high-quality blanco
or silver tequila

2 ounces sour mix

THIS IS ONE of the most refreshing drinks we have ever concocted. Don't be afraid to substitute other ingredients for the cucumber and create your own custom margarita.

1. Salt the rim of the glass, if desired.

2. Combine 4 cucumber slices, 2 lime wedges, and the simple syrup in a metal cocktail shaker.

3. Muddle gently, avoiding the lime rinds, which can add a bitter taste.

4. Add a small scoop of ice to the shaker. Add the tequila and sour mix. Pour back and forth between the shaker and a large mixing glass a few times.

5. Pour the margarita into the salted (if using) serving glass. Garnish with a lime wedge.

BOCA BEACH COCKTAIL

MAKES 1 COCKTAIL

1 orange, cut into thick wedges

1 lime, cut into thick wedges

1 lemon, cut into thick wedges

½ ounce simple syrup
(see page 256)

1½ ounces Jamaican dark rum

1 (12-ounce) bottle ginger *beer*
(not ginger ale)

1. Put 2 orange wedges and 1 lime wedge in the bottom of a highball glass. Muddle gently, avoiding the rinds, which can add a bitter taste.

2. Squeeze 2 lemon wedges into the glass. Add the simple syrup.

3. Fill the glass with ice, then add the rum. Pour half the ginger beer over the top. Use a spoon to gently swizzle, then garnish with a lime wedge and enjoy.

MANGO MARGARITA

MAKES 1 COCKTAIL

Kosher salt, for rimming the glass
(optional)

1½ ounces mango-flavored tequila

½ ounce high-quality orange liqueur

4 ounces mango puree

4 to 6 ounces sour mix

Lime wedge, for garnish

1. Salt the rim of the glass, if desired.

2. Fill a metal cocktail shaker with a large scoop of ice. Add the mango tequila, orange liqueur, mango puree, and sour mix. Shake vigorously.

3. Pour the margarita into the salted (if using) serving glass. Garnish with the lime wedge.

NOTE: *Try it frozen—simply combine the ingredients in a blender instead of a tin. Spin, blend, and relax!*

MOSCOW MULE

MAKES 1 COCKTAIL

2 ounces high-quality vodka

1 ounce fresh lime juice

1 (12-ounce) bottle ginger *beer*
(not ginger ale)

Lime wedge, for garnish

Fill a copper mug or other festive metal glass with ice. Add the vodka and lime juice. Top off with ginger beer. Garnish with a lime wedge.

NOTE: *Traditionally this drink is served in copper mugs, but I ordered a set of sixties retro multicolored metal glasses that I love to use. They also double in use as very pretty little vases.*

THE WAR EAGLE

MAKES 1 COCKTAIL

Blue Side

¾ ounce mango-flavored tequila

¼ ounce raspberry liqueur

3 ounces margarita mix

1 ounce blue curaçao

Orange Side

¾ ounce mango-flavored tequila

¼ ounce grenadine

3 ounces mango margarita mix

FOOTBALL RANKS RIGHT up there with religion in Alabama. The Auburn-Alabama college football rivalry is mythic, and parties abound all over the state for the Iron Bowl, when they face each other on the gridiron. Quite frankly, I'm happy if either Alabama team leads the SEC. Whether one wins or loses, we Alabamians will celebrate a victory or mourn a loss with a cocktail. So I decided each team needed a signature drink reflecting the schools' colors for my game-day dinner party menu. Here's to Alabama football!

1. Place the blue side ingredients in a blender with ice and blend until smooth. Pour the blue mixture into a cup or small pitcher and rinse the blender.

2. Place the orange side ingredients in a blender with ice and blend until smooth.

3. Pour the blue mixture and the orange mixture into a clear glass *at the same time* so they are side by side in the glass. War Eagle, baby!

THE ROLL TIDE

MAKES 1 COCKTAIL

1½ ounces sweet tea-flavored vodka

3 ounces fresh lemonade

3 ounces cranberry juice

Splash of grenadine

Fresh cherry, for garnish

Lemon twist, for garnish

1. Fill a tall glass with ice. Pour in the vodka, lemonade, and cranberry juice so the glass is almost full.

2. Pour the mixture back and forth between the glass and a metal cocktail shaker a few times. Float the grenadine over the top.

3. Garnish with the fresh cherry and twist of lemon. Roll Tide, Roll!

WHITE SANGRIA

SERVES 4 TO 6

1 (750-milliliter) bottle Pinot Gris or any other crisp light white wine

½ cup peach-flavored vodka

⅔ cup sugar

¼ fresh pineapple, chopped into cubes

½ lemon, cut into wedges

2 fresh strawberries, chopped

½ mango, chopped into cubes

1 (8-ounce) can ginger ale

Ice cubes

1. In a very large pitcher, combine the wine, vodka, sugar, and fruit. Stir well. Let the ingredients steep in the fridge for 2 to 24 hours (the longer, the better).

2. Add the ginger ale and ice cubes about 30 minutes before serving.

3. Place a strainer over the mouth of the pitcher and pour to order. Garnish with any leftover fruit, such as more of the pineapple, lemon, strawberries, and mango.

RED SANGRIA

SERVES 4 TO 6

1 (750-milliliter) bottle high-quality Cabernet Sauvignon

¾ cup triple sec orange liqueur

1 cup blackberry brandy

½ cup sugar

1 orange, quartered

½ lemon, halved

½ lime, halved

Handful of maraschino cherries

1 (10-ounce) bottle club soda

Ice cubes

1. In a very large pitcher, combine the wine, orange liqueur, brandy, sugar, and fruit. Stir well. Let the ingredients steep in the fridge for 2 to 24 hours (the longer, the better).

2. Add the club soda and ice cubes about 30 minutes before serving.

3. Place a strainer over the mouth of the pitcher and pour to order. Garnish with any leftover fruit, such as more of the orange, lemon, lime, and cherries.

NAUGHTY ARNOLD PALMER

MAKES 1 COCKTAIL

1½ ounces sweet tea–flavored vodka

1½ ounces fresh lemon juice

Sweet tea

Lemon slice, for garnish

1. Fill a glass with ice.

2. Add the vodka and lemon juice.

3. Top with the desired amount of sweet tea and garnish with the lemon slice.

PINK DRINK

MAKES 1 COCKTAIL

¾ ounce citrus-flavored vodka

¾ ounce mango-flavored tequila

3 ounces fresh lemonade

3 ounces sour mix

Dash of Campari

Lemon wedge, for garnish

Maraschino cherry, for garnish

1. Fill a tall glass with ice. Add the vodka and tequila.

2. Pour in the lemonade and sour mix. Add the Campari.

3. Stir well, then garnish with the lemon wedge and cherry.

RUM PUNCH

MAKES 1 COCKTAIL

1 ounce high-quality spiced rum

½ ounce Jamaican dark rum

½ ounce coconut rum

2 ounces sour mix

1 ounce pineapple juice

1 ounce cranberry juice

Splash of grenadine (optional)

Maraschino cherry, for garnish

Orange, lemon, or lime slices,
for garnish

Pineapple wedge, for garnish

1. Fill a tall glass with ice. Pour all three rums and the sour mix over the ice.

2. Add the pineapple and cranberry juice. Add a splash of grenadine (if using).

3. Stir well and garnish with the cherry, citrus slice, and pineapple wedge.

BAD DOG

MAKES 1 COCKTAIL

Kosher salt, for rimming
the glass

1½ ounces ruby red grapefruit–
flavored vodka

Juice of 4 grapefruits

1. Salt the rim of the glass.

2. Fill the glass with ice.

3. Pour the vodka and grapefruit juice over the ice and serve.

MOCKTAILS AND REFRESHMENTS

THERE IS A new movement in the restaurant business to have a menu of mocktails, cocktails without the alcohol. When I have a dinner party, I like to have a specialty cocktail to serve, but for the nondrinking folks, it's great to be able to serve that same drink as a mocktail. Nobody gets left out, and some people feel better than others the next morning!

GOOD DOG

MAKES 1 MOCKTAIL

Kosher salt, for rimming the glass

Juice of 3 grapefruits

3 ounces cranberry juice

Lime wedge, for garnish

1. Salt the rim of the glass.

2. Fill the glass with ice.

3. Pour the grapefruit juice and cranberry juice over the ice and garnish with the lime wedge.

NOTE: *See page 271 for the Bad Dog.*

COSMO NO-NO

MAKES 1 MOCKTAIL

4 ounces cranberry juice

1 ounce fresh lime juice

1 ounce nonalcoholic triple sec

Lemon wedge, for garnish

1. Fill a metal cocktail shaker with ice. Add the cranberry juice, lime juice, and triple sec. Shake vigorously.

2. Strain into a chilled martini glass and garnish with the lemon wedge.

NOTE: *To make an alcoholic version of this drink, add 1 ounce high-quality orange-flavored liqueur and 2 ounces citrus-flavored vodka to the cocktail shaker.*

RUMLESS PUNCH

1 ounce coconut milk

1½ ounces cranberry juice

1½ ounces pineapple juice

1 ounce fresh orange juice

1 ounce sour mix

Splash of grenadine

Maraschino cherry, for garnish

Orange, lemon, or lime slices,
for garnish

Pineapple wedge, for garnish

1. Fill a tall glass with ice. Pour the coconut milk, cranberry juice, pineapple juice, orange juice, and sour mix over the ice.

2. Add the grenadine.

3. Stir well and garnish with the fruit.

NOTE: *See page 271 for the Rum Punch.*

MOCK BASILTINI

MAKES 1 MOCKTAIL

4 fresh basil leaves, plus
1 leaf for garnish

1½ ounces simple syrup (see page
256), or 3 sugar cubes

2 lemon wedges

2 lime wedges, plus 1 for garnish

2 ounces ruby red grapefruit juice

4 ounces soda water

1. Combine the basil leaves and the simple syrup in a metal cocktail shaker. Squeeze the juice from the lemon and lime wedges into the shaker and muddle softly, gently bruising the basil leaves.

2. Add a scoop of ice to the shaker. Pour the grapefruit juice over the ice. Shake in the shaker.

3. Fill a highball glass with ice. Strain the ingredients from the shaker into the glass.

4. Top with soda water and garnish with the lime wedge and basil leaf.

NOTE: *To make an alcoholic version of this drink, add 3 ounces high-quality vodka or gin to the cocktail shaker.*

MOCKTAIL MULE

MAKES 1 MOCKTAIL

1 ounce fresh lime juice

1 (12-ounce) bottle ginger *beer*
(not ginger ale)

Lime wedge, for garnish

1. Fill a copper mug or other festive metal glass with ice. Add the lime juice.

2. Top off with ginger beer.

3. Stir well and garnish with the lime wedge.

NOTE: *See page 263 for the Moscow Mule.*

CHAPTER 10

SAUCES AND DRESSINGS

SAUCES were almost the end of me. The mere idea of them was a mental stumbling block. I had it in my head that I wasn't a real chef because I didn't know how to easily prepare the quintessential sauces that are the foundations of French cuisine. Sure, I could follow any recipe, but those intimidating sauces weren't in my repertoire. Somehow, I felt if I went to culinary school, it would give me the credentials to go with my well-worn street cred. So when the charter boat I was cooking on, the *Mariner III*, was about to shove off from New York City and head south for the winter season, I decided to tackle my insecurity, stay in the city, and enroll in the French Culinary Institute in Soho. Sauces be damned! I was going to earn my chef's coat!

It was late November and classes didn't start until January. It had turned a bitter cold, and my little gnarly sublet in Alphabet City literally had holes in the walls. I went to Macy's and bought all-new sheets and a duvet in red plaid flannel to make it homey. That didn't work, and as it got colder I got more disillusioned. What was I thinking?! And that's when I got the call...

The *Mariner III* had booked a charter in Antigua on Christmas Day, and the captain wanted to know if I would be able to join them. He hadn't even finished talking before I'd made up my mind—I was going south! I was going home. So I hustled over to Soho and withdrew from school, hopped into my Mustang, drove to Alabama, spent a couple of weeks with my boyfriend, and on Christmas Day boarded a plane headed for parts unknown in Antigua. No, I'd never been there; I'd barely been out of the country. This was before the days of cell phones. In true Buffett fashion, I was making it up as I went, headed to the tropics on a wing and a prayer.

Many hours later, on the last puddle-jumper flight from Miami, I descended over the silhouette of four unexpected mountain peaks and landed on a dark and desolate-looking runway. There was a smattering of lights across a mighty distance and then nothing but blackness. It was hard to tell if I was really on an island, but the smell and stickiness of the salt air helped me believe I had made it to Antigua.

I jumped into a rickety cab driven by a weathered old Antiguan man and asked him to take me to the marina. I was taken aback when we sputtered off in a direction away from the ocean and began climbing a massive hill. In broken English, the driver assured me he knew where he was going. I was headed with a perfect stranger in a strange land to a place I had never been before to a boat that may or may not have arrived. I dropped the name of a local friend my brother had given me, but the driver simply laughed. Somehow we made it back to the ocean—I could smell the salt water again. I realized we had simply gone around the island to the southern shore. It was slipping past midnight when I found myself on an abandoned curb with my suitcase. There wasn't a soul to be seen at that humble marina, much less the *Mariner III* and crew. Built in 1926, the exquisite wooden fantail motor yacht stretched an impressive 123 feet, but with only 18 feet of beam, she could be a rocker and a roller in rough seas. I knew it was possible they had caught the tail end of a front and that was why they were late.

I stood there gazing into the inky night and felt about as big as a tadpole. I thought about how I was supposed to be in New York right then and wondered if it was snowing there or if the school had sent my refund yet. Then I had one of those realizations that come faster than a sneeze flying on the heels of a pang of Catholic guilt: I was a runner, pure and simple. I had given up school and a chance to improve my skills, motivated by my fear of commitment—to sauces, no less! I was on the verge of tears, with pure panic in my heart, and yet I couldn't help but surrender to a deep belly laugh that echoed into the creosote night at the hilarity of my predicament. So I prayed…to the heavens above, with a shout-out to Neptune and Aphrodite…to the twinkling stars and the man in the moon…I paced, asking all my ancestors and my guardian angel to take care of my crazy self.

And finally, since I didn't know what else to do, I just stopped, took a deep breath, and turned it all over to the mighty Mother Ocean that had protected and provided for my family for generations. It was then that I heard a murmuring in the distance, and "I kid you not," as my son-of-a-sailor daddy used to say, a ghostly image slowly emerged from the blackness gliding toward the dock. Miraculously, it was the *Mariner III*—my little home bunk away from home—showing up just when I needed her. The stunning synchronicity humbled me, and I was greatly relieved to see my fellow crew, pretty exhausted and rough-looking but safe and sound all the same.

I caught the lines and tied her off. The crew was whipped, and the clients were due to board the boat in ten hours with their children for a seven-day cruise to St. Lucia. The boat was a mess—things get shaken loose and stirred up after a 1,300-mile straight run. It would take all night to get her shipshape again. So I jumped on board and headed straight to the galley to rustle up some warm food for the exhausted crew. Nothing like a cheeseburger in paradise to help get you through the night!

We were all sitting around the dining table on the afterdeck devouring the burgers and sipping cold beer when the captain pulled out pints of Häagen-Dazs ice cream from the freezer. Just minutes earlier I had been marooned on a deserted dock, and now I was eating high-end American ice cream on a tiny island in the Caribbean. It was one of those peak life experiences fraught with fear and victory that created an unforgettable memory.

I jumped ship in Martinique after what was to be my last charter, so any opportunity to go back to New York and re-enroll in culinary school was squelched. But it still nagged for a while, until one day when I was sharing my insecurities with

some colleagues, most of them chefs with culinary degrees. They all told me I didn't need to go to cooking school. That I had been catering these elaborate Cajun- and Creole-themed dinners in New York for over a hundred people night after night that people just loved and that I should be teaching the classes instead of taking them. "But I don't know how to make the sauces!" I exclaimed. "Well, get a book and teach yourself," they said. I hadn't thought of that.

So I did get a book and taught myself how to make béchamel, velouté, hollandaise, and plenty more, and I felt lighter. I let go of my anxiety over not having gone to culinary school, and that voice that said I wasn't good enough became fainter and fainter the more I stirred.

So don't you start thinking you can't do homemade sauces! In fact, despite your fears, most sauces are downright easy, and it's a crying shame not to make them yourself. The flavor is so far superior to store-bought sauces. If you're going to go to all the trouble of cooking and using good-quality ingredients and then you open up a bottle of store-bought tartar sauce...well, that's a crime. Your food is worth the extra effort, and so are you. Amen.

LULU'S FAMOUS
WOW SAUCE

MAKES 1½ CUPS

2 jalapeños

1 tablespoon extra-virgin olive oil

1 cup mayonnaise

¼ cup Creole mustard

¼ cup prepared horseradish

THIS SAUCE CAME by its name honestly. It was originally called Creole Mustard Horseradish Sauce, but so many people at LuLu's literally said, "WOW!" after tasting it on our fish sandwich that we felt like we needed to call it like it is.

1. Coat the jalapeños with the olive oil. Char them in a hot skillet or under the broiler. The trick is to blacken the skins evenly by turning them frequently.

2. Once the peppers are charred, place them in a plastic baggie or covered bowl for about 15 minutes. As the peppers cool, the heat and moisture will "sweat" the skins from the peppers.

3. Once the skins are removed, cut the peppers in half, carefully remove the seeds, and finely chop the flesh.

4. Combine all the ingredients in a medium bowl or airtight container. Cover and refrigerate. The sauce will keep for up to 1 week in the refrigerator. There is a reason I call this WOW sauce—you will find so many uses for this delicious sauce!

WHITE HORSERADISH
SAUCE

**MAKES ABOUT
3 CUPS**

2 cups sour cream

¾ cup prepared horseradish

1 teaspoon sea salt

½ teaspoon white pepper

1 tablespoon Worcestershire sauce

2 tablespoons fresh lemon juice

2 or 3 dashes of hot sauce

1 teaspoon chopped fresh rosemary
(optional)

Combine all the ingredients in a medium bowl or airtight container. Cover and refrigerate for up to 1 week.

CLASSIC
COCKTAIL SAUCE

MAKES 2½ CUPS

2 cups ketchup

¾ cup prepared horseradish

2 tablespoons hot sauce

¼ cup Worcestershire sauce

2 tablespoons Pickapeppa sauce

1 tablespoon fresh lemon juice

Combine all the ingredients in a medium bowl or airtight container. Cover and refrigerate for up to 1 week.

HOMEMADE
TARTAR SAUCE

MAKES 2 CUPS

2 cups mayonnaise

¼ cup dill pickle relish

2 tablespoons sweet pickle relish

½ cup finely chopped yellow onion

½ teaspoon sea salt

1 teaspoon freshly ground
black pepper

Combine all the ingredients in a medium bowl or airtight container. Cover and refrigerate for up to 1 week.

KEY LIME-MUSTARD SAUCE

**MAKES ABOUT
3½ CUPS**

---

2 cups mayonnaise

½ cup fresh key lime juice
or regular lime juice

1 cup Creole mustard

1 tablespoon prepared or
freshly grated horseradish

2 tablespoons sugar

2 teaspoons hot sauce

¼ teaspoon sea salt

¼ teaspoon LuLu's Crazy Creola
Seasoning (page xxviii) or other
Creole seasoning

KEY LIMES ARE smaller and a little sweeter than regular limes, and they ripen to a yellow rather than green color, so that is why the filling of an authentic key lime pie is yellow instead of green. As a Keys specialty, this mustard sauce is served in Key West with every fish sandwich, fritter, and stone crab, and every restaurant has its own version.

Combine all the ingredients in a medium bowl or airtight container. Cover and refrigerate for up to 1 week.

TRADITIONAL REMOULADE SAUCE

MAKES ABOUT 2 CUPS

3 celery stalks, with leaves, coarsely chopped

4 green onions, coarsely chopped

½ small sweet onion, coarsely chopped

Leaves from 4 sprigs fresh tarragon

4 garlic cloves

¼ cup fresh lemon juice

¼ cup red wine vinegar

½ teaspoon sea salt

½ teaspoon LuLu's Crazy Creola Seasoning (page xxviii) or other Creole seasoning

¼ teaspoon white pepper

1 tablespoon prepared or freshly grated horseradish

½ cup Creole or Dijon mustard

1 teaspoon hot sauce

1 tablespoon paprika

¼ cup vegetable oil

1 teaspoon sugar

1 tablespoon tomato paste

Combine all the ingredients in a food processor. Pulse several times or until the sauce is slightly smooth. Transfer to a medium bowl, airtight container, or jar. Cover and refrigerate for up to 1 week.

BAD GIRL
BUFFALO SAUCE
(SPICY!)

MAKES 2 CUPS

4 tablespoons (½ stick)
unsalted butter

1 cup hot sauce

1 cup honey

½ teaspoon liquid smoke
hickory seasoning

½ teaspoon sea salt

1 teaspoon blackening seasoning

¼ teaspoon freshly ground
black pepper

2 tablespoons all-purpose flour

MR. LOU GERMANY, a longtime, valued member of Team LuLu, came up with this incredible recipe years ago using a blond roux, which gives the sauce its deep, rich flavor. Since it's so nice, we just had to call it Bad Girl.

1. In a large saucepan, melt 2 tablespoons of the butter with the hot sauce over medium heat. Add the honey, liquid smoke, salt, blackening seasoning, and pepper. Stir well. Simmer for 15 minutes.

2. In a separate small saucepan, melt the remaining 2 tablespoons butter over medium-low heat. Slowly add the flour and cook, stirring continuously, for about 5 minutes, until the roux is a blond color and the flour comes away from the pan. It will have a pastelike consistency, but as you stir it will thin slightly. Make sure it does not burn—if it smokes and smells even a tiny bit burned, just start over.

3. While stirring, carefully add the simmering hot sauce mixture to the roux. It will sizzle! Stir until well blended. Remove from the heat and let cool to room temperature. Transfer to a medium bowl or airtight container and refrigerate for up to 1 week.

STILTON BLUE CHEESE
DRESSING

**MAKES ABOUT
2½ CUPS**

1 cup Stilton blue cheese

¾ cup mayonnaise

¾ cup buttermilk

1½ teaspoons water

1 teaspoon sugar

½ teaspoon finely chopped garlic

Sea salt and freshly ground
black pepper

1. Crumble the blue cheese into a small bowl. Stir in the mayonnaise until the mixture is creamy.

2. Add the buttermilk and water and stir well.

3. Add the sugar, garlic, salt, and pepper. Stir well, cover, and refrigerate for up to 1 week.

CHIMILULU SAUCE

MAKES 1¼ CUPS

1 cup chopped fresh parsley

1 cup chopped fresh cilantro

2 tablespoons chopped fresh oregano

4 garlic cloves, finely chopped

1 shallot, finely chopped

1 jalapeño, seeded and finely chopped

1 teaspoon sea salt

½ teaspoon freshly ground
black pepper

3 tablespoons fresh lemon juice

2 tablespoons white wine vinegar

¾ cup extra-virgin olive oil

THIS IS MY slant on a chimichurri sauce, and it's delicious on steak (see page 123), seafood, chicken, anything—it's also very pretty on the plate, adding a nice pop of vibrant green.

Combine all the ingredients in a medium bowl or airtight container. Cover and refrigerate for up to 1 week. Serve over your favorite grilled or seared steak.

CITRUS-TARRAGON
DRESSING

MAKES ABOUT
1½ CUPS

Juice of 1 large orange (about ⅓ cup)

Juice of 1 lime (about 2 tablespoons)

3 tablespoons grainy Dijon mustard or
Creole mustard

1 garlic clove, crushed

¼ teaspoon truffle salt or sea salt

Pinch of freshly ground black pepper

½ cup extra-virgin olive oil

1 teaspoon finely chopped fresh
tarragon

1 tablespoon honey

Combine all the ingredients in a medium bowl or airtight container. Cover and refrigerate for up to 1 week.

SOUR ORANGE
VINAIGRETTE

1 teaspoon orange zest

½ cup fresh orange juice

¼ cup fresh lime juice

2 tablespoons champagne vinegar
or white wine vinegar

1 cup extra-virgin olive oil

½ teaspoon ground cumin

½ teaspoon ground coriander

2 teaspoons sugar

2 tablespoons finely chopped
fresh cilantro

Sea salt and freshly ground
black pepper

Combine all the ingredients in a jar and shake vigorously to mix together. Store in the jar in the refrigerator for up to 1 week.

CREOLE MUSTARD
VINAIGRETTE

¼ cup apple cider vinegar

¼ cup fresh lemon juice

2 tablespoons Creole or
Dijon mustard

1 teaspoon finely chopped garlic

1 teaspoon sugar

½ teaspoon sea salt

¼ teaspoon freshly ground
black pepper

1 teaspoon chopped fresh basil,
or ½ teaspoon dried basil

¾ cup extra-virgin olive oil

Combine all the ingredients in a jar and shake vigorously to mix together. Store in the jar in the refrigerator for up to 1 week.

COASTING THE GULF PARTY MENUS

AS A newlywed the second time around, I went from being a single Key West hippie mom to a Daphne, Alabama, provincial housewife hosting dinner parties for friends and my husband's business associates. I taught myself how to make complicated multiple-step recipes including Asian dishes, fresh pastas, Cajun dishes I'd never tried before—anything I could read about in *Gourmet* magazine or the cookbooks I'd started to collect. I'd spread the books and magazines over my bed on Sundays and pore over them for new ideas and methods I'd never tried before.

At the time I was working as the advertising manager at a small newspaper. When I managed to sell a color ad, I got to pick the colors, and those same colors would appear on the front page. I started picking colors I liked and then using copies of the newspaper as place mats at my parties. I was doing a homespun, saltwater version of "tablescapes" before I knew they were popular. One thing for sure, my guests were always intrigued, followed by much humorous conversa-

tion and hilarity. Everyone would have something fun to discuss as we sat at the table. It was a great icebreaker. I'd caught the bug for entertaining and using food and its presentation as a creative way to express myself. Creating dinner party menus and learning how to put dishes together, considering flavors, colors, and textures, continues to be one of the most pleasurable aspects of my do-it-yourself culinary career. I always say, "I'm not the best cook out there, but I'm great at writing a menu."

Coming up with "a theme" is just plumb fun and gives a dinner party real flair. The Gulf region has no end of inspired themes, most notably the varied cultures of its entire coast—Cuban, Classic Old Florida, Cajun, Creole, Mexican, and of course a little down-home Southern. If you're cruising the Gulf Coast, you're eating mighty fine, and experiencing a whole spectrum of culture-rich flavors and techniques. But if your boat is in dry dock, then do a little virtual cruising and enjoy the ride with these party menus full of my favorite flavors from each region.

KEY WEST DINNER PARTY

Key West stole my heart in my early twenties, and I've been in love ever since. Notorious for its sunsets and casual lifestyle, most of the socializing is carried on in the many tropical open-air bars and restaurants. Locals will certainly participate for their sunset cocktail, but they tend to go home for supper. For a tourist town, Key West has a lot of tight-knit neighborhoods, and most of the homes have a courtyard, porch, or deck for entertaining, usually hidden behind lush tropical postcard vegetation. Neighbors and friends love to stop in for a bite and a drink. Key West exudes ease and breezy living, yet it's funny how one of the most laid-back, casual places on the map is a source of one of the most luxurious and luscious delicacies in the world, stone crab claws. Stone crabs prove the best things in life don't need to be dressed up.

STARTERS
Stone Crabs with Key Lime–Mustard Sauce (57)

Five-Olive Salad with Fresh Herbs (65) and Cuban Bread

Black Bean & Corn Salad Dip with Plantain Chips (67)

SALAD AND MAIN COURSE
Mango, Avocado, and Arugula Salad with
Sour Orange Vinaigrette (223)

Picadillo (151)

Camarones a la Criolla (Cuban-Style Shrimp Creole) (131)

Cuban Yellow Rice (181)

DESSERT
Chocolate Brownie Flan (17)

SPECIALTY LIBATIONS
White Sangria (269)

Red Sangria (269)

OLD WEST COAST FLORIDA PARTY MENU

I inherited my love of Florida from my mother; she was always pointing us in the direction of the good life, and any Florida beach was at the top of that list. When I cross that state line, the sun is indeed a little brighter. It's a different kind of light. The Florida of my mother's memory still exists in a few places along the west coast where sleepy fishing villages keep humming along and dark little seafood restaurants, with leatherette booths and fish mounted on the wall, serve Old Florida classics like fried grouper, soft-shell crab, and Florida lobster.

One of my favorite Old Florida haunts is the Temptation restaurant in Boca Grande, and it is the first place I go when I visit my sister each year in the early spring. I always order the same thing: the grilled fish with a citrus beurre blanc sauce served over a bed of shaved Brussels sprouts. And they have the *best* pies in the world. I've taken inspiration from their menus over the years and included some for this collection. Food for me is often inspired by nostalgia, and then I tend to put my own LuLuTwist on it to give it a new shimmer. Florida is kind of like that, too: a beautiful light that's always special and yet never quite the same on any given day.

STARTER
Crab and Corn Fritters (206) or Hushpuppies (211)

SALAD AND MAIN COURSE
Florida Lobster Salad with Grapefruit and Avocado (221)
Bronzed Yellowtail Snapper with Citrus Beurre Blanc Sauce (135)
Shaved Brussels Sprouts with Shallots and Country Ham (173)
Brown Rice Mushroom Risotto (182)

DESSERT
Buttermilk Orange Chess Pie (13)

SPECIALTY LIBATION
Boca Beach Cocktail (261)

SWEET HOME ALABAMA:
MY BUFFETT FAMILY BUFFET

This menu is a homecoming meal that celebrates Gulf Coast delicacies and the food of my childhood that I serve to my globe-trotting family when they manage to come home for a visit. It is absolutely mandatory that crab be served for my sister and brother. My mother was crazy for oysters, and my daddy made the best tenderloin in the world on his famous shipyard-made industry-grade grill, so this represents our Buffett family favorites, with a LuLu-Twist, of course! The salad is my take on the Crab Maison at Galatoire's, the classic New Orleans restaurant. Oysters, crab, red meat, creamed spinach, and floating island for dessert—we Buffetts don't mess around when it comes to eating! Sharing a meal is what keeps us connected. What better excuse is there than a family get-together? What better way to bond than while gathered around a tray of oysters or carving up a gorgeous piece of meat? I have found that food is always the great equalizer when it comes to our family. It has helped us get beyond differences and always brings us together in celebration of our heritage and deep gratitude for our ancestors.

STARTERS
Icy-Cold Gulf Oysters on the Half Shell with Classic Cocktail
and Mignonette Sauces (53)

Lucia Anna's Casa Crab Salad with Toasted Garlic
French Bread Rounds (219)

MAIN COURSE
Spicy Coffee-Rubbed Beef Tenderloin (117)

Creamed Spinach (178)

DESSERT
Floating Island (21)

SPECIALTY LIBATION
Naughty Arnold Palmer (270)

NO PLACE LIKE
NOLA

New Orleans is truly like no other place in the world. It has to be experienced. It's a place of extraordinary food and extraordinary service that's marked by layers upon layers of nuanced flavors, history, and myriad cultures. It's a place where you can drink the best champagne alongside humble red beans and rice, where some of the most exquisite strawberries in the world are on sale right next to Mardi Gras beads and gator on a stick. You can spend a thousand dollars a day or twenty dollars a day on food and eat and drink like a queen. I've lived in New Orleans two different times in my life, and the experience has fine-tuned my palate and opened my eyes to both the complexity and the simplicity of fine food. When I entertain, there's a good chance that I will use one of the dishes on this menu. I go back whenever I can, but rest assured that my time in New Orleans imprinted my heart and soul with the love of Creole and Cajun flavors that permeates how I cook, from my most elegant meals to my humble red-beans-and-rice Monday-night suppers.

STARTERS
Classic Shrimp Remoulade (37)

Gulf Oysters Brochette Drizzled with Honey
and Blue Cheese (47)

MAIN COURSE
Monday Makin' Red Beans & Rice (152)

Muffuletta Salad (225)

Crawfish Cornbread Casserole (163)

DESSERT
Strawberry Cobbler (25) with Lemon Buttermilk Sorbet (27)

SPECIALTY LIBATION
Hurricane (259)

ACKNOWLEDGMENTS

There were so many folks who had a hand in stirring this pot of *Gumbo Love*; in this case, the more "cooks," the better the broth. I am deeply grateful to all of them for sharing their own unique gifts and expertise—light and love, inspiration and humor, hard work, and gentle, yet firm wrangling of my wandering gypsy soul to "stay the course" to get this book done.

My friends and patrons of LuLu's who come back year after year—standing sometimes for hours in the heat to enjoy my Gulf Coast hospitality and the Deep South coastal dishes of my childhood—you are the champions of my world, and you have made this book—and so much more—happen for me. For that I am honored and humbled.

Sweet and savory thanks to the Grand Central Life & Style team and Karen Murgolo for jumping on the *Gumbo Love* adventure and taking a chance on a Crazy Sista with a penchant for rambling sentences and an ADD aversion to linear time and deadlines. Your patience and dedication to this project are deeply appreciated. Thank you, Gary Tooth, for finding the way to capture the complexity of my Gulf Coast culture and cuisine and translate it into the luscious design of these beautiful pages. Angie Mosier, your photography truly captured the grace, beauty, irony, and simple fun of my life and the Gulf Coast! What a treat to see just how beautiful my world is through your eyes and talent! It was a joy to work with you. Bessie Gantt, you turned my runaway sentences and nostalgic and confused ramblings into a beautiful, cohesive narrative. Your contribution of editing and project managing has been invaluable, and my appreciation is as deep and meaningful as the color of my roux! Amy Hughes, our collaboration was simply meant to be, and I'm eternally grateful that you said YES when I called. You are my true Crazy Soul Sista. I know my dreams are safe in your hands.

So many locals and friends showed up to help, contributing gorgeous food, stunning locations, and cheerful descriptions that seasoned this gumbo pot. Special thanks to Jay Poggi, oyster-shucking aficionado; Krupinski Farm; "Panini Pete" Blohme of Sunset Pointe at Fly Creek Marina; B&B Pecan Co.; Joe Patti Seafood; Henderson Park Inn; Tynes Stringfellow and the blueberry farm at Weeks Bay Plantation; Johnny Fisher and Fisher's; Ethan at Burris Farm Market; Billy's Seafood; Alabama Gulf Seafood; and Justin Taylor with Bee Natural Farms. To all of my friends whose calls or emails weren't returned or who haven't seen me in a month or a year but still answer the phone when I call and pick up right where we last left off, I am truly, madly, deeply grateful to be your friend.

My Key West peeps: Shannon Musmanno, sweet thanks for helping me turn my home into a true beautiful tropical sanctuary; thank you, Kim Caggiano, for the great props and overall assistance with the photo shoots and mainly for sharing your Keiki Love; and Esme O'Kelley, you make me smile every time you cross my threshold. My sweet thanks for being my "island gal" and helping me test recipes.

I am humbly indebted to the LuLu's team who diligently and joyfully take care of business while I now work on my writing dream, especially Natasha Milan, Gabby Barnett, Mike Butler, Gerald Tipton, Shemeika Brock, and Johnny Barranco. I have a special appreciation for those who worked on this book with me—Fred Cossens deserves mention for moving and toting the props for our photo shoots with humor and playfulness. Dustin Smith is the Beverage Manager extraordinaire for helping develop and test all of the drink recipes! (Yes, that is a job!!) Blakeli Calvert Myrick is my "Wing Gal," always showing up with a bright attitude, wearing many hats with a willingness to do whatever is needed to get any job done. My A-list LuLu's kitchen crew did a remarkable job testing the recipes for this book: Salena White, Jayson Underwood, James Archie, Sam Stanczak, Deborah Collier, and Robin Hinton. Thank you for digging deep and coming through for me with grace, enthusiasm, and sheer grit to test recipes—even into the wee hours of the night after you had already fed three thousand people that day. It is hard to come up with the superlatives that could adequately describe how much I treasure Executive Chef Dylan Feenker. You are the heart of the heart of LuLu's. I am deeply grateful for your invaluable contribution to this book and could not have done it without you. And last, but certainly not least, George Martin, our fearless leader! My heartfelt gratitude for your integrity, staunch indefatigable support, kindness, humor, and talent. You have been a bright light for me since the day I met you. Thank you for sharing your specialness and making LuLu's and me better and better.

Margaret Daniels stands alone in her absolute awesomeness and sweet devotion to my family and me. Quite simply, she is my earth angel, and without her love and tireless support, I could never accomplish what I do. Thank you, "GaGa," for your sweet care of me and the four-legged Yorkie pack: Gatsby, the boy toy; Huckleberry, the muse; and D'LiLa June Buffett, my heart!

Passed down from my Gulf Coast mother was a devotion to family. I come from an unusual tribe—all rooted in a coastal consciousness fraught with adventure, curiosity, a love of food, and a fearlessness that spurred us to dream and explore beyond the sugar-sand shores of our youth. As the youngest of three, it was to my brother, Bubba (Jimmy), and my sister, LaLa (Laurie), that I looked for direction, acknowledgment, and guiding light. You both continue to be an indelible North Star in my universe; thank you for always believing in me. Tom McGuane, my dear brother-in-law with an unrivaled talent for storytelling and a devious, delicious wit, I continue to be in awe of your gift and am honored that you wrote the foreword to this book. It means the world to me. You now qualify for membership in the very exclusive Lucy Buffett "Free Gumbo for Life" club!

My children are the greatest gifts and lessons that life has given me. Melanie Buffett, your spirit of optimism and your practice of diligence, discipline, and seeing the goodness of life are indeed inspirational. Thank you for your unwavering support and appreciation. Mara Buffett O'Dwyer, without your contribution and talented care, this book would still be floundering around in pieces and random pages. Thank you for stepping back in when I needed you the most and showering this project with your organizational magic, capturing the heart and spirit of the place we call home. I know your special touches and insights are why this book is so beautiful in so many ways. A day doesn't go by without the notion of my two grandchildren flying through my mind, warming my heart...especially during trying times. Evangeline Buffett-O'Dwyer and Aengus Buffett-O'Dwyer, your beauty, love, and innocence give me faith in life. You inspire me to keep creating, playing, and dreaming; always know your "MiMis" treasures you.

Mac McAleer, thank you for having my back, building my dream, changing my life, and loving me.

INDEX

302

INDEX

ABOUT THE AUTHOR

Lucy Anne Buffett is a barefoot bay girl born and raised on the Gulf waters of Mobile Bay in Alabama, playing in the sand, riding on boats, and soaking up all the goodness of life, food, and fun on the Southern coast. She is the mother of two grown daughters and the daughter and granddaughter of a long line of strong and spirited Gulf Coast matriarchs, sailors, storytellers, and cooks.

Lucy adventured far and wide before returning home, where she went from selling gumbo from the back of her mother's station wagon to opening her wildly successful destination restaurants, LuLu's in Gulf Shores, Alabama, and LuLu's in Destin, Florida. She hosts over a million guests a year who descend on LuLu's to savor all the flavors of Gulf Coast cuisine and the atmosphere that's overflowing with music, fun, and the freedom to be yourself. Lucy embodies this spirit wherever she goes and has shared it in her cookbooks, *LuLu's Kitchen* (formerly published as *Crazy Sista Cooking*) and now *Gumbo Love*. She divides her time between the sugar-sand beaches of Perdido Key, Florida, and the anything-goes charm of Key West.